THE STATE OF THE NATION

THE STATE OF THE NATION

The Political Legacy of Aneurin Bevan

Edited by Geoffrey Goodman

VICTOR GOLLANCZ

LONDON

First published in Great Britain 1997
by Victor Gollancz
An imprint of the Cassell Group
Wellington House, 125 Strand, London WC2R 0BB

Foreword © Tony Blair 1997
'The Soul of Socialism' © Geoffrey Goodman 1997
'A Passionate Defiance' © Barbara Castle 1997
'The Ashes onto the Wind' © Dai Smith 1997
'Political Blood Sport' © Jill Craigie 1997
'Birth of the Dream' © Charles Webster 1997
'Nye' © Donald Bruce 1997
'The Boy Who Threw an Inkwell' © Tessa Blackstone 1997
'Bevan's Message to the World' © Michael Foot 1997
'The Greasy Pole' © Alan Watkins 1997
'The Scene Shifts – the Legacy Remains' © Will Hutton 1997

P. 50: 'On Some South African Novelists' by Roy Campbell
reproduced by permission of Francisco Campbell Custodio
and As Donker Publishers.

A catalogue record for this book is
available from the British Library.

ISBN 0 575 06308 4

Typeset by Rowland Phototypesetting Ltd,
Bury St Edmunds, Suffolk
Printed in Great Britain by
St Edmundsbury Press Ltd, Bury St Edmunds, Suffolk

97 98 99   5 4 3 2 1

Contents

Contributors

GEOFFREY GOODMAN was a close friend and confidant of Aneurin Bevan. He has been a journalist all his working life on a range of newspapers which include the *Manchester Guardian, News Chronicle, Daily Herald* and *Daily Mirror*, where he was Assistant Editor and Industrial Editor. He has also been a foreign correspondent and among his awards is the Gerald Barry Award for distinguished journalism. His books include a biography of Frank Cousins, the trade union leader, and a study of the miners' strike of 1984–5. In 1975–6 he was adviser to Prime Ministers Harold Wilson and James Callaghan. He is currently editor of the *British Journalism Review*.

BARBARA CASTLE has been a member of the Labour Party since she joined the ILP Guild of Youth in Bradford in 1926. As a young MP in Labour's 1945 landslide she made her mark as a rebel and in the sixties and seventies held four Cabinet posts in Harold Wilson's governments. At the Tribune rally at the 1996 Blackpool conference she described herself as an 'unreconstructed Bevanite'.

DAI SMITH is the author of *Aneurin Bevan and the World of South Wales* (1993). He was formerly Professor of History at the University of Wales, Cardiff and is currently Head of Broadcast (English Language) with BBC Wales. He has written extensively on the history of Wales and the culture of the Labour movement.

JILL CRAIGIE was the first woman to direct films for the cinema. Her work includes the feature documentary, *The Way We Live*, on town planning following the Blitz; the satirical screenplay *The Million Pound Note*, starring Gregory Peck; and, more recently, *Two Hours from London* for TV, an indictment of the West's attitude to the Bosnian war. She is currently engaged in writing a history of women's struggle for political emancipation, *The Daughters of Dissent*.

CHARLES WEBSTER was trained as a biologist. He taught at Leeds University and has held various posts at Oxford, where he is currently a Fellow of All Souls College. His research relates mainly to intellectual history in the sixteenth and seventeenth centuries, and the modern welfare state, especially the National Health Service.

DONALD BRUCE joined the Labour Party in November 1935. From 1945 to 1950 he was MP for Portsmouth and PPS to Aneurin Bevan. He was created a Life Peer in 1974 and from 1975 to 1979 he was a Member of the European Parliament. He was Front Bench Spokesman on Treasury and DTI matters from 1979 to 1990 in the House of Lords.

TESSA BLACKSTONE became Master of Birkbeck College (University of London) in 1987 and became a Labour Life Peer in the same year. She was the opposition frontbench spokesman on Education (1988–92), and on Foreign Affairs (1992–7) in the House of Lords. In 1997 she was appointed Minister of State at the Department of Education and Employment.

MICHAEL FOOT, author of the monumental biography of Bevan (two volumes: 1962 and 1973), was editor of the *Evening Standard* in 1942 and subsequently of *Tribune*, and entered Parliament in 1945, becoming Deputy Leader of the Labour Party in 1976. In 1980 he succeeded James Callaghan as leader of the party, remaining in that position until his resignation following the 1983 general election, and retired from Parliament in 1992. His many books include *The Pen and the Sword* (1957), *Debts of Honour* (1980) and *HG: The History of Mr Wells* (1996).

ALAN WATKINS joined the editorial staff of the *Sunday Express* in 1959. Since 1963 he has written a weekly political column in, successively, the *Express*, the *Spectator*, the *New Statesman*, the *Sunday Mirror*, the *Observer* and, most recently, the *Independent on Sunday*. He is the author of several books.

WILL HUTTON was economics correspondent of BBC2's *Newsnight* and then economics editor of the *Guardian* before becoming editor of the *Observer* in 1995. He is author of *The Revolution that Never Was* (1986), a study of Keynesian economics, and the highly acclaimed *The State We're In* (1995).

Foreword by the Rt Hon. Tony Blair, Prime Minister

The Labour Party has had many outstanding members in its nearly hundred-year history. But Aneurin Bevan, for millions of people, remains a genuine hero. Until his early death in 1960, he was one of the dominant political personalities in Britain in the post-war period. He helped define political debate within the Labour Party for a generation. And since his death, his reputation and charisma have been kept alive within the party, his ideas and personality and rhetoric passed on from generation to generation. Competing biographies have sought to understand the man and his politics, and the remaining soundtracks of his speeches give people born after he died the chance to hear the power of his oratory.

Bevan's personal story – miner's son and self-educated miner to MP and Cabinet minister and Deputy Leader of the Labour Party – is testimony to his intelligence and strength of character. The force of Bevan's visceral hatred of the Tories and all they stand for came from his own life experience: aware of the extraordinary potential of many ordinary people, he could not tolerate the waste of their talent in the 11-plus exam, unemployment, poor housing and curable or preventable ill-health. Bevan's radicalism was practical as well as high-minded.

Less well appreciated, perhaps, are Bevan's managerial skills. His greatest political legacy – the National Health Service – remains the cornerstone of the welfare state and the most popular and practical living embodiment of British democratic socialism. Few politicians can have the satisfaction of seeing their work help so many people for so many years. Yet Bevan knew that the creation of the health service had been brokered by his own imagination and his own skill. He was a formidable minister who used a combination of moral suasion and personal power to bring opponents into line.

It would be wrong to skate over Bevan's ambivalent relationship with the party leadership. He was of course briefly expelled in the 1930s and he resigned from the Cabinet in 1951. He had grave qualms about the development of the party under Hugh Gaitskell in the 1950s. But it is essential to realize that the passion Bevan brought to those debates came from his commitment to the Labour Party as the only instrument capable of bringing radical change to Britain. And it was this commitment that led to his reconciliation with the leadership in the late 1950s. Someone once said that, paradoxically, the Bevanites lacked a leader. Bevan was impulsive and impassioned in his opposition to Gaitskell, but he was ill at ease as a factional leader. The reason is that he knew how much the party had done for him and millions like him; he wanted the party to do so again – and he knew that unity was essential to that.

The 1945 Labour government was the greatest peacetime government this century. Its reforms constituted a revolution: demobilization and full employment, the welfare state, significant contributions to international relations and decolonization, as well as the creation of the NHS, added up to a remarkable record. Its leaders were statesmen of enormous and enduring stature. By a combination of clarity, unity and political skill, it shaped the political agenda for a generation. And, not to be forgotten, it won the hearts and minds of millions of voters: it never lost a by-election and gained votes in 1950 and 1951.

That 1945 government was the product of many things: the experience of war, the legacy of the 1930s, the popularity and simplicity of its objectives. But it was also built on a growing consensus in the battle of ideas. The Conservatives were rejected for what they stood for and what they offered. Labour was embraced for the strength of its values and the power of its policies. In 1997, we live in a radically changed world. But once again I believe the Conservatives are intellectually and politically exhausted. And I believe Labour has the energy and ideas to take Britain forward.

Bevan's personal testimony, spelt out in his book *In Place of Fear*, was part philosophy, part policy. But his call to 'passion in action', cited below, by Geoffrey Goodman, embodies his understanding that idealism must be combined with reason to bring power. The ideals of Bevan – solidarity, social justice, co-operation – remain potent today. That is a powerful legacy for any politician.

1997

GEOFFREY GOODMAN

The Soul of Socialism

What is the relevance of Aneurin Bevan to the contemporary political scene? This book, marking the centenary of Bevan's birth on 15 November 1897, is a direct response to that question. In responding, it salutes the memory of one of the outstanding political figures of this century.

The chapters which follow will argue that, far from being frozen in history, Bevan's ideas and political philosophy remain highly relevant to the future as well as to present-day society. There was a unique quality to Bevan's thinking. In many ways it looked even more towards the future than to the age in which he lived. That may seem paradoxical in view of the pressures for change now confronting his historic creation, the National Health Service. But in fact Bevan knew all along that the NHS would be a moving vehicle on the treacherous road to improving the nation's well-being. Indeed, at the very beginning he was compelled to make compromises in his negotiations with the doctors in order to get the vehicle on the road. Nothing in Bevan's credo was based on static, unchanging notions. There was never a rigid formula, not even to his profound commitment to the rules of socialism. His socialism, albeit rooted in the deepest and oldest traditions of the ideology, was not set in concrete. The principle of his belief in socialism was unshakeable; the practice constantly subject to the realities of life.

Of course he unremittingly stood for, and defended, what he regarded as the basic ingredients of socialist philosophy: equality, justice, democracy and the power to create and enable as well as to prevent and curb; to civilize the human condition and to open it up to the grandeur that he always saw as being within man's reach and grasp. Yet there was never anything in Aneurin Bevan's credo that held to an unchanging, unalterable vision of *how* the future might unfold.

Aneurin Bevan's death in July 1960 was the watershed in post-war Labour affairs in Britain. The fifteen years since the remarkable Labour victory of 1945 had already established Bevan as an exceptional political figure, not only as leader of Labour's left, but also – to the surprise of the majority of political observers – as an outstanding minister and administrator. Even his most bitter opponents during the negotiations which preceded the creation of the NHS had to acknowledge his negotiating skills, his reasoning and even his charm. But he was also a formidable opponent, especially of those inside the Labour Party whom he regarded not as enemies but as socialists of somewhat limited imagination. He excoriated them with a passion which some of them mistook for venom.

Had it been venom and had that been accompanied by a ruthlessness of the kind associated with Lloyd George (with whom Bevan is often compared), the chances are that Bevan would have become leader of the Labour Party. But, unlike Lloyd George, he was not given to opportunism in pursuit of personal position. What rocked the Labour Party in the five years between Attlee's retirement and Bevan's death was not a personal feud between Bevan and Hugh Gaitskell – though, to be sure, there was no chemistry between them either – so much as a profound conflict of ideas and concept of history. Certainly those five years saw the entire Labour movement travel through one of its most convulsive periods since the birth of the party at the turn of the century. The upheaval was to open the door for the eventual emergence of Harold Wilson after the death of Hugh Gaitskell. Yet these brief allusions to the historic milestones conceal more than they reveal. For the unique feature of Aneurin Bevan was his vision and his understanding of power, especially its limitations. Perhaps that goes some way to explaining his lack of ruthlessness and why, certainly towards the end of his life, he sometimes seemed to view the future power struggle almost with an air of detachment.

In my many conversations with Bevan it became clear that there were two main strands of thought to his definition of democratic socialism. The first was the importance of power. Without power all else was futile posturing. It was the argument he used against his wife, Jennie Lee, when she sought to justify her continuing membership of the ILP in the early 1930s; it was the argument he used against the British communists when some of their leaders, such as Harry Pollitt, tried to persuade Bevan into their camp during the Popular Front period of the later 1930s; it was the argument he used against the unilateral nuclear disarmers when, at the 1957 Labour Party conference, he warned those who clamoured and campaigned for a 'gesture' in abandoning the Bomb unilaterally by Britain, that it would be pointless to 'go into the conference room naked'. Indeed it was the argument he often used against his own Bevanite group of supporters – of which he was always a reluctant member – when he warned them that fine phrases never moved mountains. Socialism, he proclaimed, required power and that power had to come from the people: it could be neither imposed nor manufactured by romantic nostrums. Throughout his life Bevan famously kept repeating how he had pursued the elusive goal of power – in the local council at Tredegar, in the county council of Monmouthshire, to Parliament at Westminster and ultimately in the Cabinet. Power, he later reflected, always seemed to be one reach ahead. Yet he remained undismayed. Eventually, he would muse, the needs of the people and the use of power on their behalf would fuse together. This led to his second conclusion: as nothing remained static in the social and economic territory of man's search for a power balance, this very mutability must be turned to the advantage of democratic socialism. He concluded his book *In Place of Fear*[1] with this definition:

> Democratic Socialism is a child of modern society and so of relativist philosophy. It seeks the truth in any given situation, knowing all the time that if this be pushed too far it falls into error. It struggles against the evils that flow from private property, yet realises that all forms of private property are not necessarily evil. Its chief enemy is vacillation, for it must achieve passion in action in the pursuit of qualified judgements. It must know how to enjoy the struggle, while recognising that progress is not the elimination of struggle but rather a change in its terms.

It is in this context that I would describe Aneurin Bevan as an advocate of the 'second century of the socialist idea'. How so? We must, I feel, consider the nineteenth century as the 'first century of the socialist idea', flowing as it did from the Age of Enlightenment. The theories of Ricardo, Hegel, Marx, Proudhon, Robert Owen, Heine, even Jeremy Bentham and John Stuart Mill, all evolved in the wake of the great Enlightenment thinkers, Leibniz, Kant, Voltaire and Rousseau. Democracy was struggling from its shell; liberalism mixed with civil turbulence across Europe; ideas rippled and were quelled, and from this cauldron of thesis and antithesis came Marx with his socialist synthesis. This was the first century of the socialist idea. But Marx was insufficient, vast though his influence and analysis have been. Bevan had been schooled in Marxism and in the tradition of the nineteenth-century socialist thinkers. As he observed in *In Place of Fear*:

> From Jack London's *Iron Heel* to the whole world of Marxist literature was an easy and fascinating step. The relevance of what we were reading [in the Tredegar Workmen's Library] to our own industrial and political experience had all the impact of a

divine revelation. Everything fell into place. The dark places were lighted up and the difficult ways made easy.

Yet although Bevan never abandoned his attachment to Marx's analysis of capitalism, he departed from the automatic assumptions that other Marxists drew from that analysis.

In the same way he parted company with the communists; socialism without freedom was, for Bevan, no socialism at all, though he always accepted that 'freedom is the by-product of economic surplus'.[2] He was, if the phrase suffices, a libertarian Marxist; and indeed, like Marx himself, Bevan believed in the constant movement of social ideas as economic and technological forces propelled new cycles in human development. Bevan accepted only one inevitability – the inevitability of change. In another remarkably perceptive passage in his book, Bevan described the changing character of man's relationship with society and his environment and, by inference, foresaw much that is embedded in the ambience of modern, technologically driven society:

Modern industrial society is no longer a multiplication of a number of simple self-sufficient social groupings, each able to detach itself from the others without damage to itself. It is multi-cellular not unicellular. Each part is connected as though by an infinite variety of nerves with all the others so that separation is now a mutilation. It is similar to a physical organism but with this difference: that it has no head and therefore no mechanism with which to receive and co-ordinate the vibrations.

That passage was composed in 1952. The style of language is itself instructive as it mirrors Bevan's analogy between political life and biological development. He persistently referred to the nature of socialist development as being akin to biological growth. He visualized a parallel process as part of mankind's self-protective mechanism. Whether or not this was original Bevanism is impossible to say. It so happens that in an interview shortly before he died, George Bernard Shaw told me: 'Socialism is simply an organic growth of human behaviour.' Perhaps it was pure coincidence that the two men had such similar thoughts.

If Bevan is an advocate of the 'second century of the socialist idea', how relevant is his socialist philosophy today, at the approach of the millennium? How is it possible to justify the claim that his ideas about political and social development are as relevant – or more so – to us, and to the future, as they seemed to his admirers in the past?

Consider first the political, social and cultural climate that most of us inhabit. There is a turbulence running through our society that is as disturbing as anything experienced since the first industrial revolution – and of course far more universal in its impact and implications. The technological revolution is, without doubt, the most critical single element in this. It is carrying with each cycle of its advance a menace, as well as a promise, that is often difficult to comprehend. At the same time there is a loss of confidence in 'solutions', a vacuum of belief that is without parallel. The collapse of communism and the end of the cold war (as we knew it) have not brought us to the Promised Land; quite the contrary. Indeed, the fall of communism has demonstrated, once more, just how powerfully destructive and socially divisive modern capitalism remains when it is given the freedom to behave according to its deepest instincts. The leopard has retained its spots.

If it is the case, then, that the market system, unchecked and unregulated, cannot and will not provide the basis to sustain a civilized and humane society, what are our choices? What synthesis of capitalist enterprise and socialist humanity is most likely to provide a reasoned answer? Can the socialist idea, with its historic emphasis on provision for a civilized condition, be combined with a market operation (call it capitalist or competitive or anything else) that offers efficiency without at the same time brutalizing the system? To be frank, no one can be sure. But if there is to be a hope of achieving such an aim, then the blueprint must follow very closely the philosophy and concepts of Aneurin Bevan. And to use the shorthand of the political lexicon let us describe this goal as 'democratic socialism'.

The advocates of capitalism understandably castigate controls and regulation; yet secretly they know that without such regulatory instruments the system simply would not function at all, nationally or internationally. No power recognizes this truth better than the dominant capitalist country, the United States. Indeed, where capitalist organization manifestly breaks down, the process usually follows from a removal of controlling techniques. Absolute economic freedom can no more function effectively than absolute political freedom. Civilized society requires, and demands, regulation and a measure of control. Regulation is synonymous with the very nature of the civilizing process in the same way that a legal framework of justice seeks to limit absolute free will.

The crucial argument in contemporary politics is not *whether* there should be forms of control but, much more to the point, the nature and extent of such controls; how widespread they should be and over which areas of life. It ought to be a question of degree and not of principle – and that needs to be the basis on which we have a realistic debate about the future of the socialist idea.

Again we must now consider the implications of the technological revolution. Millions of jobs have already been wiped out never to return, regardless of the levels of future economic growth. In manufacturing alone, about half the workforce has gone from British factories in the last twenty years. The speed of replacement by machines is now so great that it is feasible, at least in theory, to produce all current industrial requirements with little more than one-fifth of the current total workforce. If, in addition, we assume a relatively low growth rate over the next decade (not an improbable assumption), the prospect emerges that an increasing proportion of the available workforce, young and middle aged as well as older people, will have no reasonable hope of fixed employment in their lifetime. Even short-term contract employment will become limited to a privileged minority. Whatever the true figure of current unemployment – and it could be as high as five million – the fact is that we are still only at the edge of the revolution in technology and electronic science. It is, by definition, no longer possible for market forces to correct this situation or cushion its impact. Market forces, to be sure, have a contribution to make but, unaided, however sophisticated they may be, they cannot cope with the magnitude of the coming challenge.

Before long, most developed countries will be forced to recognize that the only opportunities open to the majority of people will be to work either in small, specialized units where high skills are essential, or in areas where public-sector intervention plays an important social role. An effective system of extended schooling, training and retraining and perpetually trying to keep abreast of a rapidly changing cycle of skills will require a completely new approach to education. Mass production in the main will be controlled (as often it already is) by a few specialists working alongside lines of robots. If that sounds like a nightmare scenario, it is no less than a realistic preview of what is ahead for all industrially developed societies. This is the real crisis of our times.

In such a situation the state cannot, and should not, remain aloof. Its role is to protect society in the same way that any state has a practical and moral obligation to defend its territories against an unwanted invader. But, of course, none of this protection can be achieved by old-fashioned, purely national, policies. By the very nature of the problem some of the answers have to be based on international co-operation and combined action. There are no longer any frontiers against the sweep of technological change and instant communication. It is now an international issue of the highest priority to try to ensure that a new 'leisured class' of workless or at best part-time, intermittent workers do not become the breeding ground for violence, aggression and an underclass culture far more threatening than anything we have experienced in the past from external enemies. With extraordinary percipience Bevan saw the future when he wrote towards the end of his book: 'National sovereignty is a phrase which history is emptying of meaning.'

Bevan, as Michael Foot illustrates below, was above all an international socialist. The idea that socialism was, or ever could be, confined by national frontiers was, to Aneurin Bevan, the argument of the politically illiterate.

It is impossible for those of us who knew Bevan not to marvel, still, at his extraordinary vision and reading of the future, as Barbara Castle describes so vividly below. He saw it not as a soothsayer or by glancing into an imaginary crystal ball but as a philosopher and a poet musing on the exceptional opportunities that could open up for mankind provided we can find the correct path. By 'correct' he naturally meant the socialist path; but, as I have already emphasized, this was not offered in any rigid, dogmatic form or as a final panacea for all the ills of mankind so much as in the shape of a reasoned, rational, 'biological' development which logic suggested. In one of our long conversations during the 1959 general election (I was with him throughout that campaign, writing for the *Daily Herald*) we sat late into the night reflecting on the problems that would face him (he was then Shadow Foreign Secretary) if Labour won that election. He referred to a world in the throes of vast change, of torment, and still wrapped in the language of the cold war. Yet he also saw beyond this to the end of the cold war, predicting the fall of the rigid communist system long before anyone had heard the name Gorbachev. Bevan even then was already contemplating the impact that a developing technology of instant mass communications would have on the ruling elites everywhere. He reflected on the complexities of operating *any* political system in such unstable conditions and he lamented that he was surrounded by 'smaller and smaller men strutting across narrower and narrower stages'. That striking phrase came out of that night's dialogue like a Shakespearean arrow and I made a note of it.

Mind you, not all the figures dancing around in his mind at that time were 'smaller and smaller men'. He had his heroes. As Michael Foot explains, Nehru was one man for whom he had a profound regard and deep affection. Tito was another. He found the Yugoslav leader an exceptionally gifted symbol of his people even though Bevan disagreed with much of Tito's tactics. Again Bevan saw into the future and often prophesied that Yugoslavia's problems would explode once Tito had gone. Bevan was convinced that the world was close to the edge of vast changes and that only a handful of its political leaders had any conception of what might lie ahead. He voiced some of these anxieties in his last great speech, to a special Labour Party conference at Blackpool in November 1959 shortly after the general election defeat:

> Our main case is and must remain that in modern complex society it is impossible to get rational order by leaving things to private economic adventure. Therefore I am a socialist. I believe in public ownership. But I agreed with Hugh Gaitskell yesterday: I do not believe in a monolithic society. I do not believe that public ownership should reach down into every piece of common activity because that would be asking for a monolithic society.

Of course it would be absurd to argue that nothing has changed in the thirty-seven years since Aneurin Bevan died. He would be the first to ridicule such a proposition. The counter-revolution against the ethos of 1945 that occurred in the eighteen years following the launch of Thatcherism has seemed to undermine much of the ground on which Bevan used to stand. Yet it has solved none of the problems he outlined – problems which he accurately predicted would intensify with the passage of time unless more rational solutions were applied. The battery of measures taken to demolish the socialist policies of the 1945 government has not solved Britain's economic problems. Privatizing large sectors of the publicly owned enterprises and promoting a (short-lived) entrepreneurial revolution have not transformed British society into a more successful, equal nation at ease with itself. It has solved very few problems – though it has certainly created new ones. Nor has the Thatcherite revolution been the *cause* of whatever increase in wealth and prosperity may have occurred; this has been due primarily to technological advance and foreign investment. Where individuals and privileged groups have benefited from this expansion, it has frequently been at the expense of substantial job losses, growing inequality and social deprivation. The physical environment has been damaged and the social climate polluted by the positive encouragement of a grasping, greedy ethos. Margaret Thatcher's comment that 'there is no such thing as society' was not a momentary aberration or even a slip of the tongue; it was a perfect description of the havoc left in her wake.

It has also to be admitted that a counter-charge can be made against socialists. Where, the opponents of socialism might well ask, has the socialist idea proved unquestionably successful? Why did the command economies of the Soviet empire collapse so ignominiously? Where, if Aneurin Bevan was correct, can we find an exemplary socialist alternative to capitalism? There is no point in ducking this challenge even if the answer is far from obvious. There are, to be sure, many and complex explanations for the failure of the totalitarian socialist economies, and Bevan himself consistently foresaw this. It is more relevant to look at the development of social democracy and democratic socialism. There are numerous examples of considerable achievement, such as the Scandinavian countries, Israel and, not least, the 1945 Attlee government in Britain. Yet all these examples contain their own cycles of success and failure. No one should ever claim – and Bevan certainly never did – that it is an easy, straight path. And while there may be no example of the absolute success of democratic socialism, neither is there any example of its absolute failure. The argument I am suggesting is in fact an unorthodox one: that the success of socialism is only now becoming feasible, as well as necessary, because of the vast social problems – and opportunities – brought about by the technological revolution. In his later years Bevan himself envisaged a combination of socialist planning and market forces, a linkage of these two elements within the corpus of a far more expansive international framework of economic development. (And this at a time when the concept of the European Union was still in its infancy.)

What we are therefore discussing here is no less than a convergence theory of political development; the merging of opposites – the utilitarian qualities of both capitalism and socialism, the market with controls and regulation, a civilizing of the conflict. It is not how Marx imagined the future – though he was always extremely vague in his serious predictions. Nor is it how Bevan, in his earlier years, had imagined the metamorphosis: and yet . . . and yet even as far back as October 1950, in an unscripted lecture delivered at the Livingstone Hall in London – and largely unpublicized since then – Aneurin Bevan was already reaching out to consider how best to preserve and advance a modern democracy. 'The first thing that we have to remember about democracy –' he said, 'it is an obvious thing to say but it is very necessary to remind ourselves of it – [is that] it is very young. The dons are so accustomed to talking about Plato and so accustomed to talking about democratic speculations of 2,000 or 3,000 years ago that they have forgotten that democracy only arrived [in Britain] about 25 years ago.' He spoke about man's struggle against physical nature, trying to establish a relationship and a home within that ambience, and then with the dawn of modern society he described man's struggle to find a social niche:

This is an entirely new situation, bringing about new adaptations and new values. So long as parliaments divest themselves of economic power then democratic institutions were bound to be always the whipping-boys for private enterprise. This happens no matter how experienced the individuals are, no matter how knowledgeable they are. That is the reason why no democracy in the modern world is safe unless it becomes a socialist democracy. There is no halfway house here at all. It may be that we are moving towards an eclectic society; we are not going to have a monolithic society; we are not going to have a society in which every barber's shop is nationalized. But we must have a society in which the democratic institutions and the elected representatives of the people have their hands on the levers of economic power.

Bevan always set the widening of democracy as the foundation stone on which he built his socialist concepts. It was this principle that lay at the root of his socialism; his coping-stone, to turn Baldwin's famous dictum on its head, was power *with* responsibility, the prerogative of the open mind throughout the ages. Many of Bevan's critics missed or misunderstood this central feature of his socialism. John Campbell in his sympathetic, albeit still critical, book on Bevan described him as 'essentially a failure' because his outstanding gifts were, according to Campbell, 'in thrall to an erroneous dogma', in other words, socialism.[3] This is a charge which must be met.

Campbell can be put into the category of those who misread Bevan's mind because he slotted Bevan into a period of political history that, in Campbell's view, had had its day. He does not accept that Bevan's philosophy of political development was expandable into the future. Campbell's book was published in 1987, when Thatcherism was in its prime and the army of political undertakers was again marking the death of socialism. He regarded Bevan as the end of the line.

Of course the death of socialism has been announced at regular intervals throughout the century; indeed it was already pronounced a corpse even before the birth of the Labour Party, and there is nothing to suggest that its burial proclamations will cease with the millennium. Rather, like Christianity, it is probable that socialism will take a long time dying. Again this is where Bevan's prescience was always in command of his daily utterances and where many of his critics, including Campbell, misunderstand him. Moreover, as he pondered the extraordinary events in the years shortly before his death, Bevan came to recognize that the socialist ethic would have to be combined increasingly with private impulses. He frankly admitted that this seemed to be a contradiction that would be difficult to work out in practice – but it would still have to be faced. His was what might be regarded, today, as a very modern view of democratic social-ism. How then can this be reconciled with Bevan's oft-quoted thesis that the 'commanding heights of the economy' must be in public hands or, at least, subject to public supervision if not outright control?

One answer is that this argument was a perfectly tenable socialist principle during his lifetime and the change has occurred because the commanding heights of the British economy are no longer under sovereign control. The internationalization of capital and capital ownership has transformed the scene. The information technology revolution now enables stock and capital transfers to take place in seconds, leaving national governments unable to influence decisions let alone control them. As Bevan discovered when he left Tredegar in search of the elusive genie of power, it frequently changes its form. Yet the man who wrote of national sovereignty losing its meaning somehow understood that this would happen in the end.

Bevan's concept of the commanding heights would, in my view, have shifted, inevitably, to where the focus of power is now: on the ability of international finance to move huge tranches of capital across frontiers at the speed of a computer signal. He would have seen the need for some form of international economic discipline as an essential ingredient in any serious attempt to tackle the vast world-wide inequalities. And he would certainly have insisted that Britain must retain an independent (in so far as that word has any significance in contemporary affairs) parliamentary voice in an increasingly interde-pendent world. Far from viewing the trans-border movement of capital

as a defeat for the socialist idea, Bevan, ever the profound inter-
nationalist, would have turned the argument on its head and proclaimed a new opportunity for socialism to seek out the commanding
heights on a world scale. I can almost hear the tone of his mockery
as he would describe the flight of capital across one border after
another in search of a greater return on investment, higher profits
and cheaper production methods. And he would warn that capital
will, before long, find that it has crossed its last frontier of escape.
His concept of the commanding heights would certainly have shifted
from a Ben Nevis perspective of the UK economy to an Everest-like
vision across the globe. Nor is this as fanciful as critics might be
tempted to assume. A problem, as Bevan frequently observed, does
not disappear simply because it becomes world-wide. He recognized
that the nature of public intervention, or control, would change as
technology developed, and that there would come an ultimate realization among world leaders that it was actually in their own interests
to try to formulate a more acceptable and civilized system. It would
become part of a universal survival kit which he always saw as a route
towards socialism. The biological concept would again be at work.

As I have already emphasized, this book does not subscribe to the
view that socialism or the socialist idea is dead, or that it was a
phenomenon of the first half of the twentieth century which history
has now left behind, stranded under the rubble of the Berlin Wall
and the fallen statues of Lenin. In this review of the life and work of
Aneurin Bevan we are not seeking to be perverse simply to register
the significance of an outstanding political thinker in British public
life. The case I am arguing in this chapter and those that others
advance in subsequent chapters are genuine attempts to establish the
relevance of socialism and socialist ideas to modern problems and,
crucially, the importance of Aneurin Bevan's concepts in their application to the future. We use the life and philosophy of Bevan to illustrate
the force of this argument. It would be quite possible to use others,

for example the late Tony Crosland, to underline the validity of the socialist idea.

Not long before he died Crosland updated his classic book, *The Future of Socialism*, with a series of essays published in *Socialism Now*,[4] in which he advanced many thoughts that would have been acceptable to Aneurin Bevan had he lived. Crosland, another former Marxist, was seriously troubled by the knowledge that, despite the great social revolution of the 1945 Labour government, Britain in the mid-1970s was still scarred by huge inequalities and class divisions. Economic power had continued to move away from the state and the working population, despite the then widespread public sector of industry, towards 'a small oligarchy of private manufacturing firms'. Far from the socialist revolution having run its course, it was Crosland's case – and it is worth remembering that he was then regarded as being on the right of the Labour Party – that the task had scarcely begun. Indeed, one of the main proposals he put forward in his updated book was for the public ownership of the land as a priority for a future Labour government. He also offered a whole range of new thoughts on the economy which, he wrote, 'should be a *genuinely* mixed economy based on a variety of ownership forms and social controls designed to provide the best possible blend of social efficiency, growth and choice'. And he wanted to see the development of 'an active policy of competitive public enterprise: that is, the establishment of state companies or joint ventures to compete with private enterprise – to act as highly competitive price-leaders and pace-setters, provide a yardstick for efficiency, support the Government's investment plans and above all produce a better product or service'.

Like Bevan, Tony Crosland wanted to move from a monolithic concept of public ownership – that is, ownership by the state on an industry-wide scale, as was the case with coal and steel – towards a broader public ownership or control by *company*. I make the point about Crosland's thesis because despite the ideological division which existed between the two during Bevan's lifetime (Crosland being a close associate of Hugh Gaitskell) there were, on reflection, many striking parallels of thought and analysis. For example, compare Crosland's writing in *Socialism Now* with Bevan's last speech to the House of Commons before he went into hospital. Crosland wrote in 1974:

Here is the basic dilemma facing all democratic socialist parties: for we owe strong moral obligations to the ordinary people who support us. The dilemma will be more easily resolved if we have a faster rate of growth. But whatever the rate of growth we can, and must, mount a determined attack on specific social evils and specific inequalities. And so we must ruthlessly select priorities. We must prepare in advance a limited programme of radical measures which do not promise more than we can actually perform, which are closely related to the needs and aspirations of ordinary people and yet which constitute a coherent egalitarian strategy instead of a muddle of bits and pieces. Diffusion of effort is the enemy of social progress.

This was very much the language of Aneurin Bevan in his last speech, a remarkable tour de force in the House of Commons at the end of 1959. It was a memorable political lecture not only to the Conservatives, after their election victory a month earlier, but also to the Labour Party. Bevan put it this way:

There is one important problem facing representative Parliamentary government – that is how to reconcile Parliamentary popularity with sound economic planning. I would describe the central problem falling upon representative government in the Western world as how to persuade the people to forgo immediate satisfactions in order to build up the economic resources of the country. Let me put it another way: How can we persuade ordinary men

31

and women that it is worthwhile making sacrifices, or forgoing substantial rising standards, to extend fixed capital equipment throughout the country? This is the problem and it has not been solved yet.[5]

Bevan was in fact harking back to an earlier, even more famous phrase (picked up by Barbara Castle, Dai Smith and Michael Foot in the chapters which follow) in which he had stressed that the religion of socialism is 'the language of priorities'.

The central problem for the future, clearly, is to seek out a rational and socially accountable relationship between public and private capital. The actual proportions of command in that relationship will be open to constant debate and changing circumstance. It may well be the case that socialism on its own, as an overwhelming controlling mechanism, has no more chance of success than capitalism on its own similarly seeking to take absolute control. The defects and impediments in both systems have been dramatically demonstrated by the events of the twentieth century. The next century therefore offers an opportunity to find a formula, whatever it may be labelled, which draws together the positive and socially creative features of both public and private capital, public and private enterprise, public and private morality and ethos; to try to combine the two strands in a far more effective and equal democracy. It will not be easy. At the extreme ends of both poles there will be powerful gravitational pulls in opposite directions. There will inevitably be periods when the pull from one end will be infinitely greater, far more appealing to the electoral psyche, than the pull from the other. That will be one of the central challenges in politics for the next century. There is no question that Bevan would have sensed all this. By temperament so different, Bevan and Crosland nonetheless shared a deep conviction that the capitalist system could not, and would not, function in an acceptable form without substantial intervention by the state and widespread changes in the democratic framework. Both of them saw the waste, cruelty, inequity and manifest inhumanity of raw capitalism – yet they also recognized its vitality.

Even so, both Bevan and Crosland underestimated the capacity of capitalism to recover from recurring crises (as, of course, did Marx). Both men had an intellectual arrogance softened – though not always – by charm, humour and, most surprisingly, the capacity to stop and to hold a question mark above their own certainties. One of the most remarkable tributes to Bevan on his death came from Henry Fairlie in, of all places, the *Daily Mail*:[6]

The overwhelming impression that remains is of a man of size, a man whose intellect was capacious, lively, and illuminating, a man whose emotions were strong and human, a man who believed greatly in his country and believed also, which is rare in these days, in the power of ideas, a man who strove to retain the predominance of politics over economics or mass-psychology. For this, in the end, is what we owe to politicians like him. A democracy cannot survive healthily without the example of individual leaders who dare all as individuals and leave, long after their failures are forgotten, the imprint of a great human being.

To pick up Fairlie's point about politics and economics, the supreme challenge for the future is not the economic balance between growth, employment and inflation, important though that balance so obviously is. Much more crucial now is to reconcile democracy with social cohesion; to handle power and the exceptional advances in technology and scientific knowledge. The broad front of technological change is helping to undermine sovereign government; complex new systems of production are removing, or have already removed, the basis for individual work and collective production; scientific innovation is constantly raising the spectre of a future of limitless possibilities coupled with the spread of human frustration and dissatisfaction on a scale never before experienced. It is a period of climax between hope and despair, belief and un-belief. And while the potential is already in place for an immense expansion of material well-being there is also, alongside these developments, a deepening crisis in the social cohesion of many developed societies. Poverty increases as wealth expands; the paradox of the opposites assaults all rational thought.

The social fragmentation we have witnessed in recent times, even the fragility of family life, comes at least in some measure from the break-up of traditional working disciplines. Where there was commitment there is now, too often, confusion and ridicule. It is not only in terms of material poverty that so many of our societies are now struggling with an underclass; it is equally due to a poverty of imagination – a phrase that frequently tumbled from Aneurin Bevan's lips.

Imagination: that is the word which captures the ethos of Aneurin Bevan more precisely than any other. He often said to me that imagination was the strongest weapon in the socialist armoury. He used it with extraordinary effect in his oratory which, as I witnessed so often, equipped people – or so it appeared – with a practical structure for their dreams. They left a meeting at which he had spoken with a new sense that change was feasible, that dreams could be realized. He gave ordinary people a vision of what he believed could be done and what they could do. He sought to inject a confidence of will into a working class that, he was always convinced, lacked faith in its own potential. But none of these dreams, he argued, could be realized within the mere status quo of political institutions, whether they were state or private bodies; nor could a broader democracy be achieved by relying on the individual benevolence or enlightened self-interest which was at the core of tolerable, humane capitalism. He remained convinced that, ultimately, progress had to come from the template of socialist ideas.

One cannot overstate the unique quality of Bevan's political-philosophical vision. To me he was one of the three outstanding political figures of the century, alongside Churchill and Lloyd George.

Nor was this allure based purely on the message of socialism that he preached. It was wider, broader than that. Jennie Lee described her husband in this way: 'Nye's socialism had the radiant, elegant quality of his own personality.' In short it was the man himself. Often he was described, and still is, as an 'aristocratic socialist' and there is truth in that. He operated high above the routine clichés of politics and the tormented phrases of history. His mind took hold of a vision, perhaps still far off, of a world of rational co-operation held together partly by self-interest as well as irrational impulses but above all united by the knowledge that that pathway holds the key to an advancing civilization. He accepted that 'mankind is not born with an insatiable appetite for political liberty. This is the coping-stone on the structure of progress, not its base.'[7] He recognized that there were clear limits to what anyone, regardless of the power in his or her hands, could do to change the world or speed up the civilizing process. And he always, finally, conceded that 'there is a question mark over our future'.

Some years ago when I was discussing Bevan with Dora Gaitskell, widow of Hugh, she confessed to me that, in retrospect, she felt that Bevan should have been the leader of the Labour Party rather than her own husband. It would have made much more sense politically, she said, because Bevan was 'a natural leader' for a socialist party. I can think of no greater compliment.

BARBARA CASTLE

A Passionate Defiance

Aneurin Bevan had his human failings like the rest of us. I have often watched in despair as, carried away by the intoxication of his own power over words, he threw away the chance to influence more timid souls and strained the loyalty of his friends. Yet it would be a tragedy for the Labour movement if we were to allow his passionate recklessness to obscure the sober political lessons he has for us today. His stormy temperament was an integral part of his giant qualities of political courage, eloquence, vision, power of analysis and independence of mind. Without them he would never have set a whole generation of Labour activists aflame.

It does not do justice, therefore, to the whole man to gloss over his weaknesses. It is the last thing he would want himself. He was always uneasy among a crowd of Nyedolators who insisted on putting him on a pedestal. To understand his contribution to the Labour movement, one has to go through all the stages of his development, even when he seemed to his disciples to be engaged in some private deviations from the straight path of socialism.

Let us consider what drove him on. He was first and foremost the product of his own economic environment – and he was proud of it. As a young miner from the Welsh valleys who went down the pit at the age of fourteen he inherited the miners' mixture of emotions: part pride in their physical manhood and part anger at the coal owners' indifference to the conditions in which their wage slaves worked. It was not only the daily physical drudgery but the exclusion from the fresh air and the daylight for eight hours' concentration in cutting coal which left the miner wrung out with a fatigue which permeated his whole being when he surfaced again.

His life down the pit instilled in him two guiding principles which had a permanent influence on his political thinking. The first was that the recognition of their interdependence is the key to survival for those who face daily dangers – a lesson millions of us were to learn in the blitzes of the 1939–45 war. It is also the hallmark of a civilized society: the very opposite of the 'everyone for himself' philosophy. Even when he climbed out of the hardships of a miner's life into the middle-class comforts of a successful politician he never lost his instinctive belief that society should bond people together in common interests, not set them against one another in a competitive struggle to survive. Aneurin was no hairshirt socialist. He was a robust man with a robust appetite for the good things of life: good food and wine, great music, great poetry, great works of art – with a good ration of sexual satisfaction thrown in. Above all he loved good talk which to him meant the clash of ideas in sometimes controversial company. It was this which led him into Beaverbrook's sophisticated social circle of the 1930s which also enthralled his young protégé, Michael Foot. It was this which led Brendan Bracken, Conservative MP for Paddington North and a Beaverbrook intimate, to denounce him as a 'Bollinger Bolshevik', although Aneurin sensibly preferred a vintage red wine to champagne. To Aneurin, enjoying these delights was one of those temptations to which true believers should submit themselves as a test of their spiritual virility. As later events were to show, it was a test from which he and young Michael Foot emerged unscathed.

The second of his guiding principles was that the individual is economically powerless in the face of corporate power. By this he meant the accumulation of wealth in a few private hands which enabled those who possessed it to buy hire-and-fire control over working people's lives. Aneurin never doubted that the answer for his class lay in workers' solidarity expressed through trade unions whose historic function was to mobilize them against exploitation. His frequent battles with trade union leaders were over his belief that they were not discharging this function energetically.

For Aneurin had not much use for well-heeled do-gooders who wrung their hands over examples of blatant worker exploitation without being prepared to probe its origin. Liberalism, he believed, had fulfilled its historic mission when universal suffrage was at last achieved and had shot its bolt. He was a Marxist in the sense that he believed that politics was a battle between conflicting economic interests: between those who owned and those who were owned. Unless this was grasped, politics became mere jousting with empty words. The Liberals' function had passed to the party of the dispossessed.

What mattered to him was to give working people some economic control over their own lives. This made him a collectivist. Individual freedom of choice was a mirage for working people in his young days. There was only one career open to them: to work in the pits, steelworks, foundries, textile mills and other factories. For them, he wrote in *In Place of Fear*, 'the hope of individual emancipation was crushed by the weight of accomplished power'. None of his fellow workers could by their own efforts capture any of the power and wealth which these great industrial empires conveyed. 'The question therefore,' he wrote, 'did not form itself for us in some such fashion as "How can I buy myself a steel works or even a part of one?" Such possibilities were too remote to have any practical import.' And he added: 'The streams of individual initiative therefore flowed along collective channels already formed for us by our environment.' This was the great case for public ownership.

But he kept his feet on the ground. Like most working people in those harsh days he was also a pragmatist. He could identify with the priority needs for a job, a home, a living wage and enough to rear a family decently which preoccupied the class from which he sprang. Ideology had to be tested in the light of practical experience. His aim was to arouse a spirit of revolt against a system which denied these basic necessities to millions.

To the theorists of New Labour, Nye's revelation of the influence on him of his industrial environment in his early years proves that his doctrines are now out of date. Has not the role in our economy of the once great traditional industries – coal, steel, textiles and the other manufacturing giants – shrunk almost to vanishing point? Must not any political analysis based on them become irrelevant in an age of electronics in which manufacturing has given ground to service industries and in which the development of information technology, from the word processor to the Internet, calls for different skills? Has not the dream of workers' solidarity organized in trade unions become a piece of romantic nostalgia at a time when group working has been fragmented by a 'flexible' labour market and the facility for people more and more to do a job just as well by working individually at home? In short, has not 'Bevanism' become part of the ideological baggage which we must shed if we are to convince the electorate that we are fit to form a government?

What this argument reveals, of course, is that its advocates have never read *In Place of Fear* or grasped the lesson its author was trying to drive home: principle matters more than methodology. The astonishing thing about the book, written in 1951, just after Aneurin had launched the Bevanite revolt, is its flexibility. Nye had no use for rigid ideologies. He was a free spirit with too creative a mind ever to be trapped in any dogma which prevented him from questioning its validity.

His credo, summarized in this passage in his book, might surprise some of Labour's latter-day modernizers: 'The student of politics must seek neither universality nor immortality for his ideas and for the institutions through which he hopes to express them. What he must seek is integrity and vitality. His Holy Grail is the living truth, knowing that being alive the truth must change.' Before the New Labourites triumphantly claim him as their own, they should read on: 'If he does not cherish integrity then he will see in the change an excuse for opportunism and so will exchange the inspiration of the pioneer for the reward of the lackey.' Adaptability must never be confused with expediency. Debate and the right to dissent were sacrosanct.

It was the majesty of this freedom of thought which made Bevan's followers overlook his blemishes. He was intoxicated by ideas and his determination to follow where they led him got him into endless trouble with the politically correct, including some of us who called ourselves Bevanites. That did not worry him unduly because the last thing he wanted was to become the leader of a cult, using it to forward his political ambitions. He wanted to be free to be himself at whatever cost. If people followed him, it was at their own risk. Inevitably it was a stormy ride.

This flexibility of thought was demonstrated most clearly in the evolution of his attitude to the role of trade unions. His belief in the principle of solidarity never wavered, but he was prepared to let experience teach him the best way of applying it. As a young man imprisoned in the harsh restrictions of his environment he was obsessed with the need for power to enable him and his fellow prisoners to break out of their cramped lives. 'It was no abstract question for us,' he wrote. 'The circumstances of our lives made it a burning luminous mark of interrogation: where was power and what was the road to it?' Strong trade unions were clearly part of it.

From the beginning he participated eagerly in the activities of the South Wales Miners' Federation, becoming chairman of its leading Tredegar lodge, the youngest member to occupy that position in the history of the union. He was also profoundly influenced by the books to which he had access in the Tredegar Workmen's Library, 'built up by the pennies of the miners' he tells us proudly. It was 'given its distinctive quality by a small band of extraordinary men, themselves miners and self educated'. They made available on its shelves a far wider range of books than was found in most schools or colleges: not only the Marxist writings, but the works of orthodox economists, political historians of varying views and philosophers. It was through his wide reading that Aneurin developed his critical faculties. His flirtation with syndicalism was short, if intense.

In those days Parliament did not seem to offer much hope, dominated as it was by wealth and privilege: (full adult suffrage at twenty-one was not achieved until 1928). Inevitably he felt the lure of the argument that workers were wasting their time and strength trying to win power through a still unrepresentative Parliament, and that they must rely on their own industrial might.

This belief was fuelled by his reading in the Tredegar Workmen's Library. To the frustrated young miners of South Wales, impatient at the tepid leadership they were getting from their own federation, the Marxist-syndicalist doctrine seemed to tally with their own experience. Aneurin responded eagerly to the doctrines spread by the Irish leader, James Connelly, by Jack London in *The Iron Heel* and by the American IWW (Industrial Workers of the World) who were all in their different ways urging that 'they who rule industrially rule politically'. One of the strongest influences on him was Noah Abblet, a syndicalist leader who impressed Aneurin with his intellect. Abblet dismissed the parliamentary road to power with the words: 'Why cross the river to fill the pail?' Industrial action was the quickest way.

Yet as always Aneurin remained a realist. The Triple Alliance of miners, railwaymen and transport workers had been able to exercise industrial muscle during the 1914–18 war, but once it was over wartime controls were removed by Lloyd George's coalition government and laissez faire brought depression and unemployment immediately. Unions became as powerless as the demobbed soldiers who had been condemned to selling matches in the streets. It may have left Aneurin angry, but it cured him of any flirtation with direct action. 'Mass unemployment', he wrote in his book, 'was a grim school. Industrial power was just what the unemployed did not possess. To render industry idle as a means of achieving political victory was hardly an effective weapon in such circumstances. Capitalism had already done it for us.'

But it was not only political expediency which drove him to pin his hopes on Parliament. He was by every instinct a free-ranging individualist and therefore a democrat. He was one of the first to see that industrial power must be a supplement, not an alternative, to parliamentary democracy. *In Place of Fear* contains an illuminating account, which he obtained from Robert Smillie, miners' leader in the Triple Alliance, of how David Lloyd George diverted the threat of a crippling strike in 1919. The coal owners wanted to cut the miners' already low wages and the Triple Alliance rallied to their defence. Lloyd George called the union leaders in to No. 10. They went in, Bob Smillie told Aneurin, determined not to be won over by Lloyd George's seductive Welsh eloquence, but were taken aback by his unexpected line: 'Gentlemen,' he said to them, 'you have fashioned in the Triple Alliance of the unions represented by you a most powerful instrument. I feel bound to tell you that in our opinion we are at your mercy. The army is disaffected and cannot be relied upon. We have just emerged from a great war and the people are eager for the reward of their sacrifices and we are in no position to satisfy them. In these circumstances if you carry out your threat and strike, then you will defeat us.'

Disarmed by such frankness, the union leaders sat silent. Then came the coup de grâce. 'But if you do so,' went on Lloyd George, 'have you weighed the consequences ... For if a force arises in the state which is stronger than the state itself, then it must be ready to take on the functions of the state ... Gentlemen, are you ready?' 'From that moment on,' Robert Smillie told Bevan, 'we were beaten and we knew we were.'

After this, Bevan wrote, 'The general strike of 1926 was really an anti-climax. The essential argument had been rubbed home in 1919.' Its leaders, he wrote, 'had never worked out the revolutionary implications of direct action on such a scale. Nor were they anxious to do so.' They were reacting emotionally to a mood of frustration against Lloyd George's coupon election of 1918 in which voters had been conned by the promise of a 'land fit for heroes', which promise had proved fraudulent. 'Nevertheless', Aneurin continued, 'the authority of Parliament is part of the social and political climate of Britain.'

By this time the Labour Party had begun to exert an influence on the public consciousness. In 1924 it had clawed its way into office as a perilously insecure minority government which fell an easy prey to the 'Reds under the bed' bogus scare of the Zinoviev letter. But public opinion had grasped that Parliament offered an alternative to industrial power and Aneurin, the most instinctive of politicians, realized that industrial action could only succeed if it was sanctioned by the subjective reactions of the majority of the men and women who would be affected by it.

I was a schoolgirl living in Pontefract, the centre of a mining area, when the miners were locked out in 1920. I was brought up in a family which had no doubt as to whose side we were on. My father, though a socialist, was a senior civil servant who had to keep his mouth shut in public, but that could not prevent my mother from opening a feeding centre for the miners' children in our modest home. I remember the copper in our little kitchen being used to cook vast quantities of nutritious soup for the queue of hungry youngsters. When the miners were forced back to work, we went into mourning.

Yet I also remember how uneasy I felt when the general strike was called in 1926. I had not heard then of Lloyd George's victorious argument, but I vaguely sensed that this was a showdown with govern-ment that the unions could not – and perhaps ought not to – win. For some years after the unions' defeat I felt I had been an ideological coward until Aneurin's analysis made everything fall into place – and not for the only time.

In switching battlefields Aneurin had not given up the battle. All his life, he used to tell us jokingly, he had been tracking power to its elusive source: first through the Tredegar lodge of his union, then the district council, then the county council, only to be told it was somewhere higher up. At last he had arrived in Parliament, to which he was elected as MP for Ebbw Vale in 1929. He was not going to let the prize slip out of his grasp yet again.

He went to Westminster, therefore, determined to use this new instrument to shift the balance of power and wealth in favour of the working people he represented. Politics, he believed, was a struggle between three conflicting forces in society: wealth, poverty and democracy. He still believed it twenty-three years later when he wrote in his book: 'Poverty, great wealth and democracy are ultimately incompatible elements in any society.' If parliamentary power was not used to redress the great gulf between rich and poor, faith in parliamentary democracy would diminish. 'People have no use for a freedom which cheats them of redress.' And he concluded, 'If freedom is to be saved and extended, poverty must be ended. There is no other way.'

Bevan went to Westminster, therefore, like a boxer, ready for a fight. Like the majority of us he was deeply shaken by Ramsay MacDonald's surrender to the aristocratic embrace which led to his betrayal of the 1929 Labour government. Aneurin never underestimated his enemy and the subtle seductions that the privileged under duress would offer to the newcomers from the ranks of the dispossessed who had managed to penetrate their sanctuary. The newcomer's only hope was to be mentally prepared for it.

He had some warnings for the new member arriving in Parliament bruised by the struggles of his working life. 'His first impression is that he is in church,' he wrote. The vaulted roofs, the stained glass windows, the busts of great statesmen round the walls, the semi-ecclesiastical ritual, the soft-footed attendants, the hushed voices all conspired to make him feel he had not come to challenge but to worship and what was more, at the most conservative of all religions – ancestor worship. So Aneurin reminded him grimly that these were not his ancestors. He must create his own gods, not inherit them.

With a touch of personal bitterness he warned that passionate language would be shrugged aside as a breach of etiquette.

The atmosphere of Parliament today is, of course, very different. The hushed voices have given way to rowdy exchanges across the floor of the House with Labour members joining in lustily. Ancestor worship has taken refuge in the House of Lords. But what exactly are you challenging? Bevan would ask today. Noise is not enough.

'The first essential in the pioneers of a new social order', Aneurin wrote in 1951, 'is a big lump of irreverence.' No one could deny that he practised what he preached. In those early days in Westminster it was a stony road and often a lonely one. In the election which followed Ramsay MacDonald's defection to form a National Government Labour's ranks in Parliament were shattered and demoralized. The number of Labour MPs was reduced from 288 to 52 and of their erstwhile leading figures only Clement Attlee, Sir Stafford Cripps and George Lansbury survived. The sense of failure inhibited many MPs in fighting back.

The atmosphere was made worse by the fact that discipline in the party was in the hands of a National Executive Committee dominated by a few big unions who had no hesitation in reminding party conferences that 'he who pays the piper calls the tune'. They had no patience with ideas of fundamentally changing an unjust society, preferring private deals with employers behind closed doors to the open assertion of their members' rights. They also claimed their prerogative to be kingmakers, a right which they exercised blatantly later when they set out to replace Attlee as leader and Prime Minister by Hugh Gaitskell whom they considered they could rely on to be tougher with the left.

There are many lessons which Labour today can learn from this period. The first is how unwise it is to lump 'old Labour' together as an ideological whole. In fact this period was one of conflict between left and right in which recent developments have shown that it was the right which was antediluvian.

Looking back, for instance, it is ironic to note how complacent the party's leadership and its press allies were about the union block vote as long as it was in right-wing hands. They could even stomach the situation in which the trade union bosses and their subservient delegations to party conferences not only elected the trade union and women's sections of the NEC but decided who should represent the constituency parties, making a mockery of democracy. It was the left, through the Constituency Party Association backed by *Tribune*, who eventually corrected this anomaly. I remember with some amusement that it was I, together with another left-winger, William Warbey,[1] who pioneered the idea of 'one man one vote' as long ago as 1943 by circulating to every member of the National Executive a document arguing that part at any rate of the trade union votes should be cast through local parties, though we were in favour of some of the union votes being cast nationally in order to retain a trade union's corporate identity. Our document did not receive even an acknowledgement from any member of the NEC. The press ignored it as a left-wing irrelevance, only changing its tune when left-wingers like Frank Cousins were elected to the leadership of powerful unions such as the Transport Workers. Frank even had the audacity to say he must be guided in his actions by the votes of his own union conference.

In such a political climate Aneurin's abrasive challenges to the status quo inevitably got him into trouble. He affronted the trade union bosses by the undiscriminating enthusiasm with which he took up the cause of the unemployed, joining with communists and anyone else who cared enough to come along on protest demonstrations, rallies and marches of the unemployed. The official view was that these protests should be organized by the trade unions on behalf of trade unionists. Unemployed non-unionists were no concern of theirs.

Aneurin was deeply concerned at what was happening in Germany. He had always seen unemployment with its accompanying poverty and above all loss of status as the greatest threat to democracy. As he wrote later in his book, 'either poverty will use democracy to win the struggle against property or property, in fear of poverty, will destroy democracy'. The rise of fascism seemed to be proving him right. With his usual unorthodoxy he argued that neither the Versailles Treaty nor the weakness of the Weimar Republic was the sole cause. 'The Weimar Republic had survived the Versailles Treaty,' he argued. 'It could not survive both the Versailles Treaty and unemployment for six or seven million Germans. The decisive factor was the unemployment.'

Whether or not his analysis was correct in every historical detail, what mattered was the sense of urgency it conveyed and the belief that a properly organized society could and should do something about it. Like many others on the left he had watched in despair as economic timidity had destroyed the 1929 Labour government. They knew that it was the financial orthodoxy of Philip Snowden as Labour's Chancellor which had brought the government down by insisting that Britain must stay on the gold standard at whatever cost to the three million unemployed. Yet within three weeks of taking office the National Government took Britain off the gold standard and unemployment began to fall.

With hindsight most commentators now admit that Snowden misled the Cabinet. Even Hugh Dalton, who was to become Chancellor in the 1945 Labour government and one of Aneurin's bitterest critics, argued in his autobiography that the 1929 government fell because it lost its economic nerve and listened to bad advice.[2] 'Our adverse trade balance in 1931 was not serious,' he wrote. As for going off gold, 'we should certainly have faced this possibility much sooner and not let ourselves be dragged so far down the deflationary slope'. Dalton himself proved an unorthodox Chancellor with his 'cheap money' policy which saved the government millions of pounds in interest payments. More recently Labour's advisers seem to have ignored the lessons we learned in 1931 by supporting the Tories' move to take Britain into the modern equivalent of the gold standard, the Exchange Rate Mechanism – with disastrous results. A touch of 'old Labour' might have helped us here.

Another source of conflict between left and right in those early days was Labour's official timidity in trying to halt the fascists' relentless onward march. The most conspicuous example was its endorsement of Britain's non-intervention policy in the Spanish civil war. It seemed obvious to most of us that Franco's armed uprising against the elected government was the trial run for a wider war against the Western democracies. Hitler and Mussolini so regarded it as they poured in arms to help the insurrectionists. But appeasement-ridden Britain chose to stand aside, denying arms to both sides and therefore, in effect, to the legitimate government which had no other source. The party's rank and file was horrified as their leaders meekly acquiesced in this policy. Their gut instinct was aroused in support of Spain's elected Republican government as was that of a wider non-political circle. 'Arms for Spain' resolutions poured on to the party's conference agenda. 'Aid for Spain' committees raised money in every locality and found homes for Spanish refugees. A few brave souls, such as Jack Jones of the Transport and General Workers' Union, went out to fight side by side with the disorganized forces of the Spanish government, inspired by a spirit of international solidarity, a phrase which we seldom hear today.

No one should pretend that all was angelic in the Republican army's ranks. Aneurin was too much of a realist not to know that the forces ranged against Franco were torn by enmity between the communists and the Trotskyists organized in POUM. He was instinctively against schism and never lightly gave himself to the frantic efforts of left-wing groups such as Stafford Cripps's Socialist League, set up in 1932 to correct the Labour Party's policies which had led to the disaster of 1931 and which were doing so little to fight fascism. When the League launched the Unity Campaign of working class forces, i.e. League members such as Michael Foot and myself, the communists and the ILP, to combat the drift towards appeasement he put only a tentative toe in the water. He assessed correctly that its base was too fragile to succeed.

Nonetheless his hatred of appeasement remained undimmed and when the success of Victor Gollancz's Left Book Club showed there was a wide-ranging public realization of the dangers Hitler posed to us, he enthusiastically joined Cripps's new project for an all-party Popular Front of anti-fascist forces, inspired by the setting up of a Popular Front government in France. In the event only one daring Liberal spirit was to join.

It is no part of my thesis to argue that the left was always correct in its analysis. It was no doubt a tactical misjudgement for Cripps, Bevan and their allies to oppose the rearmament programme proposed by the Chamberlain government. They suspected, and rightly, that a government of appeasers could not be relied on to use those arms against Hitler when they quite openly preferred to turn him against the Soviet Union. Munich and Chamberlain's rejection of the Soviets' offer just before war broke out to form a Triple Alliance with France and Britain proved that the left's suspicions were justified, but in politics it is important to keep the issues simple and the left's politically sophisticated attitude muddied the waters for some of their followers.

Nonetheless the purism of the left in opposing rearmament was out-matched by the purists on the NEC who insisted on enforcing the strict letter of the party constitution even when Hitler was marching across Europe almost unchallenged. They interdicted all 'fronts' with whomsoever they might be formed or for whatever cause. The Unity Campaign had clearly to be proscribed because it meant consorting with communists. It made no difference that communists had led the resistance to Hitler in Germany and had paid a heavy price – nor did the fact that in Britain, too, at that time communists were in the van of protest against appeasement. Both the Unity Campaign and the Socialist League had to be wound up. Another object of suspicion was the Left Book Club, but even the sternest disciplinarians on the Executive realized they could hardly throw people out of the party for reading books. Stafford Cripps's switch to a Popular Front fared no better. The Labour *virgo* must be kept *intacta*, even with the enemy at her gates.

Looking back on those days I am often reminded of one of my father's favourite quotes from a book on South African writers he had read in the 1930s to which the poet Roy Campbell contributed the following satirical verse:[3]

> You praise the firm restraint with which they write—
> I'm with you there, of course:
> They use the snaffle and the curb all right
> But where's the bloody horse?

In March 1939, with Hitler in Prague and menacing Poland, Bevan, Cripps and a few key allies including George Strauss and Sir Charles Trevelyan were solemnly expelled from the party for unlicensed anti-fascism.

Six months later Britain declared war on Germany. Even Chamberlain had not been able to resist the pressure of public anger which followed Hitler's invasion of Poland. Aneurin was anxious to be at the centre of the political struggle in the only body which he believed could influence it and he was readmitted to the party, together with George Strauss, four months after war broke out. They had every reason to believe that they had won the argument. Stafford Cripps remained outside the party until 1945.

It took another six months to get rid of Chamberlain. Aneurin welcomed his replacement by Churchill, but he was not going to suspend his critical faculties. He did not trust Churchill to fight the war in order to create the new social order which he, Aneurin, believed was the only secure basis for democracy. He was worried when Churchill invited a number of leading Labour figures – Attlee, Bevin, Morrison and Arthur Greenwood – into his War Cabinet, suspecting with some reason that they would be given the unpopular jobs while Churchill remained the glamorous figurehead. He complained that the Tories would be in charge of the ideological war while Labour was given the responsibility of waging the material one. As a fellow orator Aneurin was second to none in his admiration of Churchill's defiant speeches in June 1940 when the capitulation of the French government to Hitler left Britain standing perilously alone against the enemy. Nonetheless he was not blinded by the words: it was the deeds which mattered.

So Aneurin pursued a stony and lonely road in Parliament. One of his most admirable characteristics was the moral courage which enabled him to stand up against an emotional tide. It must have influenced me without my realizing it because when some twenty years later I entered Harold Wilson's 1964 Cabinet, I was imbued with the instinctive belief that any worthwhile politician must be prepared to be unpopular in the right cause and must resist what I came to call the 'companionable embrace' of the civil service. After a few years of political battering on such issues as the breathalyser and my White Paper on trade union reform, 'In Place of Strife', I used to joke that ministers ought to pin over the door to their ministerial room a bannerette with the words: 'Abandon love all ye who enter here'.

But I have never had to face the hostility which Nye met when he dared to criticize Churchill's conduct of the war. Then indeed the atmosphere of Parliament was like being in church: it was not only treachery, but heresy to suggest that the great war leader was not infallible. Aneurin remained suspicious of Churchill's political motives to the end. Churchill may have deplored Chamberlain's failure to take up the Soviet Union's offer of a Triple Alliance in August 1939 which, he wrote later in his war memoirs,[4] might even at that late stage have averted war. But this in Aneurin's eyes made it all the more culpable to include Chamberlain and his fellow appeasers, Simon and Halifax, in his first War Cabinet when he took over in 1940.

Churchill also admitted in his memoirs that it was Chamberlain's coolness which decided the Soviet Union to seek self-preservation in the Ribbentrop/Molotov Pact. When Hitler broke the pact by invading the Soviet Union in the summer of 1941, Churchill formally welcomed his new ally – as well he might, for Hitler's folly had greatly relieved the pressure on Britain and her dwindling band of friends. Nonetheless Churchill's military staff continued to keep the Soviet military mission at arm's length.

As freezing winter gripped besieged Leningrad where one million people slowly starved to death the demand grew at home that we should come to her aid by opening a Second Front. Following Japan's attack on Pearl Harbor in December 1941 America had come into the war and we had room for manoeuvre. But Churchill remained unmoved. Aneurin believed the reason for his refusal was as much political as military and led the campaign in the Commons and *Tribune*, while Michael Foot promoted it in Beaverbrook's *Evening Standard* of which he had become editor. As Aneurin's attacks grew more strident Churchill dismissed him as a 'squalid nuisance', an epithet which was privately echoed by some on his own side.

But Aneurin was now thoroughly alarmed. He was convinced that Churchill was planning to put himself at the head of a post-war coalition government which would reflect his own political prejudices and he feared that Labour ministers, accustomed to the cosy confines of the War Cabinet, were inclined to go along with it. There was talk of the electoral truce being extended beyond the war and of the formation of a National Government with Churchill at its head. Hopes of a new social order were under threat.

The first danger signal came when Arthur Greenwood, one of the party's most respected socialist veterans, was dropped from the War Cabinet. Churchill gave no explanation for this move either then or at any time, but the instinct of backbench Labour MPs alerted them to the reason why. As Minister without Portfolio, Arthur had been given a roving commission to produce reports on post-war reconstruction plans. In this capacity he had appointed the eminent Liberal, Sir William Beveridge, to examine the rickety pre-war structure of 'social insurance and allied services' and to advise what should be done. The very terms of reference clearly alarmed the Conservative-run government and Greenwood was sacked even before the report appeared. Labour MPs promptly elected him chairman of the parliamentary party.

Beveridge's report, together with a later one on full employment, issued a challenge to the ruling orthodoxy of laissez faire. Poverty and mass unemployment, he argued, were not dictated by natural law, but could be cured by the state taking responsibility for the proper organization of the country's resources. A comprehensive system of contributory national insurance could give everyone a basic level of security when their earning power was interrupted, whether by sickness, industrial injury, child-bearing, unemployment or old age. Mass unemployment could become a thing of the past if governments would accept the duty of keeping demand at the appropriate level to preserve jobs.

Beveridge's message filled the Labour movement with new hope. Dedicated enthusiasts spread it through innumerable little meetings of local Labour parties, co-ops and trade union branches which were held up and down the country. Thanks to the Army Bureau of Current Affairs it even penetrated the fighting forces who were fired with new confidence that the carnage of war need not have been in vain.

But would it be carried out? Fine-sounding generalizations were not enough for the party's rank and file. They wanted clear commitments which would not allow any post-war government to wriggle out of them. When in February 1943 Labour MPs forced a debate on the Beveridge report the government tabled the expected anodyne motion welcoming the report as a valuable contribution to the discussion of how post-war reconstruction might proceed: no pledges. Aneurin led a backbench revolt, proposing an amendment demanding the immediate setting up of a Ministry of Social Security to start implementing Beveridge's plan. Herbert Morrison resisted it on behalf of the War Cabinet while Kingsley Wood, Tory Chancellor of the

Exchequer, gave the familiar 'we have to wait until after the war to see if we can afford it' argument. No fewer than fifty-seven rebel Labour MPs voted for the amendment, but inevitably the government got its way. The danger that the scheme would be watered down, or even abandoned, was obvious.

The battle moved to the party conference of 1943. Arthur Greenwood used his traditional duty as chairman to submit an annual report on the doings of the parliamentary party to warn delegates that in the famous debate the government had not shown 'any great enthusiasm' for the Beveridge report. Delegates were dismayed when the only response of the trade union heavyweights was to criticize the fifty-seven Labour MPs who had shown 'disloyalty' to the wartime government. But the rebels stood their ground. I made my debut as a conference delegate in a speech demanding Beveridge NOW. It was to win me the selection as candidate for Blackburn a year later. Party activists were in no mood to compromise and a commitment to implement duly appeared in Labour's election manifesto which swept them to victory in the election of 1945.

The Labour leadership was surprised by the warmth of the voters' response to the welfare state. Without this Big Idea it is doubtful whether the party could have offset Churchill's charisma as the war leader who had led his country to victory. When the election was declared Churchill came out in his true colours, savaging his former colleagues in the War Cabinet and claiming that if a Labour government were elected, it would introduce a 'Gestapo'. The attack was counter-productive as voters could not visualize the mild Major Attlee as an autocrat. Churchill seemed a likelier candidate for that role. Most important of all, the voters' personal experience justified the radical reforms Labour was promising. Virile policies will always stand out more strongly than personalities.

Beveridge had always advocated the creation of a National Health Service as part of his war against the five giant evils: ignorance, disease, squalor, idleness and want. To him it was economic common sense to keep people as fit as possible by giving them access to the best medical care. This appealed to Aneurin's mixture of pragmatism and vision, his need to combine what was possible with his sense of what the good society should be like. It was a sign of Clement Attlee's innate decency that he should have brought into his Cabinet in 1945 this 'squalid nuisance' who had alienated so many of his colleagues with his abrasiveness. He showed even greater vision when he made him the custodian of one of the key items of Labour's Big Idea: the establishment of a National Health Service.

The job was to give Aneurin one of the most fulfilling periods of his political life. Other people, notably Michael Foot and John Campbell, have set out in their biographies the details of Aneurin's struggle with the medical establishment.[5] As a backbencher in the 1945 Parliament I could only sense at a distance how intense his struggle was, but the message seeped through that Nye was proving not only a highly competent administrator, respected by his civil servants, but a brilliant tactician. His critics watched amazed as the abrasive agitator was transformed into the smooth operator. He played off one section of the medicos against another, detaching Lord Moran, President of the Royal College of Physicians, from the body of consultants by accepting his advice to allow consultants to treat their private patients in pay beds in NHS hospitals. This was not in accord with the pure socialist doctrine, but the left accepted it pro tem as a small sacrifice to make for the realization of Nye's revolutionary concept of a comprehensive national service paid for out of taxation and free at the point of use, giving everyone the right to expert medical treatment from the cradle to the grave.

The political struggle was a tough one. The Tory opposition soon showed that their idea of a health service was very different from Nye's comprehensive one and that they still yearned for voluntary hospitals supported by flag days and charity. A favourite line of attack was that Nye was planning to rob GPs of their clinical freedom by turning them into the salaried servants of the state. Nye could – and did – beat these arguments into the ground, arguing that there was no clinical freedom for doctors who dare not prescribe treatment for their patients for which they knew they could not afford to pay. He also met some resistance inside the Labour Cabinet to his proposal to nationalize the hospitals. Herbert Morrison, for one, put up a vigorous defence of municipal hospitals, a battle which Aneurin won by pointing out that universal health care needed the nation's resources to make it a reality.

With power at last to help build a new social order, Aneurin's temperament mellowed and he showed a side which few people had realized was there: a tender love of humanity with all its frailties. I remember reading the press reports of a speech he made to a conference of nurses who were a little nervous of the radical development in health provision he was preparing. He won them over by talking to them as one human being to another, lifting the argument to a new level. They sensed that this was no party political ploy, but a crusade.

I met many examples of Nye's capacity for good-humoured tenderness, even at the most stressful moments of his stormy life. On one occasion at the height of the Bevanite row he was due to address the Young Socialists' annual conference. His train was late and a young delegate was put up to hold the fort. Aneurin found him purple with embarrassment as the loudspeaker was playing him up. So Nye opened his speech with gentle self-mockery: 'I would say to my young friend he should not worry because the loudspeaker fails on him. If it had only failed on me more often I should not be in the trouble I am in now.'

But he had not gone soft. In his bitter battle with the GPs, led by Dr Charles Hill, President of the BMA, who had gained a considerable following as the radio doctor with the plummy voice and who had been a Conservative candidate in 1945, Aneurin made any concession he felt he could in all conscience without undermining the fundamentals of the scheme. He yielded, for instance, to their hostility to a salaried service and offered a capitation fee instead. He rejected, however, their persistent attempts to amend the Act he had got through Parliament. Ignoring their threats to boycott the new service, he decided to gamble on the public support he was sure was there and announced that the Act would come into operation on the appointed date: July 1948. It was a breathtaking risk but it paid off. With the GPs still declaring they would have nothing to do with the NHS, their patients invaded their surgeries demanding that they should. Within a few weeks the vast majority were signing up.

It was a famous victory. Aneurin had kept his nerve and he had won. He could be forgiven a little burst of pride. Had he not proved that socialist principles, sensitively applied, were not alien to the British character as some of his colleagues feared? Events were to prove him right. The public's loyalty to their health service deepened with the years and no government dared seriously challenge it. When Margaret Thatcher came to office in 1979 with the harsh doctrine that everything and everyone must pay their way in an unbridled market economy, she was forced to beat a tactical retreat when she tried to apply it to the NHS. One of the most dramatic testimonies to Aneurin's triumph came in the 1997 election campaign when John Major made a bid for last-minute popularity by making financial and ideological commitments to the NHS which a cautious Labour leadership was afraid to make. Aneurin would have enjoyed the irony of this Tory Prime Minister's conversion to the flagship of socialist principles to save his electoral skin.

When in late 1950 and early 1951 first Stafford Cripps then Ernest Bevin had to give up office on the grounds of ill-health, Aneurin had every right to expect to move higher up in the Cabinet hierarchy. He had his sights on the Exchequer and failing that on the Foreign Office, but the bosses of the big unions with whom he had done battle for so long planned otherwise. They had picked Hugh Gaitskell, the up-and-coming junior minister who had become Cripps's right-hand man at the Treasury, as the man who could be relied on to slap down the red rebel from South Wales. They even plotted to oust Attlee. With such allies Gaitskell's star was bound to rise and Nye's to sink. Gaitskell became Chancellor of the Exchequer and Herbert Morrison followed Bevin as Foreign Secretary – by common consent a disastrous choice. Aneurin was sidelined into the Ministry of Labour. A few months later he resigned from the government.

Gaitskell's promotion was to plunge the Labour Party into thirteen years of internecine war. Aneurin's critics put the blame squarely on him. Did he not prove himself a vanity-ridden egoist who was prepared to wreck a brilliantly successful Labour government from personal pique? There was little sympathy among his Cabinet colleagues for the issue which provoked his resignation: his refusal to accept Gaitskell's demand that the NHS should make up a shortfall of £13 million by charging for false teeth and spectacles. To a government under pressure this was a small sacrifice to make, so it was assumed his stated reason was an excuse rather than the genuine cause.

There can be no doubt that personal resentment entered into it. There was a chemistry of hostility between him and Gaitskell but often in politics a clash of personalities hides a clash of policies. Aneurin was no wrecker. He was immensely proud of the achievements of the Labour government and used his great gift of words tirelessly in its support. He was never defensive about the short-term austerity which a Labour government bent on long-term economic recovery was bound to impose. He made a virtue of it, pointing out that rationing granted everyone an adequate, if not very exciting, diet. Above all, it put first things first. I remember how inspired I was when he explained how even a cash-strapped Treasury had found the money to give every baby in the land free orange juice, free cod liver oil and cheap milk. He encapsulated a drab post-war situation in an illuminating phrase: 'If you want to see the prosperity of Britain, look in the perambulators.' Agnostic as he was, he managed to turn politics into a faith. Indeed his most famous phrase became: 'The religion of socialism is the language of priorities.'

It was his belief which, together with his personal resentments, created the explosive mixture which led him to blow the government apart in 1951. It was not only that Gaitskell, in his budget of that year, had insisted on lopping £13 million off NHS expenditure, but the purpose for which he wanted the money. If Bevan had become Chancellor of the Exchequer instead of Gaitskell he would undoubtedly have been just as tough in facing the economic realities, but his priorities would have been very different. He had already had a bitter battle in Cabinet to preserve the party's manifesto commitment to the nationalization of the iron and steel industries, a battle in which Herbert Morrison had been his leading opponent and Attlee had proved weak. Now Aneurin was faced with Gaitskell's demand for the first inroad on the principle of a free health service in order to finance an unrealistic rearmament programme under pressure from America. It was his breaking point.

There has been a lot of argument as to how far Aneurin's resignation was motivated by anything more rational than injured pride. Certainly his pride had been deeply wounded by his exclusion from the Cabinet's inner circle: Attlee, Bevin, Cripps, Dalton and Morrison. Now his continued exclusion in favour of the rapidly promoted Gaitskell was hard to bear. Despite this he hung on, accepting a series of compromises, first over iron and steel and next over rearmament, a display of moderation with which he was later taunted. It was when Gaitskell refused to make the slightest gesture to keep him in the government that his bitterness boiled over. It was to distort his political judgement in the ensuing years.

Nonetheless his gut instinct had been right. The Cabinet was beginning to divide into two distinct camps. On the one hand there were those like Morrison who argued that the government's sweeping reforms had gone far enough and that it was time to 'consolidate'. On the other there were those led by Bevan who believed it was folly to call a halt until Labour had won control over what he was to call 'the commanding heights of the economy'. The rift was to be exacerbated by the different attitudes to American policy. Even Churchill had been shocked when, seven days after the Japanese forces surrendered, President Truman cut off without warning the Lend-Lease help in food and materials America had supplied us with during the war to enable us to concentrate on making munitions. He could not believe, Churchill told the House heavily, that a great nation like the United States would so treat her 'faithful ally who held the fort while their own American armaments were preparing'. The mild-mannered Attlee was goaded into using the strongest language the House had heard from him. Worse was to come when stunned MPs learned the terms on which the Americans insisted on a loan for which we had been obliged to apply in order to save us from bank-ruptcy. Among other things, sterling was to become convertible in two years – long before we had any hope of rebuilding our export trade. Among the twenty of us who went into the No division lobby against the terms, I found Aneurin's wife, Jennie Lee: a sure sign of the opposition Nye had voiced in Cabinet though he himself was silenced by collective responsibility.

Once again the rebels against the party's official policy were proved right. The impossible convertibility goal had to be abandoned. Through all this Gaitskell remained stubbornly loyal to America, not least in her foreign policy, which was increasingly dominated by cold war hysteria. The climax came with the Korean War which the Americans saw as proof that the Soviet Union under Stalin had a cunning plot to achieve the political and even military conquest of the West. Saner observers doubted this, as Denis Healey – a one-time cold warrior and Ernest Bevin's right-hand man – has belatedly admitted in his autobiography.[6] Aneurin was one of those who argued that a conquest policy was logistically impossible for a country like the Soviet Union whose major manufacturing industries had been crippled by war. When the United States demanded as the price of its continued economic help that Britain should adopt a massive three-year increase in its arms spending, Aneurin used the same logistical argument. He reluctantly accepted the first stage of increase to £3,600 million, a piece of loyalty which was to be used against him as showing he had no objection in principle, but when, in February 1951, Gaitskell agreed to boost the three-year programme to £4,700 million and levied charges on the NHS to help pay for it, Aneurin's patience snapped and he resigned.

In a sense his misery at this break with what he considered the first government to use parliamentary power positively was to prove his greatest handicap. In the debate which followed his resignation he lashed about like a wounded animal, making a disastrous personal statement in the House and alienating colleagues of the parliamentary Labour Party by his bitterness.

It was left to more calculating strategists such as Harold Wilson and Dick Crossman to exploit the reasoning behind his case. Harold Wilson and John Freeman, who resigned with him, made personal statements of impeccable moderation, though insisting that war-ravaged Britain had neither the skilled manpower nor the materials to make the inflated rearmament programme a reality. The Labour government, they argued, would merely drain its resources in a futile attempt. Gaitskell would not listen, but others were impressed. One of Winston Churchill's first acts, when he took office again following the general election of October 1951, was to abandon the target as unattainable and cut the rearmament programme down to a manageable size. In announcing his decision to Parliament he mockingly rubbed salt into Aneurin's wounds with a back-handed compliment to 'The Rt Hon. Gentleman, Member for Ebbw Vale, . . . for having, it appears by accident, perhaps not for the best of motives, happened to be right.'

But Aneurin had done more than win the logistical argument. He had put himself at the head of a growing protest against the cold war policies which threatened to plunge the world into another war at a time when nuclear weapons were being developed by both East and West. This was the major theme of the Keep Left group of which

Dick Crossman, Michael Foot and Ian Mikardo were the instigators. It was this issue which split the party far more than any mere temperamental tantrums could have done.

In the ensuing years of conflict Nye twisted and turned between acts of passionate defiance on behalf of the policies he believed were being betrayed by the leadership and expressions of his deep-seated yearning for party unity. Gaitskell, untroubled by doubts, continued his unremitting campaign to get Aneurin expelled from the party, but without success. Every year the constituency parties elected Bevan top of the poll for their section of the National Executive, while rejecting Gaitskell, but Aneurin was unsatisfied. He wanted the whole party to give him the recognition he felt was his due. He achieved this at last in 1956 when he was elected party treasurer by a respectable majority of the votes of the whole conference. The scenes when his election was announced were extraordinary. Delegates not only cheered and waved their papers, but clambered over the seats to shake his hand. The mood was not so much one of triumph as of relief – shared even by the most hostile of the trade unions who at last realized the party could not afford to dispense with this brilliant man.

Nye's election was a turning point for the party and for Bevan himself. With his wounds assuaged he turned all his energies to winning the next election under Gaitskell's leadership. When Harold Macmillan pulled a Tory victory out of his showman's hat again in 1959, Aneurin continued his healing role. At the inquest held by the party conference a few weeks later the press sat poised, notebook in hand, for the anticipated row. How could the left allow Gaitskell to get away with this second ignominious electoral defeat under his leadership? As current party chairman, flanked by Gaitskell and Nye, I opened the proceedings from the chair with a left-wing speech. Gaitskell followed with one of familiar insensitivity, blaming the defeat on the unpopularity of nationalization and all left-wing works. When Aneurin rose to wind up the debate everyone waited expectantly for a counterblast. It never came. Instead he proceeded to tease his audience both inside and outside conference with gentle wit. The press, he told us, had forecast a party terminally split, but how could that be? Here was Barbara in her chairman's speech quoting with approval his argument that 'socialism in the context of modern society meant the conquest of the commanding heights of the economy'. And here, too, was Gaitskell quoting the same phrase. Even as a board school boy, he had been taught Euclid's deduction that if two things are equal to a third thing, they are equal to each other. So, far from being split, we were a kind of trinity. And to the delight of delegates he added mischievously: 'What does that make me – the Holy Ghost?' Everyone relaxed in laughter.

It was the last speech Bevan was to make to a party conference and it gave him a moral ascendancy over his clumsy former antagonist. Never again was Gaitskell able to ride roughshod over his views.

His last great speech to the House of Commons had been made some three weeks earlier in the debate on the Queen's Speech. Aneurin had been given the job of winding up for the opposition and I remember thinking how nervous I would have been at such a responsibility: I would have been in the Commons library to the last minute, checking up on the statistical ammunition I was going to fire at the enemy. I was therefore taken aback to discover Aneurin, relaxed and unperturbed, having a drink with his coterie of political cronies round their usual table in the corner of the Smoking Room. I joined them and sat bemused as they parried each other's jokes. An attendant came in to tell Aneurin the minister was about to begin his winding-up speech for the government. Reluctantly he left us and arrived at the opposition front bench just in time. He sat there without a note, nor did he take any as the minister gloated over his party's 'You've never had it so good' victory. The Tory benches behind him were crowded with triumphant MPs flushed with post-prandial determination to wreck Aneurin's speech.

The scene which followed was unforgettable. It was as though the lions had turned on Nero instead of on the Christians. Quietly

Aneurin admitted that the Tories had won a spectacular electoral victory, but went on to warn that both parties had failed to solve the outstanding problem in a modern democracy: how to persuade the people to forgo immediate satisfactions for future economic strength or, as he often put it, 'how to persuade the people not to eat the seed corn of tomorrow's harvest'. The post-war Labour government had failed to solve the problem because the austerity it had to impose in order to build up the country's resources had cost it power. His indictment of the Tory government was that it had not even tried.

Tory backbenchers listened uneasily. There were mutterings of protest but no serious heckling. Despite themselves they were impressed by Aneurin's warning that Britain was enjoying a 'shallow affluence' which would leave her ill-prepared for the economic struggles which lay ahead. It was a message which is of even greater relevance to the consumerist society in which we live today.

In December Aneurin had an operation for stomach cancer and lived only for another six months. Gaitskell did not survive him long, dying of a mysterious illness in 1963. I was not the only one who believed that if Bevan had outlived him he would have become party leader and in due course a great Prime Minister.

Among the many lessons Aneurin Bevan can teach the Labour Party is the virtue of tolerance. We must respect other people's ideas, even if we disagree with them, provided they are honestly held and not just a sham to hide the holder's real purposes. 'Politics', Aneurin wrote in his book, 'is an art, not a science'; the art of working with fallible human beings, of applying one's principles to a given situation and learning from the result, with a view not to abandoning those principles but to applying them more effectively. Freedom to explore, to challenge, to test and to criticize must be sacrosanct.

The tragedy of Aneurin's political life, apart from his lasting memorial in the NHS, was that other members of the Labour Cabinet did not share this doctrine in the crisis of 1951. If Bevan had not been forced out of the government by Gaitskell's rigid arithmetic, he could have forged a creative partnership with Gaitskell much earlier. The magnificent political drive of the post-war Labour governments need not have petered out in defeat and the years in the wilderness need never have taken place.

Contrary to appearances, Aneurin was capable of unsuspected intellectual humility. 'The influence of ideas on social events is profound', he wrote in *In Place of Fear*, 'and is no less so because things turn out differently from what we expect.' And he added scathingly: 'Disillusionment is a bitter fruit reaped only by the intellectually arrogant.' One just picks oneself up and tries again.

For Aneurin was above all a realist. In the 1945 government he even advocated an incomes policy on socialist grounds, believing that you cannot plan an economy without planning wages: an approach which was vehemently attacked by the left when Wilson tried it in the 1960s.

Nor had Nye any patience with industrial action which threatened the economic recovery being promoted by the trade unions' own Labour government. He was still harping on this theme when inquests were being held in the party on its electoral defeat in 1959. In a discussion on the NEC he rejected the facile assumption that nationalization was to blame and argued that the growing number of disruptive down-tool strikes was the more likely cause. Turning to the trade union representatives on the Executive he told them gently: 'I say to my trade union friends that the trade unionist votes at the polls against the consequences of his own industrial anarchy.'

I had these words in mind ten years later when, as Secretary of State for Employment, I had the responsibility of advising Cabinet on what we should do about the Donovan report on industrial relations. In my White Paper, 'In Place of Strife', I balanced a charter of trade union rights with their need to accept some responsibility in helping a Labour government to deal with unofficial strikes. My proposals drew down on my head a shower of vilification from both

Labour MPs and the unions. What angered my critics even more than the proposals was the title I had chosen. They suspected, and rightly, that I was calling Bevan's own views in aid and I still do.

That is why I believe that Aneurin, if he were alive today, would be irritated by New Labour's claim to have a monopoly of ideas for bringing the party and the unions up to date. All his life Aneurin had pioneered new ideas with which the 'modernizers' are only just catching up: democratizing the unions, abolishing the old-style block vote, giving individual members of the party a greater say, recognizing the need to accept a mixed economy. He even pioneered the televising of Parliament in order to break down its secret-society atmosphere. When he launched this idea in his famous speech in 1959 it was greeted with groans of dismay from many quarters of the House, but he profoundly believed that without the political education which Parliament ought to provide, we should never be able to build up a strong economy by persuading people to accept the importance of long-term investment and spending on essential infrastructure as against the short-term satisfactions of tax cuts, consumer credit booms, government bribes to go private and arbitrary leaps in share dividends: to say nothing of the escapist enticements of the national lottery.

But the premises on which Aneurin's proposals were built remained stubbornly socialist. The individual could only fulfil himself or herself in the context of an enabling society, in which collective action organized by the state gives everyone a chance. Economic strength could not be built on the existence of a deprived underclass. We must not allow the ethic of consumerism to condemn the producers to the sweated labour conditions dictated by capitalism at its most savagely competitive.

Above all Aneurin would have mistrusted the modern politician's verbal flourishes. Misty phrases would have left him cold, whether John Major's talk of 'family values' or the rhetorical generalization of the new Clause IV. What mattered to him was action. 'Social institutions', he wrote, 'are what they do, not necessarily what we say they do. It is the verb that matters, not the noun.' One firm, specific commitment was worth a thousand purple passages.

So he warns politicians of both left and right against the 'old words' of which they are in danger of becoming prisoners: phrases which persist even when the reality behind them has changed. 'For', he warns, 'if they are out of touch with reality, the masses are not.' They judge the validity of Labour's rhetoric by the extent to which their own conditions change.

Not least, Labour must not succumb to the values of the materialist society. Apart from anything else, Tories would always beat socialists in playing that card. It would be fatal to try to outbid them. All his life Aneurin had had his ear to the ground, sensing undercurrents of protest which went wider than most politicians realized. He would have sensed the tide of revulsion against the Tories in the 1997 election as he had done in 1945. Of course people wanted a better life for themselves but most people, he believed, were unhappy at living in a country dominated by a 'pull up the ladder, Jack, I'm all right' morality. The effects of such a philosophy surround and menace us on every side. I am confident that he would today be urging Labour to harness that negative revulsion to a positive demand for a new social order based on zero tolerance of poverty, inequality and joblessness. Beveridge's five giant evils still remain to be overcome.

DAI SMITH

'The Ashes onto the Wind'

Bevan and Wales

> The student of politics must . . . seek neither universality nor
> immortality for his ideas and for the institutions through
> which he hopes to express them. What he must seek is integrity
> and vitality. His Holy Grail is the living truth, knowing that
> being alive the truth must change.
>
> Aneurin Bevan, *In Place of Fear*

In 1944, famously or infamously, Aneurin Bevan, MP for Ebbw Vale
since 1929, rose in the House of Commons during the first ever
Welsh Day debate to declare there was no 'Welsh problem' as such
– only those social ills and economic difficulties which beset Wales
as they did other, similar parts of the British Isles. In the summer of
1959, as the Labour Party prepared itself to fight the last election in
which Bevan would play a part, he surprised some of his Welsh
parliamentary colleagues by not only supporting Llanelli MP Jim
Griffiths's plea for a Welsh Office but logically arguing that having
a minister meant having a seat in the Cabinet with full Cabinet
responsibilities for the specific duties to be undertaken in Wales. And
those duties were, largely, those already devolved administratively.
Labour fought and lost that election with the proposal for a Welsh
Secretary of State as one of the planks of its manifesto. Before the
summer of 1960 had ended, Bevan was dead. In 1964 James Griffiths
became that first ever Welsh Secretary. Since then, as commissions
deliberated and devolution became the oval ball of Welsh politics –

run with, fumbled, kicked to touch, kept in the stands – Bevan's fragmentary opinions have mattered and have been claimed, justifiably given their seeming self-contradiction, by both sides in the ongoing debate. All this would be a futile exercise in hero-citation, and one which Bevan would have scorned, if it were not for one other factor, one very particular to this politician: he had a philosophy of political action that went beyond the merely contingent. An apparently contra-dictory stance may be the result of a change of mind or of circumstance over a fifteen-year period or it may conceal a stunning indifference to the actual form democratic politics takes, provided it remains accountable and the outcome liberates more than it controls.

The Welsh Day debate had taken place in October 1944. Bevan's contribution was typically brisk and unsentimental, sardonic even. Historians have since cited Jim Griffiths's autobiography *Pages from Memory* for its view that Bevan's long-standing doubt about the cre-ation of a Welsh Office stemmed from an antipathy to 'nationalism which divided peoples' and a concomitant fear that Welsh 'political activity' might be divorced 'from the mainstream of British politics'.[1] This is clearly a fair assessment. However, in the context of earlier and later pages in that same autobiography Bevan's actual position is always qualified by the other possibilities he also accepted. In July 1943 Bevan was Vice-Chair (with Megan Lloyd George) of the Welsh Parliamentary Party (representing all MPs in Wales), a body which had Griffiths as its secretary. They wrote to the Prime Minister to indicate that, with the unanimous support of the members, a sub-committee was being established to consider 'the problems of the future government of Wales, and in particular the establishment of a Welsh Office with a Secretary of State'. Undoubtedly Bevan was one of those who would disagree about the desirable extent of 'administrative devolution' but, equally, his signature on the letter indicates he was not far, if at all, from the prevailing view that what should be trans-ferred were 'those departments . . . in which there was already some degree of devolution in the form of the Welsh Department of

Education and the Welsh Board of Health'. This limited devolvement, after all, is precisely what he also signed up for in 1959. We can interpret his all-Wales health service administrative machinery (along with Griffiths's identical social insurance system) in the same light: not sentiment but being sensible of the widespread, existing pattern (seventeen government departments with Welsh administrative units by the late 1950s and under, since 1951, a Conservative Minister for Welsh Affairs).

By 1959 there was no conceivable reason why Bevan should have opposed the main planks of a proposal which, in principle, he had accepted as possible in 1943. Admittedly, neither he nor the Labour governments of 1945–51 had made 'the government of Wales', in a separate sense, any kind of priority. Bevan could not have minted his dictum 'the language of priorities is the religion of socialism' with any better cause in mind than the specific legislative drive of the Labour government during those years and besides, he was clearly on a flood tide of Welsh approbation for his political actions. The Council for Wales, established in 1948 with an old friend of Bevan's at the helm, the trade union leader Huw T. Edwards, was not especially favoured by Bevan who, rightly, regarded it as a superior talking shop which was neither accountable nor responsible. If you were to have proper responsibility you needs must be accountable. This was the logic Bevan applied in 1959.

The longer term question of his views on further devolution and some kind of elected Welsh political forum is strictly unanswerable. We know that Bevan was a clear, consistent opponent of the Parliament for Wales campaign inaugurated in the 1950s and led by, among others, Welsh Labour MPs such as Goronwy Roberts and S. O. Davies. But Jim Griffiths was just as committed an opponent of that initiative. Bevan did not live to see the growth in Welsh Office powers under both Conservative and Labour governments. There is no reason to assume he would have been concerned since the same question of Cabinet responsibility and parliamentary accountability would have been in place and was answered. Where he would have stood in the referendum debate of 1979 is more of a moot point: his friend and successor as MP for Ebbw Vale, Michael Foot, offered support and loyalty to the Labour government's scheme; his fellow townsman and, by common consent, the nearest thing to an heir apparent we had seen, Neil Kinnock, then MP for Bedwellty, was, along with Leo Abse, MP for Pontypool, a scathing denouncer of the democratic inadequacies of the proposed Assembly; in my view Bevan would have been unlikely to be swayed by the 'patriotic' appeals that Michael Foot could resist less easily and, if at the height of his own powers, more likely to take a scalpel to the flabby arguments used to dress up the proposal. What I think is unarguable is that Bevan would have railed until he dropped at the manner in which an incremental growth in devolved powers, through the 1980s into the 1990s, went hand-in-pocket with a superstructure of unelected, unrepresentative bodies and the downgrading of local government power. That might have led him to consider the whole matter of electoral politics with a distinct Welsh dimension in a different manner from the one he certainly professed in his lifetime.

In those days, the imperatives of class politics, in and beyond Britain, was what exercised his mind and he consistently depicted Wales, or rather his significant part of it, as at the forefront of those 'advanced movements'. In other words, as with most of the Welsh over the whole period of his life, the question of Wales, *per se*, was not one to which he gave much thought in isolation. It was what had taken place inside Wales through its industrial history which concerned him and, by extension, how the people who had undergone that experience might make dynamic social capital out of their material exploitation. Those factors could not be kept within national boundaries, whether Welsh or any other kind.

However, Bevan was an acute reader of the specificities of lives on the ground and a stern critic of those, whether on the left or the right, who would deprive people of the requirement of self-definition.

He would not have failed to notice how, for many, that had come to include a deeper sense of their Welshness. Provided this was in an inclusive rather than excluding sense Bevan would surely not have applauded the shallow thinking, as evinced by some recent members of his own party, which scorns the only thing we really know about ourselves: the past. He would have been at one with those, on both sides of the argument within his own party, who would wish to restore some measure of control over socio-economic trends, however powerful and trans-national, to the people whose lives are otherwise bent to their impersonal and ahistorical whim. That would not have seemed utopian to him. That was the essence of his political rationale. It is not so abundantly obvious exactly how it is to be done that we should second-guess the way in which Bevan's own stance might have shifted. If, on the other hand, we can tease out what Aneurin Bevan might have preferred in place of the Wales that has actually emerged since 1960 we might come closer to answering a more pressing conundrum: and that is, how do we restore the insights Bevan's life and work have left us to the debate on an emerging Wales.

There are two ways to examine Aneurin Bevan's actual response to the leading issues of his own time and his projected attitude to those of the immediate future: first, by considering his practice and, secondly, by sifting his views. As so often with Bevan, that reviler of 'romantic biographies', his cool irony had anticipated and deflated the practice. A full year before the war ended, and with Churchill ready for a peacetime dividend that did not come, Bevan reflected: 'This is . . . the immortal tragedy of all public life, that the *hero's* need of the people outlasts *their* need of him. *They* obey the pressures of contemporary conditions while *he* strives to perpetuate the situation where he stood supreme. *He* is therefore overwhelmed by a nostalgia for past glory whereas *they* are pushed on by new needs, impelled by other hopes and led by other nascent heroes.'

Since Bevan pointedly dismissed hero-worship as an immature pursuit it is clear where his own instincts lay – with contemporary conditions, change and hope. It is a measure of his continuing importance, now as icon more than influence, to note how, even at the blushing rose-pink dawn of New Labour, his own authority and glory is still claimed across the spectrum and the decades. It was scarcely surprising that Tredegar-born Neil Kinnock, as modernizing leader of a torn Labour Party, should invoke Nye's name, quote his words and assume his mantle at conference after conference in the 1980s: it was a tribute and a comforting necessity so to do as his own name was linked to the legacy of Gaitskell. If, under Tony Blair, that battle was decisively concluded with the refutation of Clause IV and the rewriting of the party's constitution, there might seem little space left for the man who did, after all, say he owed more to Marxism than any other political creed and never apologized for telling the world in 1948 that so far as he was concerned Tories who had, in the inter-war years, 'condemned millions of first class people to semi-starvation' were 'lower than vermin'. Such remarks might have once underpinned the anathema with which Bevan was regarded by Cabinet colleagues such as Herbert Morrison but Morrison's highly influential grandson, Peter Mandelson, M P, had no hesitation, in 1996, in placing Bevan and Blair on the last page of *The Blair Revolution*.[2] Bevan is quoted for asserting that 'Free men can use free institutions to solve the social and economic problems of the day.' The index tells us to look up the word 'socialism' under the heading for 'New Labour'. As contemporary politicians seek the advantage of a past authority and achievement, Bevan has become cut off from the contemporary conditions which his own life had attuned him to meet.

Aneurin Bevan's own emphasis in *In Place of Fear* was that his whole life had been shaped and circumscribed by the factors (iron, coal, steel) which had industrialized Tredegar, South Wales and, of course, comparable places in Britain.[3] His concern was to use the condition as a catalyst to effect change, not to see it as a genetic code to excuse stasis or deference. In my *Aneurin Bevan and the World of South Wales*,[4] I argued that imagining his culture – the whole way of life that had formed him, not only the spotlight of biographical facts but also its penumbra of social existence – was an essential precondition to comprehending his politics. I had not quite understood how much of a social closure I had implied by so integrating South Wales's greatest political figure with a declining cultural formation. In a stimulating and challenging essay review in *History Workshop Journal*,[5] Dr Chris Williams reminded me both of that factor and of the further necessity of turning the narrative lacuna into a social and political caesura. He wrote: 'the challenge for the next generation of Welsh historians . . . is to come to terms with the South Wales that Bevan, dying in 1960, would never see.'

The full weight of those remarks, however, goes way beyond the historical profession even if it is they who will need to clear the social waters we have let grow stagnant with suspended ambition. It is the practice of politics, of defused common purpose as in the miners' strikes of the 1970s and 1980s and of diffused civic intentions as in the palpable turning away from political faith, which has helped atrophy the culture which once gave South Wales its local vibrancy and its wider significance – the culture that moulded the public and representative Bevan as its finest exemplar. Of course, the primary, forcing factors have been de-industrialization, the decline of heavy, male-dominated single industry communities, the coming of service industries, of white collar work and in-migration, of inward capital investment and the de-skilling of a significant part of the working class, of spotted but long term unemployment and social–spatial differentials. A sociological, socio-linguistic, socio-economic profile written as bullet points in managerial landscape-style, with the demographic shifts of the politely named Groups A–E clearly outlined, is nowadays an essential snapshot analysis of our new world. Shot from space, naturally, or wherever minds once were, for all this is to allow Bevan's famous noun (of description) to subvert his desired verb (of action). Societies of purpose are what they choose to become, not what they settle to be.

Through his own formative period, down to the early 1920s, the dominant regional politics all around Bevan were very different from those that would be espoused in his heyday. This was true of both the trade unions and of the county councils whose committees, in turn, he would join. Nor was he ever a great believer in the inviolability of political institutions. He had a sceptical notion of Parliament and its traditions: not even democratically elected, he felt, until 1929 (when he entered the House of Commons) and whose televising he ardently promoted in debate decades before it became remotely fashionable to do so. That was in order to maintain a bond between the voters and those they elected. He had no time for tradition if tradition's purpose only served to keep corners of public life away from the democratic gaze. At the same time constitutionalism was a sterile game played by those who had proved incapable of joining in the potentially fertile process of political power-seeking: what he did by accepting a Secretary of State for Wales was cold-eyed, pragmatic, almost indifferent to the nature of the change provided the practice brought results. And that was what his culture, his deep social formation, had taught him.

This, above all, is what continues to make an understanding of Bevan, in all his complexity, relevant to us today – that he fused attachment to a core of principles (his libertarian, democratic and socialist creed) to a politics aligned to the practicalities of what was achievable (for that majority who were not privileged). Where the tension between the two became unbearable he did not retreat from the former but he did resign from the latter. Power had to have meaning beyond itself if it was to be renewable. You could do little without it. You did less if you simply held it. That was what caused him to resign in 1951 and that was also why, after 1955, however reluctantly, he supported Gaitskell. It was the Welsh dimension to his politics which made him want to root that democratic branch in a wider British life.

The Wales of his first decade was recognizably the Wales of his last decade. Momentous changes had occurred but a visitor to Tredegar or Rhondda or even Cardiff in 1956 – the first year of that city's existence as a capital – would have seen the same basic infrastructure as in 1906. Half a century of coal boom and bust, of a thriving export trade in the huge docks of Barry, Cardiff and Newport, mass unemployment and out-migration of the Welsh people so that population did not rise between 1921 and 1961, and even the welfare security of the 1940s and the shallow affluence of the 1950s had not altered the basic dependency of the Welsh economy – from Brymbo to Bedwas – on coal extraction and steel production. What had been lost in the thrusting economic terms of a madcap capitalism had been replaced by a really deep sense of societal ownership. Nationalization was not, as Bevan the old syndicalist well knew, the panacea – and he had been an early advocate of a mixed economy in which public and private partners took their designated roles – but it was not an advance which would have been rejected at the time. In a sense it was an anchored world, moored for the foreseeable future against the kind of storms which had buffeted it so hard. Only the future was scarcely foreseeable.

A decade after Bevan's death two Labour governments had reduced the coalmining workforce in South Wales from 100,000 to 38,000 and thus, themselves, paved the way for the social defiance which the increasingly militant mining communities, not just the affected workforces, would offer as their sole defence against 'higher' economic wisdom. Now, in 1997, there is, after a perhaps avoidable maelstrom, only one deep-coal mine left as a working pit in South Wales, and that is a worker co-operative. This is still quite unimaginable stuff to those who thought South Wales and those particular communities – whether in coal or any other heavy industry – would always be synonymous. The phrase 'cultural materialism', a concept which encapsulates the profoundly liberating argument (and actual outcome) that men and women could create their own civilizations out of intractable reality, was given vivid life by the history of these people. And, let us be brutal about this, it has been submerged in the years since Bevan's death. We have instead been inhabiting an archipelago of historical vanity ringed by coral reefs of nostalgia.

We can, of course, blame Bevan and those he represents for much of this. How can we live up to them? Why weren't they more perfect? How could they be so ambitious? Why did they fall so short? Two men I admired greatly spent large parts of their lives lamenting the fallen City of Dreams that once was South Wales: the writer Gwyn Thomas (1913–81) who wrote two unperformed plays about Bevan and the historian Gwyn A. Williams (1925–95) who tried to fashion Bevan into the unlikely form of a Welsh Gramsci (a Doppelgänger role in which Gwyn played the more vocal part). The novelist was in his teens by the time of the General Strike and, essentially, the world had already fired his imagination: after the traumas of 1921 and 1926 survival was the only vitamin deficiency South Wales did not have. Gwyn A. Williams's generation twisted any number of ways in the winds of sectarian fashion, eager to escape the bad news that 1945 And All That was a tidying-up job, not a blueprint for further advance. Bevan was central to their dreams. Indeed, he not only shared them, he lived them. He too felt the despair at what might have been; as he so poignantly told Geoffrey Goodman in 1959 – 'History gave them [the British working class] the chance – and they didn't take it.' Though, to be sure, and as Michael Foot's biographical masterpiece makes clear by context and by quotation, that mood could drift away and even at the very end of his life the challenge to enlarge expectation was to the forefront of his mind. At the Blackpool conference, an electoral post-mortem, in his last great speech Bevan informed the delegates but only reminded himself that:

The fact is . . . that a very considerable number of young men and women in the course of the last five or ten years have had their material conditions improved and their status has been raised in consequence and their discontents have been reduced, so

that temporarily their personalities are satisfied with the framework in which they live. They are not conscious of constriction;
they are not conscious of frustration or of limitation as formerly
they were, in exactly the same way as even before the war large
numbers of workers were not sufficiently conscious of frustration
and limitation, even on unemployment benefit, to vote against the
Tories.

What is the lesson for us? It is that we must enlarge and expand
those personalities, so that they can become again conscious of
limitation and constriction. The problem is one of education,
not of surrender.

It had been an opportunity for the man who was then the elder
statesman of the Labour Party to indicate, however gently, that he
(born in 1897) had been this way before. For Bevan had the memory
of a real landscape, in political terms, that had not been mapped out,
and so reduced in the mind, at all. This was especially true of Tredegar
and Monmouthshire where Labour political domination was not
secured, at either district or county level, until the late 1920s. The
county of Glamorgan, with more intensive and breakneck industrializ-
ation behind it and, except on its southern extremities, devoid of
countervailing influence, was embroiled by then in debates about the
efficacy of *which* 'socialism' – the communist or the Labour kind.
Both the geography and the sociology of Bevan's patch were more
diverse. The social and economic constrictions, as he later put it, were
nonetheless obvious. They were to be met, by those of Bevan's fiery
persuasion, down to the 1920s by a 'direct action' outlook, via the
South Wales Miners' Federation, and its local offshoots. Behind that,
at least for the minority who were consciously attempting to channel
the workforce's disgruntlement (some 270,000 coal miners in South
Wales by 1920), was a programme of working-class education (vari-
ously in the Plebs League classes and the Central Labour College) of
which Bevan partook voraciously.

There had been no national Labour governments. The Labour administrations in South Wales had been, at best, patchy and scarcely at all of socialist intent. A philosophy of Lib-Labism was deeply ingrained. Autodidacticism and union activity were elemental but heavily dependent, for effectiveness, on an almost impossibilist combination of constant mass strife and self-sacrifice. Bevan and various colleagues, maybe by dint of necessity in the company town of Tredegar, began to forge a political culture or rather, as time went on, to let culture shape the political formations they neither possessed nor inherited. Between the rock of the great strikes and the hard place of the welfare state they found a place for the individual life.

Labour lost its temporary control of Monmouthshire County Council in 1923 and in Tredegar Urban District Council did not regain it until 1928. These intervening years were crucial. How would a new Labour Party root itself in these drifting and uncertain communities? It was a question the young Bevan directly addressed. Neither the economy nor the social fabric of industrial South Wales was established, as it had been since the 1840s, any more. Clearly a people, defined by religious persuasion and social custom as much as by aimless aggregation, had not become a proletariat, and in the classically defined sense never would. The brilliance of Bevan's earliest foray into political endeavour lay in his capacity to see the issue as an ethical one that had to be underpinned by a cultural commitment. Defining the latter would not be done in a study – though, notoriously, Bevan read incessantly in these years and, later, was instrumental in building the Tredegar Institute Library into the finest in a coalfield whose every pit village and township would strive to provide access to the information technology weapons of the day – books, films, journals, newspapers and radio. Education, to succeed as Bevan wanted it to succeed, could not have the whiff of the schoolroom about it; it should not degenerate into a solo voice and a megaphone of righteousness. He would, therefore, have approved of the Carnegie Trust's plan in 1930 to provide wireless sets in fourteen centres across the coalfield where people could gather and listen – to drama, variety theatre, sport and news. Their report said:

> The wireless set has brought much pleasure and variety into the lives of many people who, before it came, had little to talk about except the perennial subjects of how to make ends meet. As one man remarked, wireless had brought 'happiness' into the place. [The sets are] . . . intended to be used for amusement and recreation as well as for instruction. It would be entirely wrong for anyone to suppose that the wireless set was to be looked upon as a kind of schoolmaster. Such an attitude would show a complete misapprehension of the whole business. The thing which wireless can do is to bring into every Institute the living voice . . . discussing all kinds of subject, subjects which have a broad human value and are not confined to any one way of life or any one attitude towards it.

Now we can grasp why Bevan was not being frivolous when he made one of his earliest interventions as a Monmouthshire county councillor in 1928 – he wanted local cinemas to be allowed to open on Sundays (thus, his critics alleged, 'ushering in the worst excesses of the Continent'). Popular culture was not an opiate. On the contrary, the pleasure principle was a release trigger that exposed what constriction and frustration really were. Enjoyment of life was a necessity for socialists. Articulation of that necessity became Bevan's mission.

They knew they inhabited an old iron and coal town in a depressed industrial area in the very maw of the world capitalist slump. What should they put in its place? Bevan and the circle of friends in the Query Club – always a question – acted with the intensity of those short of time and behind in the race. Soon they outstripped the rest of South Wales, and thereby Britain. At least they could show the skeleton of ambition. Flesh was for later bones, ones put in the right order of priority. Bevan presided over a range of unprecedented activity, all radiating from the Labour Party. Events proliferated, big and small, from teas and dances to the Labour Players' amateur dramatic group, from jazz bands and street carnivals to sports days and choral meetings, from cinema showings of all manner of films, from Europe as well as America, to whist drives and brass band parades. There were regular Sunday evening lectures on socialist culture throughout the winter months of 1924 and an array of visiting speakers. Bevan was justified in boasting that 'in Tredegar they could congratulate themselves upon organizing a Labour movement second to none in South Wales and they had every phase of the movement provided for even to an orchestra which was promising to become a very fine one.'

A hallmark of his thinking was heard as early as 1925 when he told fellow councillors, with Independents and ratepayers in the majority, that a 'rabbit warren home led to a rabbit warren life' and that their plans to squash sixteen homes to an acre in blocks of six (instead of the previous Labour council's decision for blocks of two with twelve homes apiece and an extra room downstairs) would create 'slums of the future'. He was scornful of the cost cutting which had no regard 'to the artistic and aesthetic aspect of the scheme'.

Throughout this time he built with words a picture of a town in which amenities were shared and the beauty of a man-made landscape treasured as much as the wilder hills he adored walking. No one has unearthed the detail of this more effectively than Dr Sue Demont in her work on Tredegar politics and society in Bevan's formative years.[6] Her summation rises to this climax:

It was no accident that this surge of extra-political activity occurred in the years following the miners' defeat in 1921 and the local electoral setbacks of 1922. It was clear to Aneurin Bevan, if less immediately to others, that if the Labour Party were to run and retain power on the basis of its ability to act as the vehicle for working people's aspirations then it had to root itself much more firmly in its communities of origin by becoming involved in as many different aspects of local life as possible – sport, the arts, light entertainment, hospital administration, the library, the Workmen's Institute, even the governing body of the County School . . . [and] by 1929 he had held the chairmanship of the Miners' Welfare Committee, the Workmen's Library, the County Omnibus Committee, the Unemployment Committee and the vice-chairmanship of the Hospital Committee. He had represented Tredegar on the Monmouthshire Association of UDCs, the Western Valleys Sewerage Board and the Court of Governors of the University of South Wales and Monmouthshire . . . [He presided over] not merely political meetings, . . . but also benefit concerts and cultural occasions such as the first dramatic performance by the 'Labour Players' and a recital by a visiting Russian violinist. His engagements [from January to March 1926, a typical run] . . . included . . . an address to a thousand children of the unemployed of Tredegar at a special tea party, speaking at the opening of the Dukestown Workmen's Institute and acting as one of two judges of the Sirhowy Valley heat of the Miners' Road Race . . . [And] on all of these occasions Bevan was present not in an individual capacity but as a representative of the Labour Party, of both its political and industrial wings, which in turn was the representative of his class.

The flamboyant insolence which this representative Bevan exhibited, as an MP in London, and for which he was much mocked by colleagues and enemies (in his case the distinction was often blurred), was no foolish affectation. It was necessary to have 'enough energy to be rude', he told Durham miners in 1948, in order to 'be rude to the right people'. By then he was at the peak of his confidence in a Labour Britain he saw as only a move in the right direction towards the world he had imagined, and partly created, through his cultural initiatives of the 1920s. If we remove the film over the mind's eye that the powerful images of the Hungry Thirties have induced in Wales we might see that we now have more in common with a Wales that had not been so overdetermined. Aneurin Bevan responded to that challenge in his own time.

In our own we could find a ready tick-list of the aspects of life in the 1990s he would rage against – and unnecessary, deep-seated family poverty would be high on that list. Nor would he have any patience with that half-baked and quintessentially passive macro-economic theory, of globalization and money markets, which bypasses uncomfortably persisting notions of exploitation and resistance. He would, after the economic history of his own country in this century, stand amazed at the failure of some political experts to identify self-preening as the parrot's alternative and, at least, self-taught trick. For the rest, my guess is that his own political waters would find their own appropriate levels whether over the idea of Wales as a European region or on the question of a single European currency. It is not so much that you *could* claim him for both sides as which side will answer his persistent question about community empowerment and individual freedom. Of course they are hard questions. That is why he would have quizzed them long and hard from within his party. Evasion was never his style.

But it is upon his lifelong quest for a personal voice, a style if you will, with which to express the human dilemmas he first found in Wales that we must settle for proof of his continuing worth to us as thinker and doer. It is that example, more than anything, which we should use as a signifier of how mature citizens should face contemporary uncertainties – not by clutching at identities, antique or freshly drawn, but by embracing our culture, achieved and changing, so that we can celebrate the shape of our humanity in the places where we live.

Bevan's credo was based on such distinctiveness. How he would have despised the shallowness of those who promoted the consumption of the culture of others without supporting the production of our own. It was Bevan who signed on Alun Lewis, the young Welsh poet and short story writer, for *Tribune* in 1942 and Bevan who pulled George Orwell into that orbit. Israel Sieff recorded his friend, the philosopher-politician, shyly reading his unpublished poetry out loud and Jennie Lee emphasized, more than once, how dearly Nye would have enjoyed the equivalent of a university sabbatical. He would scarcely have had difficulty in agreeing that, in the late twentieth century, his fellow citizens will need retraining and re-skilling to find a niche in the global markets so transformed by the new, and coming, technology; nor would Bevan have rejected for an instant the drive to sustain economic well-being; but he would, surely, have asked then as he always did: for what purpose beyond the material do we propose these measures? Confronted by the quantum leap in the technology of communications made since 1960 Bevan, above all others, would have been amazed at the indifference or cynical disregard with which the elected have treated English language broadcasting in Wales for Wales. Here still is the most potent opportunity to articulate the voices of the people he chose to represent decade after decade. Amid the post-industrial uncertainties of South Wales in the 1990s, held afloat by no indigenous industry and on a geographical margin where once it had been a hub-and-spoke centre, Bevan would not have been content with the necessary support of one dependent, linguistic culture while a majority languished as cultural supplicants. One of his favourite novels was Stendhal's *Scarlet and Black*, perhaps because of its exquisite dissection of greed and snobbery, perhaps because in the character of Julien Sorel, conformist rebel and sexual predator, he detected the ambiguous careers of any number of Welsh parliamentarians, but, for certain, because he would see in that prophetic book the need for a rounded society to express its individuality by allowing its individuals social expression in a common pursuit.

Naturally, with Bevan attached to a project this could be no narrow pursuit. Nationalism was never a perspective he would adopt. To an extent his opening salvo in the Commons against David Lloyd George was directed against the facility of the professional patriotism employed by the ex-Prime Minister as much as against his chicanery in the miners' strike of 1919. Emblematic of Bevan's own relationship to a specifically Welsh culture was his pride in welcoming Paul Robeson, whose civil rights cause had been upheld by the South Wales miners, to the National Eisteddfod when that peripatetic body visited Ebbw Vale in 1958. Bevan then said that the Eisteddfod, an all-Welsh-language occasion which had caused controversy by going to 'anglicized' Ebbw Vale, was 'a monument to civilization'. Civilization was here rooted in one of Wales's languages; like all creative human acts it was to be cherished. It was an eisteddfod which did seek to unite the linguistic communities of Wales. Bevan was there on equal terms, symbol of what could be done if Wales 'spoke to the world'.

Despite financial losses since bad August weather caused poor attendance, it was a triumph. Not least for Bevan himself who was, for once, lauded in both the Conservative and the Welsh-language press. It seemed he could do no wrong and, one year before he shelved all formal doubts about the proposal for a Secretary of State for Wales, he responded to the focus of a Welsh-language world with warmth and generosity. Perhaps his geniality had been inspired by the presence of Robeson whom he introduced to a crowd of eight thousand in the Eisteddfod Pavilion, with another thousand in an overflow venue to hear, if not see, the two together. But, completely at ease and among his own in every sense, he went further and, in welcoming the festival to his constituency, as the *Western Mail* reported on 4 August 1958, he stressed that although 'We in Monmouthshire . . . speak English and no Welsh we are essentially a part of Wales [for] . . . Its characteristics are Welsh, its legends are Welsh.' So how should the duality of 'Wales and Monmouthshire' be ended? Why, by ignoring the foolish distinction and striking it out of official documents. And that done, he appealed to local authorities to use the parliamentary Act 'which gave them the power to spend money on cultural purposes . . . [to lead] to an artistic revival in Wales'. Vintage Bevan on his own patch.

Full circle. Gwyn Thomas caught that echo in the title of the first play he wrote on Nye – *Return and End* (1963). His second attempt in 1975 was *A Tongue for a Stammering Time* and, again, he returns Bevan to his beginnings, to the open moorland of the Waun above Tredegar where his three memorial stones now stand in perpetuity.[7] This Aneurin is not looking to make his own end any kind of terminus for others. His past is what should help us to a future. The play's time is 1958:

> It began here. I feel I'm hitting a new stride. I give you a pledge . . . I'm going to live another twenty years. I'm going to catch the world's ear. I'm going to switch the light on in rooms that have been dark for ages . . . Let us improve the slum of our beginning. Let us put contempt for others at the top of the list of deadliest things. We shall unclench our fists and minds. Let's stop frightening each other to death in shadows of our own creating. Let's make a happy morning and make a new kind of fuel of joy.

Almost uncannily, except that it penetrates to the essence of the meaning of Bevan, another distinguished socialist playwright, Trevor Griffiths, was drawn to a connected imagery of renewal. He closes his 1997 screenplay for BBC Wales by having Jennie Lee reconsider her actual words about Nye being born old.[8] She is addressing the large crowd gathered to hear her speak at the commemoration of the stones erected to his memory:

> 'For years and years, I would say that Nye Bevan never had a childhood in the conventional sense, that somehow he came into this world full grown. But I see now there is something to add

to that judgement; for if it is true he was born a man, it is equally true he died a boy . . .'

She turns, takes the urn . . . spills the ashes onto the wind.

In place of the Wales that was, Aneurin Bevan imagined the Welsh who might show the world how to live fulfilled lives in a country of their own making. His flaunted style of highly conscious being did not take away a people's sense of their own worth; it suggested what was latent in their wider consciousness. In place of Wales as an abstract entity he offered up a subtle, endlessly modulated language of citizenship to hold the quicksilver nature of a changing society. In place of a Wales which suffocated in provincial garb in either of its languages he stressed the links between 'a rich local life and a wide cosmopolitanism' since the one 'gives meaning and particularity to the other'. In place of Wales as a country which possesses us he taught us to create the Wales we desire.

JILL CRAIGIE

Political Blood Sport

My husband, Michael Foot, was Aneurin Bevan's best friend and close political ally long before we married; consequently much of our free time was spent with him and his wife, Jennie Lee. Nye's former constituents of Ebbw Vale, the ever-articulate Welsh, loved to talk about him long after his death. 'Aneurin', they would say, 'was like a great glowing furnace. You warmed yourself in his company and he lifted your spirits.' He could also scorch. Nye suffered fools badly, very badly; but still a snub from him could be a compliment. He expected everyone to be as intelligent as himself. The contrast between Nye, the man, and the Bevan of the headlines could be so extreme as to astonish people who met him for the first time. Those were the days before TV had entered the home, when press reports could be even more misleading than they may be today. He was wonderful company, witty with a brooding, soaring imagination and, as often as not, he had something fresh to say. The mere thought of him conjures up vivid scenes like a montage in a film.

First, to Handel's *Love in Bath* pouring out of the radiogram, Nye and Peter Ustinov, who happens to be present, spring to the parquet floor each to play at conducting their own imaginary orchestras. They interpret the joyous certainties of eighteenth-century England, implicit in the composition, with their feet, bodies, imaginary batons, even with their facial expressions. Both give fair imitations of the real thing, especially when first one then the other unexpectedly swivels round on his feet to point his baton for no more than a second at a couple of imaginary players. Only when a suggestion of poignancy flows into the music do their efforts teeter on the edge of farce. Neither could quite assume the air of the lovelorn. Whatever Peter's cogitations, Nye's capacity to lose himself in the music and with so much delight amazed us. Just at that time he was the victim of the most vicious smear campaign ever inflicted on an honourable politician.

Next snapshot: Nye in a fashionable restaurant, the focus of furtive attention from everyone in the room. People strain their ears to hear what is going on at his table, only to wonder, no doubt, at the sudden bursts of laughter.

I see him at Stratford-upon-Avon, in the theatre at the height of its glory, with Peggy Ashcroft playing Cordelia to John Gielgud's Lear. At a special dinner arranged by my friend Dot Hyson, wife of the actor-director Anthony Quayle, leading members of the cast half expect to meet a boorish buffoon who might tuck his napkin round his neck and eat from a knife. Nye's beguiling courtesy, appreciation of the performances and, especially, his sparkling exchange of views on the merit of *King Lear* – Shakespeare's warning to parents, according to him, not to relinquish their patrimony to their offspring before being safely tucked in their graves – almost made Bevanites of them all. On the river the following day, I remember Nye on a mountain of pillows half mocking, half admiring Michael's 'decadent, bourgeois' ability to handle a punt.

In a darker mood, during their only quarrel: Nye slowly raises my precious Sheraton chair as high as he can reach, intent, apparently, on bringing it crashing down on Michael's head. To add to the horror, a glimpse of Jennie revelling in the prospect. As it happens, Nye resists the temptation and wreaks his anger instead on the antique and the floor.

Finally, the memorable sight of Nye on the platform, a commanding presence, erect, facing his audience with confidence; an audience, whether hostile or not, likely to fall under his spell.

When Labour won the general election of 1945 the people had

voted unequivocally for a new world, for no return to the bad old days of mass unemployment; in short, for the better Britain defined in the Beveridge report. The report aimed to conquer the five giant evils – want, disease, ignorance, squalor and idleness. Under the heading 'Disease' a plan for a National Health Service had already been drawn up before Nye entered the Ministry of Health and Housing; but the plan included so many conflicting suggestions to appease vested interests of one sort or another that it pleased neither the doctors nor the minister.

Nye considered the gargantuan task afresh. To create a National Health Service available to all free of charge and, no less important, reasonably accessible to all – many of the specialists resided in Harley Street, London – clearly required a comprehensive redistribution of medical facilities and treatment combined with a co-ordinated plan for the location and status of the hospitals, many of which were solely dependent on charity. Having consulted various sections of the profession, Nye decided to put the hospitals under state control, in other words to nationalize them, besides abolishing the cash relationship between patients and doctors without interfering with clinical freedom – revolutionary decisions.

Nye's historic fight for the National Health Service is covered elsewhere in this book; suffice it to say here that, although he won with sensational speed the loyalty and admiration of his civil servants and some eminent medical practitioners, throughout his negotiations he had to contend with a real timidity on the part of some of his Cabinet colleagues, a grotesque distortion of his intentions by leaders of the BMA, dogged obstruction from the Tory opposition, and a continual stream of personal abuse from the press.[1] He was also under intense pressure not to introduce the service on the date of his choice, 5 July 1948. Even as late as June, *The Times* launched an impressive correspondence urging postponement on the grounds that 'it is quite impossible for the Minister to provide the facilities required'. Sir Frederick Menzies, an influential name within the profession, followed: 'The truth is nothing is ready. Nor will it be ready for another two or three years. We are a nucleus of people trying to point out that the Government has sold the public a pup.' The weight of medical opinion on the state of unreadiness incited laymen to take up the cry. Under the heading 'The New Health Swindle', the Vicar of St Gabriel's, Cricklewood, advised his parishioners 'not to fall ill before July 5 or they might make a job for him'.

Headlines in the news such as 'LONG QUEUES OF OUT-PATIENTS LIKELY TO SWAMP HOSPITALS' accompanied calls for the minister's resignation or replacement. Accusations of ministerial inexperience, incompetence, hot-headedness and reckless impatience seemed mild compared with the enraged taunts of opponents who called him 'a medical Führer, who sought to impose National Socialism on the people, for which we had just defeated Germany'.

Nye remained unmoved. 'If we wait for everything to be ready,' he said, 'it will never be ready.' He wanted the health service 'to be growing, changing, improving all the time'. 'Expectations will always exceed capacity,' he told a meeting of nurses. 'If there is a shortage of doctors on July 5, when the cash relationship between doctors and patients will disappear, it is very much more important that the doctors who are in short supply should spend their time looking after patients who really need to be looked after than that they should spend their time looking after a lot of hypochondriacs who can afford to pay.' Nobody knew for certain how many doctors would join the service nor to what degree it might receive public support. Nye alone appeared to be buoyed up by an inner confidence.

At last the great day came, and on 5 July three-quarters of the population entered their names in the doctors' lists as they had been directed to do. Over twenty thousand general practitioners, 90 per cent, joined the service at its inception. It amused Nye to be told that the pupils of the great public schools, Eton, Harrow and Winchester, had also signed on that day. Before the end of the year 95 per cent of the population had joined the National Health Service.

The Jeremiahs had been confounded. The Tories had been routed. They had voted against the second and third readings of the National Health Bill. Soon they would start rewriting history in the hope of living down the ignominy of having attempted to strangle at birth the most popular piece of legislation ever to have passed through Parliament since the repeal of the Corn Laws.[2]

Of course there were deficiencies and difficulties, but none so catastrophic as to cause a scandal, nor so serious that the worst effects could not be eased with temporary solutions. Apart from the potential benefit to the nation's health and the immediate mitigation of a tremendous amount of undeclared suffering, a most pleasing aspect of the bold experiment from Nye's point of view was the proof that the middle classes could accept a purely socialist measure.

Lest it be supposed that a 'WELL DONE, BEVAN' might now appear in the headlines, it should be understood that, of all the privileges enjoyed by politicians, a tender regard for their egos is not one of them. On the great day of 5 July the press was more concerned with a broadcast to the nation delivered by the Prime Minister, Attlee. In it he paid tribute to 'the other parties' for their contribution towards helping to bring to fruition the new social services. Since 'the other parties' consisted mostly of Tories, Nye regarded the tribute as somewhat misplaced. He decided to put the matter in a truer perspective at a Labour rally to be held that evening in Belle Vue, Manchester, where he was due to speak.

On the platform Nye was known as a 'soft-spoken man'. His voice, a pleasant tenor with a Welsh lilt and slight stutter, surprised those who came to his meetings expecting to hear the loud-mouthed demagogue of the press reports. He never shouted, not even to get the better of hecklers; rather he tended to lower his voice so that they had to lean forward to catch his replies. He wanted people to understand the complexities of government, how in a thickly populated, industrialized, democratic country, decisions affecting their lives might involve choices, not between right and wrong but between two rights;

but never forgetting that the ultimate goal must be kept in mind. To him, the test of democracy was whether poverty could win the fight against property. He could put the case *against* a measure he favoured, indeed could build it up by adding one point after another so brilliantly as to surprise its supporters with the efficacy of their own convictions. At the Guild Hall, Devonport, then Michael's constituency, we heard him subdue a hostile audience by just such a method. 'I am going to talk about the nationalization of steel,' he announced quietly. Uproar! Groans, jeers, boos, cat-calls and strident chatter. The bewildered chairman looked across at Nye indicating his hammer as if wondering whether to bang it and call for order. Nye shook his head and stood waiting for the noise to subside. Not until there was complete silence did he add, just as quietly, 'From the Conservative point of view.' He then began to state the case against the controversial measure, in effect defending laissez faire economics, free trade, call it what you will, till the hall resounded with 'hear-hears' from opponents. Michael and I began to wonder how he would get out of it. By the time he came to the little word 'but' he had captivated his listeners. He interwove his intellectual arguments, for and against the measure, with asides, jokes and ironies. By thinking out loud, searching for the right word, he appeared to be taking his listeners into his confidence, even sharing their perplexities, thus creating a mutual bond of empathy. 'If you want to win an argument,' he advised friends, 'forget your opponent's weak points. Concentrate on the strong ones.'

Returning to the Belle Vue rally, he claimed for Britain the moral leadership of the world. Despite economic difficulties left by the war, the country had put the succour of the needy and the care of the sick above other considerations. He paid tribute to those who had served in the voluntary hospitals, but insisted: 'charity can never be a substitute for organized justice'. Every choice between awkward alternatives in the allocation of scarce resources posed moral questions: 'Labour demanded that the succour of the needy should come first, but

Churchill preferred a free-for-all, so what is Toryism but organized spivery?' Nye had made his point. Churchill was no more a lover of the Health Service than most of his party had been before 5 July.

Nye then turned to what he regarded as the most important part of his speech, the aforementioned nationalization of steel; a matter of special concern to him because, as Minister of Housing, the output of steel had its effect on his building programme. It was Nye's responsibility to ensure that, unlike the soldiers who returned from the First World War, those who had fought in the Second really would come back to homes 'fit for heroes'. The steel industry had failed the nation during the war by restricting pre-war production; sailors and merchant seamen had lost their lives importing steel from abroad. Steel nationalization had been included in the Labour Party's election manifesto of 1945 much against the will of Herbert Morrison, now Home Secretary, and other Cabinet colleagues. Despite improvement in the output of steel, the industry still required massive investment, beyond the capacity of private enterprise with its demand for quick profits, to increase production sufficiently to meet the nation's needs. Fearing with justice that Morrison and his friends might renege on their election pledge, Nye announced: 'In 1950 we shall face you again with all our programme carried out, and when I say all I mean all . . . I mean steel, though every obstacle will be put in the government's path including that battered old carcass, the House of Lords.' Nye was well aware that his Cabinet colleagues would not thank him for recommitting them to steel nationalization. He knew that in some quarters the statement would be regarded as political dynamite. But so long as the party carried out its election pledge, he was prepared to face any amount of lay fury his comment might cause.

It only remained to round off his address. What better than to compare the vigorous, reforming, post-war Labour administration with the sluggish, defeatist, pre-war Tory government? The thought brought back bitter memories of his youth spent on the dreaded Means Test; memories likely to have been shared by many among his audience. 'That is why no amount of cajolery can eradicate from my heart a deep burning hatred for the Tory Party. As far as I am concerned they are lower than vermin. They condemned millions of first class people to semi-starvation. I warn young men and women: don't listen to the seduction of Lord Woolton. He is a very good salesman. If you sell shoddy stuff you have to have a good salesman. The Tories are pouring out money on propaganda of all sorts and are hoping by this organized mass suggestion to eradicate all memory of what we went through. But I warn you: they have not changed – if they have, they are slightly worse than they were.'

Most of those who heard him knew what he had been talking about. Judging by his rapturous reception, it seemed not to occur to them that anything had been said likely to cause offence. Moreover, Nye's manner, his characteristic way of speaking, could be so much at variance with the impression given in the press that even if his words were accurately reported they could almost amount to a lie. In oratory, as in daily life, it is not so much what is said that matters as the way of saying it. A friend, Hugh Delargy MP, who had heard the speech warned Nye of trouble to come. Yet Nye felt sure that he had said nothing of consequence except about steel. Politicians were not expected to like their opponents. People were accustomed to hearing them slating each other.

The press gave fair reports of the Belle Vue speech and though the phrase 'burning hatred' appeared in various headlines no one seemed inclined to make anything of it. *The Times* alone mentioned the fatal word: 'Mr Bevan's "Burning Hatred". Attack on Tory "vermin".' Again, it passed off apparently unnoticed. When almost a week went by it seemed as if Delargy's misgivings had been unfounded. Suddenly, a Tory MP for Hornsey, Captain David Gammans, called Bevan 'the Conservatives' best propagandist', adding, 'even in a moment of crisis socialism will still appeal only to class hatred and inferiority complex.' Next day in the House of Lords, Lord Reading described Nye's speech as 'the most deplorable that he had ever read'. More ominously, four days later in a published letter Lionel Heald, KC protested that he had recently agreed to continue as a governor of Middlesex Hospital, but since he was a Conservative, did the minister require his services? In his published reply, Nye regretted that remarks made at a political meeting should be taken so much amiss, while insisting that, of course, the health service required the assistance of all irrespective of party.

That night someone daubed in big black letters across the cream-painted exterior of Nye's house, 23 Cliveden Place, SW1, 'VERMIN VILLA — HOME OF A LOUD-MOUTHED RAT'. The storm had broken. 'Politics is a blood sport,' Nye often said. The *Sunday Dispatch* blew the horn. Printed in huge black type right across the front page were the words 'THE MAN WHO HATES 8,093,955 PEOPLE', that being the total of Conservatives who had voted at the last general election. The message set the tone for what was to come. Henceforward, the word 'vermin' would drill into Nye's ears not just for a few days but for weeks, months, even years. Leader-writers pontificated on the difference between 'free and frank' expression and 'disgusting abuse', on 'words that foul the air we breathe', on 'words that bring politics into disrepute', on 'words that undermine democracy itself', on 'words too insulting ever to be forgotten'. Prime Minister Attlee sent his minister a letter of rebuke. Labour colleagues accused him of costing them the next election. Conservative Associations throughout the country formed Vermin Clubs and distributed vermin badges. They invaded Nye's meetings yelling, 'vermin, vermin'. A semi-fascist underclass dropped obscene notes, dead mice, dead rats, animal droppings, even human excreta into the letterbox of 23 Cliveden Place. Jennie crept downstairs in her dressing gown early every morning to collect the disgusting missiles lest they be discovered by her secretary, her mother or Nye. The *Daily Express* set up a photographer with a telephoto lens at the window of the second floor of a house directly opposite No. 23 to spy on the occupants and to keep track of the visitors. When Nye was out walking one night along the Embankment, as he was wont to do, a prostitute accosted him, and at the same time a flashbulb from a camera lit him up. He knocked it down with his walking stick. Fearing that he might be compromised, thereafter Nye persuaded Jennie to accompany him on his nightly wanderings which she was most loth to do.

For those of us who were close to Jennie and Nye in those days the normal connection between cause and effect was so disrupted and our belief in democracy so shaken that life became surrealist. One evening we were waiting with Jennie and Ma Lee for Nye to arrive for dinner. He turned up late looking jubilant. Having poured out a drink for himself, he told us, 'Tomorrow tens of thousands of people will hear who cannot hear today.' He had assembled a team of aural technicians to test every hearing-aid on the market. They varied in price from £2 or £3 to £30; enormous sums in those days, mostly beyond the reach of the poor. The technicians produced a hearing-aid as efficient as the best and at a tenth of the cost. Having secured the approval of the ear specialists, Nye had the new aid mass-produced and distributed free on the NHS. His modest pride in this achievement derived, as we knew, from a deeply felt compassion.

The name 'Bevan' was news. Where he had his hair cut, where he dined, whether he would wear a dinner jacket, how much money he earned – especially how much money – was news. The newshounds questioned his relatives, scoured every circumstance of his private life, including school reports, in search of items of gossip. But the tale of the deaf enabled to hear was not news.

Understandably, Jennie and Nye began to develop an obsessive hatred of the press. At the best of times, Nye loathed to see political issues discussed in terms of personalities. They saw no justification for the importunities and intrusions into their private lives. If a journalist dared to telephone Jennie for information, friend or foe, she would reply brusquely, 'This is a private house,' and slam down the phone. One day I remonstrated with Nye: 'You know very well you only have to take some of these journalists or editors out for a meal and butter them up a bit and you would have them eating out of your hand.' 'What do you take me for? A political gigolo?' he retorted. We pointed out that they did have some friends on the press. 'What about Jimmy Cameron and Vicky with his wonderful cartoons always in your favour, and Geoffrey Goodman, and Andrew Shonfield on the *Financial Times*?' But Jennie and Nye seemed unimpressed, which Michael thought rather hard on their friends. It was not until he became leader of the Labour Party himself that we began to understand how they must have felt. Most people take no more than one or two newspapers a day and perhaps a couple of weeklies. A Cabinet minister or party leader arrives at the office to see all the national newspapers, a huge quantity when seen in the mass, neatly spread out across a wide table or desk with the headlines clearly visible. To see oneself lambasted or ridiculed in so many headlines can have a devastating effect.

The worst development of the vermin period was yet to come: Winston Churchill had been holding his fire, waiting for his moment. Suddenly, in one of those beautifully polished speeches to the nation launched at a time when nothing short of a train crash or an earthquake was likely to wipe his precious words off the front pages, Churchill launched his own idiosyncratic attack. 'The National Health Service has been marred and prejudiced in its initiation by the clumsy, ill-natured hands of the Minister of Health to whom it has been confided.' Churchill went on to denounce the minister for his bad manners, class hatred, spite and much else besides, all based on that single gaffe, until he came to: 'He has chosen this very moment to speak of at least half the British people as lower than vermin. We speak of the Minister of Health, but should we not rather speak of the Minister of Disease, for is not morbid hatred a disease . . . and a very infectious form? Indeed, I can think of no better step to signal the initiation of the National Health Service than that the person so obviously in need of psychiatric treatment should be among the first of its patients.'

The blow struck hard. Churchill was out for the kill. Politics is a blood sport. The speech released an underlying viciousness endemic in a certain type of well-off Londoner. A friend took Nye to dine at White's Club, one of the most exclusive clubs in London. A gang of toffs threw him down the steps. We took Nye to see *The Galloping Major*, an Ealing comedy directed by a friend. In the foyer, a man roughly jostled Nye and shouted, 'You haven't a clue.' Everyone within hearing laughed. Nye might have sat through the show seething, but he refused to allow the ill-mannered Londoners to ruin his evening. He gave himself to the film and during its absurd climax he laughed and laughed and laughed and laughed as uncontrollably as a child. Indeed, an endearing streak of childishness formed part of his multi-faceted nature.

Nye *did not* hate the Tories. The health service had been established for the benefit of all. He had been scrupulously fair in his appointments of those who were to run the service. Many Conservatives, including Conservative consultants, found themselves very well off under the service. Some of Nye's friends – he would not say best friends – were Tories. He ate their food and drank their wine if their conversation was good enough. But in politics words speak louder than deeds, unless, of course, the deeds are outrageous. 'When I speak of Tories,' Nye said at the Durham miners' gala, 'I mean small bodies of people who, whenever they have the chance, have manipulated the influence of the country for the benefit of the privileged few.'

Nye never underestimated the power of the Tories to stage a comeback. The country enjoyed near full employment during those early Labour administrations, thanks partly to the application of Keynesian economics. Most of us believed, to our intense relief, that the old scourge of mass unemployment had been conquered for ever. Nye alone feared that it might return, along with the vulgarity of extreme wealth living side by side with extreme poverty. 'The Tories are soft on the outside but hard inside,' he often remarked, adding, 'with our people it is the other way round.' The people he likened to vermin were not Tories in the mass. He had been thinking of the dreaded inquisitors who invaded the homes of the colliers during his youth. Perhaps a glimpse of the Means Test, as it operated throughout the coalfields, may help to account for Nye's 'burning hatred'.

Before drawing unemployment relief a miner had to contend with a visit from a clerk, an inquisitor, usually a woman. It fell to her to ensure that he received no money from the state so long as he retained in his possession anything which might be sold, other than the necessities for his daily life. That meant that his wife would have to give up any jewellery she might possess, maybe a brooch or pendant. Fine china inherited from grandparents or great-grandparents would have to go; the same applied to articles kept for purely sentimental reasons though worth a price on the market. The miners' wives loved Staffordshire ornaments, Toby jugs and lustre ware. The mining communities were almost denuded of these common ornaments as a result of the Means Test. The inquisitors also had the right to search the cottages. Imagine the distress and the bitter arguments arising out of an inquisitor's visit. But the ordeal was not completed with the confiscation of everything the family most valued. The questioner then had to discover as best she could whether the miner received any money from anyone at all. If a woman lived at home and went out to work a proportion of her wages would be deducted from the amount allowed under unemployment relief to go towards the cost of food. Many a miner's daughter aged no more than thirteen or fourteen worked in a local factory. For the miners, the most macho of men, to have to live on the wages of their daughters, as they saw it, was the ultimate humiliation. Even when the distressing transaction was completed, the family received little more money than was needed for mere subsistence; it was indeed semi-starvation, as Nye had claimed. The government recruited its staff for the odious task in the coalfields not from local residents, who might be sympathetic, but from the South.

In the light of hindsight, we may wonder whether Churchill's Minister-of-Disease speech was not in itself an outburst of morbid hatred greater than that attributed to Nye, especially as the great man was aware that the Bevan he attacked was not the man he knew him to be. Proof of this assertion came in February of the following year.

After an enormous outlay on spectacles, false teeth, wigs, medicines and the running of the Health Service in general, an extra £52 million was required to meet the expense. Huge headlines forecast a political crisis, an imminent collapse of the service. The Tories believed that at last they had got the Minister of Health on the run. Churchill stirred a parliamentary uproar. He demanded a three-day debate, an event without precedent in time of peace, on account of the 'wildest miscalculations' and the 'enormous addition to the burden of the nation'. He suggested there might be a vote of censure. 'Hear, hear, let the opposition come along,' said Nye. But on the great day there was no Churchill – he had sent a not very distinguished member of his team to take charge. True, the expenditure amounted to more than anything Nye had dreamt of; at the same time he had been canny enough to argue that no worthwhile estimate could be made of the service's cost until there had been practical experience of its working.

Anyone reading this thrilling debate in full would understand why Churchill preferred to attack Bevan only from a safe distance. Bevan's mastery over the House of Commons was absolute: it took him no more than a minute or so to put the opposition on the defensive. We may refer only briefly to a section of his speech:

> Who would have suspected that we would have 95 per cent of the population registered with general practitioners by the end of the year? . . . As these people came into the service naturally the expenditure went up. But that mounting expenditure was an admission of administrative success, because if they had not come in I would not have had a deficit, I would have had a surplus, and I would then be praised by the opposition for being a financial success and an administrative failure as a Minister of Health. It is just because these services expanded so quickly, so

harmoniously, and so fruitfully that we find ourselves with this deficit. Of course the service cost money. But was there not some compensation in the relief provided for the vast amount of inarticulate misery and pain uncovered by the service? Why don't the right honourable gentlemen opposite start ceasing to be so sour? Why is it that as the health of the population goes up their spirits go down? The Tory Party used to represent themselves as a jocund party. [Hon. Members: What?] They cannot understand English now. I will give them a clue: 'How jocund did they drive their teams afield.' [From Grey's *Elegy*.] Pale and miserable lot, instead of welcoming every increase in the health of the nation, the buoyancy . . . the vitality . . . they groan at it . . . What they are saying to the country is 'We were never against it [the NHS]. It is quite true that we voted against it . . . agitated against it . . . plotted against it, but we were really in favour of it all the time.'

This and variations in a similar vein produced second thoughts on the opposition benches. When it came to the vote on the Supplementary Estimates, the Tories sat tight on their seats, silent and glum.

Two unexpected advantages came out of the press persecution of Nye. The more he was pilloried the greater the crowds who flocked to his meetings.[3] He filled the halls and the streets outside the halls, so that loudspeakers had to be erected to avoid disappointment. No other politician was such a draw. Many of the people arrived more out of curiosity than for enlightenment, but left in a spirit of excitement and elation and far better informed on the art of the possible than they could ever have expected.

Nye joked to his constituents in Tredegar: 'I have been represented as an ogre, as a man animated by hate and malice. I think the Tories came along to my meetings expecting to see someone with sabre teeth, a dagger at his side and wearing a red sash. I noticed expressions of surprise flitting across their faces when there appeared on the platform a comparatively mild-mannered individual – not too bad-looking perhaps – not handsome perhaps – but not hideous either.' When in other parts of the country Nye's audiences formed a similar opinion, they resented the deception played on them by the press. That in itself awakened sympathy for the speaker. No other politician commanded such widespread support throughout the Labour movement, nor has any leader done so since.

The second unexpected boon to come out of the press persecution was private. Nye and Jennie were drawn more closely together than they had ever been before. Jennie felt a great compassion for Nye, admired his courage and resilience, especially his firm adherence to principle. She subordinated her own interests to care for him as a wife; a considerable sacrifice, for Jennie possessed no small ego. I think too she fell in love with Nye at that period, perhaps for the first time.

Neither of them believed in monogamous marriage. Marital fidelity was certainly not among their priorities. Nye did not scruple to make passes at his friends' wives or at anyone else whom he hoped might be available. But if any woman attributed his advances to her own special attractions, she would have been flattering herself. Nye wanted nothing more than a doll on top of a bed to play with for a couple of hours, but pure dolly types were rather rare in Bevanite circles. Driving past Sonia Orwell's house one evening, I saw Nye leaving her front door. She was a friend whom I admired. We compared our experiences with Nye in the wicked way women do. We agreed that his style and manner made him a natural aristocrat, that his power to make dreams come true made him a political genius, but we had to admit that, even if we had fancied him, his overtures were too explicitly crude to tempt – and neither of us were prudes.

Nye told me that he thought 'tenderness killed sex' and, strangely, that 'an element of antagonism kept sex alive'. But whatever he said or did, there was really only one woman for him. While in India he wrote to Jennie of 'their secret happiness', adding romantically, 'I paid my respects to the Taj Mahal and whispered your name in the moonlight.'

If Nye had wanted children, as he may have done, he believed that the decision must be the woman's. He was a very good feminist. Who but Nye would have objected to a man sharing his life between a wife and a mistress purely on feminist grounds? He considered the situation an insult to both women, and what is worse, a public insult, as it usually is. For that reason he disapproved of his friend and Labour colleague, George Strauss, for leading a double life and even more so of Hugh Gaitskell, whose mistress was a Tory.

Recently, some historians have suggested that there was not much difference in the policies advocated by Nye Bevan and Hugh Gaitskell; one of the most curious assumptions to have come from the pens of academics. Nye was a socialist who wanted to change society; he sought with all his strength and wits to bring about a redistribution of wealth. Gaitskell was a man whose favourite word was 'moderate', usually preceded by 'if I may say so'. Nye wanted to bring 'the commanding heights of the economy' under state control. He toyed with all kinds of ideas, such as whether by taking over the commanding heights the consequent profits might not be used to abolish income tax altogether, since taxation makes 'Jekyll and Hydes of us all'. He did not want anything under state control to be run by faceless men. 'People do not work for money alone, they work for status and honour.' If Nye had had his way every little local gas station would have been run by a person accessible to the public, whose name was known and to whom people might have taken their complaints.

Gaitskell was an administrator; he might have made an excellent headmaster of a public school or a colonial governor. Nye had immense personal magnetism, star quality, charisma, as did Churchill. Gaitskell struck people outside his immediate circle as remote.

It has also been suggested that there must have been some serious flaw in Bevan's personality for him to have aroused so much acrimony.

Perhaps the following well-known incidents will help to clarify the main reason for the acrimony.

One summer's evening a journalist managed to take a photograph of Gaitskell slumped on a pavement in Chelsea, obviously drunk, with his arm round a lamp-post and with his mistress standing nearby. To the journalist's surprise and disappointment, not a single editor would publish the picture. Yet almost every editor would have snapped up the photograph of Nye beside the prostitute if it had been sufficiently compromising. The press lords saw Nye as a real threat; he meant business, he was a socialist. Gaitskell was tame. The next best thing to a Tory government, for the privileged few who own more than their fair share of the nation's wealth, is a Labour government tamed.

When Nye fell ill a curious change of mood came over the nation. Everyone talked about him, in the shops, the tubes, the buses. 'Will he get better?' 'What is the latest news bulletin?' People asked the same questions wherever we went. I remember meeting Bernard Levin and feeling surprised that he seemed almost as upset about Nye as we were. It was as if the nation suddenly realized that they were losing a great man; it was as if they had repented.

Most of the leading politicians whom I have met fall into the category of having had greatness thrust upon them; that applies even to some Prime Ministers. A few of the clever ones do achieve a kind of greatness, but Nye was one of the rare ones who was born great. He should have been leader of the Labour Party; he was cheated of his destiny. When Harold Wilson took over the leadership shortly after Nye's death he raised his glass in a toast: 'To the man who should have been in my place.' Those are the finest words Harold ever spoke.

CHARLES WEBSTER

Birth of the Dream:
Bevan and the Architecture of the National Health Service

Although recent academic investigations into the origins of the National Health Service vary in their emphasis, most recognize the importance of the Labour movement, and almost universally they confirm Michael Foot's conclusions about the crucial importance of the personal role of Aneurin Bevan.[1] There is diminishing support for the revisionist view, originating with Eckstein, which discounts the contribution of 'doctrinaire politicians of the Left', and presents the NHS as essentially the work of the medical profession, especially the BMA.[2] The successful launch of the NHS on its appointed day, 5 July 1948, the immediate success of the new service and its rapid consolidation as a national institution commanding the support and affection of all sections of the community are now recognized as owing a great deal to the creative genius of Aneurin Bevan. For this reason, long after most politicians of his generation have been forgotten, Bevan is remembered, and as long as the NHS persists, it will be associated with his name.

Most aspects of Bevan's work as Minister of Health have been described in detail. Particular attention has been attracted by his marathon confrontation with the medical profession, especially before the appointed day. Although the crucial formative phase, when Bevan was determining the administrative outline for the new health service, has also been particularly actively researched, there are still some important gaps in our knowledge and opportunities remain for the exploitation of little-used evidence. In this short essay, I will re-examine two related issues: first the sources for Bevan's ideas concerning the nationalization and regionalization of the health service; secondly the immediate personal impact made by Bevan in the course of gaining support for his ideas among his ministerial colleagues and with members of his department. It is hoped that this short investigation will provide a fuller understanding of the rationale for Bevan's great creative experiment in health care. If the following construction of the prehistory of Bevan's plan for the health service is correct, then his already strong reputation is further enhanced, since I suggest that he showed a high order of political and analytical judgement in circumstances where most other politicians would have opted for safer but much less credible alternatives, the outcome of which was likely to be disastrous for the health service and its consumers. The health debate in which Bevan participated is not merely of antiquarian interest; it involved the consideration of fundamental issues, as relevant now as when they were originally debated. The issues confronting Bevan were of permanent importance, and it would be unrealistic to claim that they have been resolved by his successors.

It is recognized that Bevan's most original and audacious intervention in the field of health policy was to nationalize the municipal and voluntary hospitals, and place the entire hospital system and associated consultant and specialist services under a new regional administration dissociated from local government. Nationalization and regionalization established the hospitals as the strongest feature of the new health service. This represented the area within which the most substantial progress was made and it absorbed two-thirds of the resources available to the NHS. The high degree of support for the new system recorded by the medical and nursing leadership within the hospital sector and the regard for the NHS among the public were largely founded on the innovations and successes associated with the new consultant and specialist services.

In the course of the labyrinthine preparations for a comprehensive health service during the Second World War nationalization seems to have been an almost unconsidered option, largely because of the known opposition of two of the chief vested interests, the voluntary hospitals and the local authorities, who between them administered the existing hospital system. Regionalization was better regarded, but it meant entirely different things to the various parties. Few envisaged the emergence of regionalization in the form adopted by Bevan.

It is well known that from the earliest point in his policy deliberations, the new Minister of Health was dissatisfied with all previous schemes for health service organization, with the consequence that already in August 1945 he was giving serious consideration to nationalization and regionalization of the hospitals. In the face of opposition from some senior civil servants within his department, Bevan adopted nationalization and regionalization as the chief working principle for the new scheme, which was first presented to his Cabinet colleagues in a memorandum dated 5 October 1945.[3] The Cabinet was persuaded to accept Bevan's scheme, but not without prolonged and vigorous opposition from a group of ministers headed by Herbert Morrison. This first major confrontation with his colleagues of his ministerial career counted as a resounding triumph for Bevan and a decisive humiliation for Morrison.[4]

Recent commentators have repeatedly pored over the limited evidence relating to Bevan's first reflections on policy, without discovering any conclusive leads concerning the direct source for the nationalization/regionalization proposal. This problem therefore remains unresolved. The experts are generally uncategorical, but most express a marginal preference: Bevan himself remains the principal contender, but there is also strong support for J. M. K. Hawton and J. E. Pater, his chief policy assistants within the department. There is also a case for Sir Wilson Jameson, the Chief Medical Officer, while Stephen Taylor suggests his own involvement. Finally, some attention is drawn to the claims of Lord Moran. Of course, it is also conceded that various of these individuals acting in combination were likely to have influenced Bevan's policy reorientation.[5]

Rather than examine these paltry entrails yet again, I would like to propose a different avenue of approach, by suggesting that Bevan was likely to have drawn upon an alternative source, little considered by writers on the origins of the NHS. For understandable reasons, such writers tend to be preoccupied by the not inconsiderable body of evidence relating to the immediate exchanges on health policy between the planners, relevant professional groups and other vested interests, of whom the most aggressive and vociferous was the BMA. The lively debate between the government and these interest groups had been in full swing for at least three years by the arrival of Bevan; indeed the parties had taken up their basic alignment even before the Second World War. Every conceivable permutation had been considered. The alternative of nationalization of hospitals was sometimes mentioned, only to be dismissed as completely impracticable.[6] Regionalization remained on the agenda, but as a concept it lacked clarity; to local authorities it was taken to coincide with their schemes for joint boards; for the voluntary hospitals, it was taken to coincide with their proposals for loose co-operation, not entailing loss of independence in ownership. Even the plans for more radical change were chary about interfering with ownership. Consequently, the imaginative scheme advocated by Medical Planning Research, which proposed the establishment of a National Health Corporation to supervise the new health service and the division of Great Britain into twelve regions for health service purposes, conceded that 'while it is in theory desirable that all hospitals and other health buildings should ultimately be the property of the National Health Corporation, we recognise the need for a compromise. The actual ownership of the fabric need not change.'[7] Consequently, in the increasing heat and turmoil of debate, the alternatives of nationalization and regionalization in the form adopted by Bevan were lost from view in the main policy deliberations, well before 1945. Recent commentators are therefore justified in considering that Bevan was unlikely to have been influenced from this source.

The Social Reconstruction Debate

The health debate waged during the Second World War revolved around questions of great technical complexity. It was very much a matter for experts; few politicians were conversant with more than the main outline of the issues in contention. Bevan was preoccupied by other problems; apart from a handful of brief interjections, he was not a participant in the detailed deliberations on health policy. However, he was completely conversant with the wider context: the arguments about the implementation of the Beveridge social security proposals (which famously involved an Assumption B relating to the establishment of a comprehensive health service), or the general issue of post-war reconstruction, many aspects of which possessed implications for the health service. The reconstruction debate was of central political importance; success on this front was essential for credibility and for the electoral prospects of the main political parties. As Bevan appreciated, the electorate required practical guarantees that the fiasco of the First World War reconstruction programme would not be repeated. Accordingly all planners approached the problem of reconstruction with particular seriousness; of the main parties, Labour led the field with its large social reconstruction policy apparatus. This wider reconstruction programme inevitably involved consideration of the future health service; I suggest that this source provided Bevan and his colleagues with the outline of the argument concerning nationalization and regionalization of the health service.

It is of course beyond the remit of a single chapter to consider the reconstruction debate in detail. Consequently, I will draw attention to the major relevance of this debate as a source for the idea of abandoning local government administration of the health services, and considering nationalization and regionalization as preferred alternatives. To underline the wide currency of such ideas, I will refer mainly to the course of the discussion in *The Economist*, which was one of the most influential journals of the day, fundamental to the reading of both planners and politicians.

The first hint that the government was being forced to consider major reform within the health services came with a ministerial statement on 18 October 1941, when it was announced that ways would be sought to bring the municipal and voluntary systems of hospital administration into more effective alignment. The government's formal proposals were not made known until the White Paper, 'A National Health Service', was issued in February 1944, and this was itself a tentative document. In the meantime the debate over reconstruction had moved forward rapidly.

It was increasingly appreciated that radical improvement in services after the war would be severely handicapped by the existing system of local government and its finances. In its major review of this problem, *The Economist* pointed out that pre-war experience underlined the dangers of continuing with the existing system. Local government areas were anachronistic; local authorities had failed to provide services of adequately uniform standard; and their efforts were encumbered by the rating system, which penalized the poorest authorities. The system had failed during peacetime; its weaknesses were further exacerbated during the war; it was therefore patently inadequate to perform the onerous task of post-war reconstruction. Hospital services were cited as a casualty of this system. Since it was accepted that there was a strong case for nationalization and regional administration in such areas as gas, electricity and transport, all examples where a high degree of technical expertise was involved, it was suggested that consideration should be given to treating the similarly technical health services in a similar manner. It was argued that this would bring about substantial economies of scale, would provide a more attractive career structure for highly qualified staff, and lead to more effective management.[8]

Apart from its commentary on the growing tide of health service planning documents, and about the increasing signs of militancy on the part of the medical profession, *The Economist* kept up the pressure for the reform of local government and it addressed these questions in considerable detail. It was alarmed that the government was approaching the task of reconstruction in a piecemeal fashion, without confronting the limitations of the current system of local government and its finances. It castigated ministers for failing to appreciate the importance of local government reform. *The Economist* warned that the government was repeating the pre-war mistake of burdening local government with tasks for which it was unfitted. The journal was firmly convinced that local government was incapable of taking on everything required during the period of reconstruction. Local authorities had no means of raising the resources to support the services for which they were responsible and were not organized in units capable of undertaking these services. *The Economist* warned that the likely result would be the breakdown of the system. It was therefore necessary to consider whether any functions could be transferred elsewhere. *The Economist* welcomed the fact that the Labour Party had produced planning documents on the reconstruction of the health services and local government in tandem. It agreed with Labour's proposal to introduce a regional tier of local government, with hospitals, health centres, ambulances and the school medical service being administered by this tier. *The Economist* was, however, disappointed that Labour had not accepted the case for financing regional services by a form of local income tax.[9] It favoured a more radical approach.[10] One alternative envisaged that 'a brand new regional tier should be inserted between the central government and the present local authorities, which would take over from the local authorities a number of the present services and finance them out of a regional income-tax, the rates being correspondingly reduced'. Education was one candidate for transfer to the region; the obvious second choice was health, where a 'regional medical service could similarly be a rounded and balanced whole in a way that few county medical services can be'. Alternatively, a politically easier choice was nationalization of some services currently provided by local authorities. Once again education and health were regarded as prime candidates for nationalization and funding from the Exchequer. It was accepted that the new health service was the more obvious choice for application of this principle:

> the balance of advantage would seem to lie with nationalising the health services . . . and leaving education with the counties and county boroughs, as proposed in the [education] White Paper. Health services on a national standard are only just coming into being; the educational system is a going concern. Standards of service are more easily measured in objective terms, and therefore more susceptible to central control, in medicine than in education. Though a certain variety in methods is desirable in both, it is more desirable in education. The teachers are accustomed to employment by local authorities; the doctors would resent it. Health services are already connected with nationally administered social insurance; education is not.[11]

Thus, by the end of 1943 *The Economist* had firmly concluded that the future health service should not be entrusted to existing units of local government, and that nationalized and regionalized organizations were preferred alternatives. This accounts for the lukewarm response to the 1944 White Paper, the failings of which *The Economist* attributed to continuing refusal by the Ministry of Health to accept the need for attaching priority to local government reform. In basing the new health service on existing local government structures, the White Paper was forced to resort to elaborate ad hoc devices, and it was entirely unclear whether the government believed that the proposals were workable. *The Economist* was not surprised when the new proposals sank into an imbroglio of controversy. Encouraged by an absence of firm commitment on the part of Henry U. Willink, the

Conservative appointee as Minister of Health, and continuing general lack of confidence in the government's health service scheme, *The Economist* continued to press the case for local government reform, and for nationalization and regionalization. The health service remained the favoured candidate for nationalization and regionalization. It was pointed out that local authorities would be unable to sustain the cost of the new health service on the basis of the current rating system of finance. The awesome tasks facing local government after the war therefore required as an absolute necessity the transfer of one large service away from rate funding. Health was the obvious choice: 'there can be little question that a sufficiently large saving in rate expenditure could only be made by transforming public health, the highest single charge on local funds after education, into a national service'. It was recognized that such a move would be opposed on the grounds of erosion of local democratic responsibility, but *The Economist* retorted that otherwise the local authorities would be 'financially incapable of maintaining their present degree of democratically controlled responsibility in any sphere. Better a complete surrender in one sphere than an almost complete surrender in all.'[12]

In the months before the 1945 general election, in the context of the continuing impasse over future policy in the fields of local government and health service reform, *The Economist* lost no opportunity to reinforce its message on nationalization and regionalization. The journal was unrepentant that 'the case for transferring the health services to central administration' was 'frequently argued in these columns'.[13] When the government finally refused to contemplate the general reform of local government, *The Economist* insisted even more strongly on the merits of the case for nationalization of the health service. This was seen as the only way to prevent hopeless overloading of local authorities, to place the health service on a sounder financial and planning basis, and to make the scheme more palatable to the medical profession. In January 1945, *The Economist* called for the creation of 'the new Medical Service on a national basis, wholly financed from national resources and embracing part or all of the health services which form so large a part of the local authorities' total expenditure. This would have the additional and important merit of meeting the strongest objection that the medical profession has to the Government's proposals.'[14] In February 1945, in the course of its review of the unsatisfactory nature of existing units of local government and its critique of the government's proposal for a Boundary Commission, *The Economist* concentrated its attack on the system of joint boards, which it described as 'hybrid bodies devoid both of taxing powers and of direct election', unsuitable for dealing with such services as health.[15] In its review of the depressing findings of the regional hospital surveys in May 1945, *The Economist* again insisted that in view of the 'considerable reorganisation, rebuilding and new building that will be necessary', it would be well to 'nationalise the service from the outset'.[16] Finally, in June 1945, in its critique of a speech by Sir John Anderson to local government treasurers, *The Economist* insisted that local authorities would not be able to undertake bold schemes of reconstruction if they were saddled with responsibility for the new health service.[17]

Unsurprisingly, immediately after the general election, *The Economist* returned to its traditional theme, insisting that the Labour government would be ill-advised to revert to the White Paper proposals. After ambiguous and inconsistent impressions given by Labour ministers, *The Economist* warned that the medical profession would not accept transfer of the voluntary hospitals to local government. Given the strength of feeling within the medical profession, the only viable way forward was to 'transfer the whole service to the state and cut out the mutual jealousies of doctors and local authorities at one stroke'.[18] The general argument for transfer of the new health service, including voluntary hospitals, to the state was repeated on the occasion of the local elections in October 1945, upon the first rumours of Bevan's intentions to nationalize the hospitals in the following month, and finally in its exhaustive three-part review of the rate system, which concluded with four proposals for immediate reform, of which the third was the transfer of financial responsibility for the new health service to the Exchequer.[19]

Aneurin Bevan in Power

The above brief review of health policy from the perspective of *The Economist* establishes decisively that nationalization and regionalization of the new health service were central to the debate on social reconstruction taking place during the Second World War. Policy deliberations ranged across the entire field of social provision. With respect to public utilities such as gas and electricity, undertakings such as highways and transport, or personal social services such as housing, education and health, it was necessary to decide on the most effective mechanism for providing modern and efficient services. This inevitably raised the questions of the suitability of the inherited mechanism of central and local government, and the types of taxation associated with them. The vested interests within central and local government were naturally inclined to favour the least interference with the existing system, but across the board it was pointed out that technocratic needs suggested that other alternatives would be superior, hence the demand for administration of services by public corporations, or the interpolation of a regional tier of government, and substantial reform of the system of local taxation. Since the largest range of health services was provided by local government, including more than 80 per cent of hospital beds, it was essential to consider whether this form of administration offered a viable basis for a future comprehensive health service.

The Ministry of Health placed its confidence in the existing system. The 1944 White Paper and subsequent planning documents assumed the incremental advance of municipalized services, retaining rate funding, and with minimum interference in the administrative system. It was also assumed that the voluntary hospital system would be maintained in its current form. Labour at first came out strongly in favour of regional government and for placing most of the health service under its control, but without a reform of the rate system or a direct assault on the voluntary hospital system. As the 1945 election approached, Labour lost confidence in local government reform; it therefore fell back on the White Paper proposals, but with greater insistence on the role of existing local authorities, and employment of doctors on a full-time salaried basis. As noted above, *The Economist*, reflecting more radical opinion among local government experts and economists, favoured a radical overhaul of local government, but in the absence of this it insisted that, to prevent the breakdown of the existing system, it was essential to establish the new health service on the basis of state control and Exchequer financing.

By the date of Labour's great election victory these arguments had been debated at length and in great detail. The outlines of the argument were particularly clear in *The Economist*, but they were reflected elsewhere in the press. Any politician concerned with social reconstruction would of necessity have considered these issues, and would therefore have been familiar with the case for nationalizing the new health service. If by any chance Bevan had not become fully acquainted with these arguments, he would have been introduced to them soon after his appointment as Minister of Health, which was of course the department responsible for health, housing and local government. As a matter of urgency he needed to advise on the new administration's policy on local government reform, and about the administrative structures appropriate to the large new developments expected in the fields of housing and health. This represented a formidable policy challenge, and it was essential to view the problem as a whole. In order to reduce it to manageable proportions, and enable his department and local government to handle their responsibilities, Bevan opted for the compromise advocated in the columns of *The Economist*, which entailed shelving the question of local government reform, placing the housing programme with existing local authorities with funding shared between rates and central support, but placing the greater part of the new health service with purpose-designed regional authorities, supported by funds from the Exchequer. This formula averted the conflicts with powerful vested interests that would have attended any attempt to disturb the existing system of local government; it left local government with sufficient exciting responsibilities in social reconstruction in such fields as education, housing and planning, and ultimately even residual health service activities, including the provision of health centres; but it removed the most expensive item in the new health service, permitting the hospital, consultant and specialist services to be developed by new regional authorities. This raised the prospect of superior planning, greater equality of service, and more adequate provision of resources. This solution was politically persuasive as it was more palatable to the medical profession, and at least tolerable to the voluntary hospital interests.

I would argue therefore that the scheme adopted by Bevan was not the result of his fishing around in the dark, or dependent on his own or some particular adviser's idiosyncratic imagination. He was not launching health care into a wild experiment, or even opting for a little-considered alternative. I would claim that Bevan was, on the contrary, subscribing to one of the most effectively argued alternatives available at the time, which was the scheme carrying the greatest amount of credibility, and calculated to stand the greatest chance of success. Also, with respect to political challenges, it was calculated to incur the least amount of damaging criticism. By adopting the option canvassed by *The Economist* and expert opinion subscribing to its views, Bevan was therefore aligning himself with some of the best-informed and most imaginative analysts among the technocrats writing on problems of social administration. This accounts for the warm welcome given by these experts and by more advanced thinkers within the medical profession when Bevan's plans for the new health service were made public. Not for the first time, by happy chance, the aspirations of socialism and enlightened opinion coincided in their conclusions.

The above construction helps to explain why Bevan possessed the confidence to abandon the White Paper plan completely, to evolve a radically different alternative without delay, and to push forward with his scheme without further negotiation with the parties involved. Of course, before his scheme could be brought to fruition, it was necessary for Bevan to negotiate a minefield of opposition to his ideas from much less forward-looking figures within the Attlee administration and his own department. The outline of the debate within his department and in Cabinet has been often recounted, and need not be repeated in detail. But it is helpful to cite some hitherto unexploited sources, which fill out the picture of Bevan's early reception within his department and confrontations with his colleagues.

Particularly vivid and helpful insights may be derived from the letters of Enid Russell-Smith to her brother in Somaliland, which have fortunately survived. Enid Russell-Smith was an able civil servant whose entire career was spent in the Ministry of Health, where she rose to the rank of Assistant Secretary.

In August 1945 Russell-Smith was surprised by the scale of the Labour victory, but she regarded the outcome with satisfaction. She and her colleagues expected Ellen Wilkinson or Edith Summerskill to be appointed Minister of Health, and they were taken by surprise by the appointment of Bevan, who was largely unknown to them. To the civil servants he had 'chiefly distinguished himself for his hostility to Churchill', which at least suggested that he was likely to carry weight and judgement as a minister. She was immediately impressed by his ability, quick brain and fighting instincts, all of which, she noted, had been lacking in Willink and were desperately needed in the Ministry of Health. She was nevertheless apprehensive about his reputation for being lazy, which seemed to be confirmed by his overweight appearance.[20]

In practice, Russell-Smith's fears were dispelled and she reported favourably on the performance of the new Minister of Health. With a characteristic taste for clinical detail, she described her first impression of him as being of 'great drive, and able and clear mind and a capacity to listen. In appearance, he is a big, heavy man, not very tall but thick set, with very powerful arms and shoulders, dark, round headed, and beetle-browed with eyes, nose and chin all rather prominent and large, speaks with a lisp and a Welsh intonation.'[21] Russell-Smith was not directly involved with high-level policy decisions, and she was mainly concerned with housing at this stage, but she was impressed that Bevan 'really cared about the way in which the people lived'.[22] Her first long engagement with Bevan was delayed until March 1946, when she visited Doncaster with him. She reported that 'here and there among the audience one sees that beatific expression on a worn old face which means that some pioneer in the Labour movement is seeing all Heaven in a Labour Minister in a Labour Government expounding a Socialist policy'. This meeting suggested to Russell-Smith that there was a real prospect of the nation achieving an 'inner unity between classes and individuals', a unity of spirit which younger socialists in Bevan's audience took as the prospect for a millennium.[23]

Bevan was ably assisted in framing the scheme for the new health service by J. M. K. Hawton and J. E. Pater. As the records indicate, he was not helped by other senior officials, who attempted to block progress with Bevan's preferred scheme and force him back to the compromises of the 1944 White Paper. Of course Bevan swept aside these obstacles, and soon his scheme was prepared for presentation to colleagues. In order to speed up discussions and overcome likely objections, Bevan submitted his proposals for nationalization and regionalization of hospitals to the Cabinet without delay. His memorandum was submitted on 5 October, and the scheme was discussed on 11 and 18 October. These discussions are well known, but the fragmentary report in the Cabinet Secretary's notebook has not been previously cited. Since this includes a short paraphrase of the statement by Bevan, which differs significantly from the final Cabinet Conclusions, this part of the report is worth transcribing in its entirety:

> No real difficulty in getting agreement with Scotland: for I don't intend to leave the teaching hospitals as voluntary hospitals in old sense of the term.
>
> No other way of getting proper hospital service. – or efficient nursing service.
>
> Can't entrust to local authorities because (even in London) the local authority areas are not natural hospital areas. Resistance of voluntary hospitals to being entrusted to local authorities couldn't be overcome. White Paper had to resort to Joint Boards, which is worst form of local authority.
>
> Argument: equal service for equal contributions.
>
> Voluntary hospital system has broken down. Success of Emergency Medical Service due largely to its breaking down local boundaries.
>
> Revenue. 100 per cent in some cases will come from rate and state funds: in other cases 60 per cent upwards. Ruling out endowments, less than 8 per cent will be provided by voluntary contributions.
>
> Protection versus centralisation?
>
> My conversations with doctors lead me to suppose that this will be welcomed by them and will reduce their opposition to rest of the scheme.[24]

Comparing this paraphrase with the much fuller account in the Cabinet Conclusions (included at the end of this chapter as an appendix), it is striking that the latter is by no means an extended version of the former. The sequence of the presentation is completely different and there are minor differences in content. The statement recorded in the Cabinet Conclusions is in reality a summary of Bevan's Cabinet memorandum. The four other recorded contributions to the debate on 11 October show better correspondence between the two sources. Unfortunately, the main body of the debate occurred on 18 October, for which there is no record in the Cabinet Secretary's notebook. However, the Cabinet Conclusions are very full, and they have enabled historians to gauge the balance of forces among ministers over this issue.[25]

The discussions on 11 and 18 October represented a major test for Bevan. It will be noted that almost all the arguments he used in favour of nationalization and regionalization had been anticipated in the columns of *The Economist*. But Bevan was a skilful exponent, and all his powers of persuasion were required to overcome the opposition of Morrison and his allies, who argued for the retention of the White Paper scheme.

Bevan's next big test came on 20 December when his full scheme was discussed by the Cabinet. Unfortunately the Cabinet Secretary's record of this meeting omits the first half-hour of the discussion, and therefore does not include the opening statement by Bevan. The Cabinet Conclusions, hitherto cited as the source for this meeting, give a full account of the debate from the perspective of the main protagonists, but the actual event was considerably more disjointed than suggested by the Conclusions. Despite its omissions, the Cabinet Secretary's notebook includes the majority of the exchanges, and once again demonstrates the strength of opposition facing Bevan. The new minister was impatient to introduce his legislation and conduct discussions with relevant interests. He insisted that 'when I start these negotiations I shall make up my mind to concede nothing'. Unless prompt action was taken to regain the initiative, he believed that the momentum would be lost, and that there would be infinite regress of the kind witnessed during the Coalition administration. As a precondition for the success of this bold initiative, he required the full backing of the Cabinet, and this proved extremely difficult to obtain. Morrison and his team reiterated arguments in favour of the 1944 scheme; as delaying tactics they proposed further investigations on such subjects as the financial implication of Bevan's scheme, further negotiations with outside parties, and detailed scrutiny of the draft legislation. Bevan responded with frequent interjections, many of them betraying signs of exasperation with what he took as carping and destructive criticism from his colleagues. When the Prime Minister seemed to support the calls for postponement of legislation, Bevan intervened: 'Here is our chance to do something big. Are we to sacrifice that chance for fear of parish-pump? But unless I have firm support of Cabinet, I am beaten from the start.' He refused to agree to 'Cabinet reviewing heads of Bill and modifying them in the light of opposition. It will be only in detail that I will give way.' In the acrimonious exchanges, Bevan was generally supported by George Buchanan (representing Scotland), Hugh Dalton (Chancellor of the Exchequer), Ellen Wilkinson (Minister of Education) and Viscount Addison (Secretary of State for Dominion Affairs, who had been the first Minister of Health in 1919). Unhelpful to Bevan were Herbert Morrison (Lord President of the Council), James Chuter Ede (Home Secretary), Arthur Greenwood (Lord Privy Seal), A. V. Alexander (First Lord of the Admiralty) and Tom Williams (Minister of Agriculture). Dalton's support was by no means unequivocal; he expressed some serious reservations on the grounds that the government was facing over-commitment on its public services, while Attlee inclined to caution and procrastination.[26] The opposition to Bevan was therefore more formidable and the issue more finely balanced than is generally estimated. The Cabinet Secretary's account provides no indication of the outcome of this tense debate, but the final Conclusions record results generally favourable to Bevan. The Minister of Health was forced to present his draft legislation to colleagues for ratification, but in practice this was no more than a formality and it involved no substantial delay.[27] The NHS Bill was published in March 1946 and it reached the statute book on 6 November 1946 without being subject to substantial amendment.[28]

Conclusions

Improvements in health care were an unavoidable commitment for any post-Second World War administration. The precise nature of these changes was by no means a foregone conclusion. Without the personal intervention of Aneurin Bevan, it was quite likely that the nation would have been provided with a health service only marginally different from its pre-war antecedents, and therefore without the resources or system of administration needed for the establishment of a modern health service. Bevan spurned the compromises favoured by fellow politicians and by the vested interests, and in the crucially important hospital sector opted for nationalization and regionalization. This placed all hospitals under common ownership and established a rational basis for planning, so enabling the new health service very rapidly to build up a comprehensive consultant and specialist service. By transferring the financial burden of hospitals from the rates to the Exchequer, Bevan provided for the first time a system of resources for the hospital sector that was capable of bearing the burden of this massively expensive undertaking.

I have suggested that Bevan's solution involved remarkably astute political judgement. He recognized that the most effectively argued solution among the technocrats was also subject to the least political objection among the personnel of the health service. By confining nationalization and regionalization to the vital and pre-eminent hospital sector, where the greatest planning effort and most substantial injection of resources were required, Bevan was able to conciliate general practitioners and local authorities. He allowed their essential services to continue under their traditional forms of administration, which also enabled the new health service to continue to draw to a minor extent upon funding from the NHS Contribution (the 'health stamp') and the rates. Bevan's ingenious solution, combining both radical elements and strategic compromises, was not only fruitful for the advancement of health care, but it was also beneficial to the social reconstruction programme more generally, by alleviating pressure on the rate-funded services. Bevan's National Health Service soon proved its worth by demonstrating its capacity to provide hugely expanded services and meet all the essential demands of modernization. The unified hospital service demonstrated efficiency savings on a substantial scale, and thereby proved able greatly to increase the volume of its services without increasing the number of beds or receiving more than modest increments to its budget.[29] The new health service produced a high degree of confidence and satisfaction among both its consumers and its workforce.

The appropriateness of Bevan's formula is suggested by its immediate successes and by the difficulties experienced in arriving at a more satisfactory alternative. With respect to the method introduced by Bevan to finance health care, the switch to central taxation has become accepted as a principle that has withstood frequent critical scrutiny. Bevan himself admitted that the system of organization adopted was a compromise that needed to be re-examined in the course of time. Once the NHS was consolidated, neither Labour nor Conservative could resist the temptation to try for a greater unification of services than was practicable for Bevan. This problem proved more intractable than was originally anticipated; it was left unresolved by the Wilson administration during the 1960s, while the Sir Keith Joseph reorganization of 1974 was universally admitted to be a failure. Many of the changes introduced during the 1980s were addressed to resolving difficulties created in 1974. Notwithstanding all the twists and turns of policy, between 1948 and 1989 there was broad continuity on most fronts, and general consistency with the principles established by Bevan. Indeed, with respect to the general goals of unification, rational planning, and integration of purchasing and provision, developments during this period were consistent with a mainstream of thinking about health care extending back to the Victorian sanitarian movement.

It was only in 1989 that the Thatcher administration threw away the learning process of a century and a half, took the knife to Bevan's scheme, and set about the systematic dismemberment of the health service in the interests of imposing a market mechanism. Of the main administrative structures existing in 1974, only the Community Health Council has escaped abolition or transformation. Every step has taken the health service away from the ideals of unification and rational planning of the kind advocated since the days of the Victorian sanitarians, promulgated in the columns of *The Economist* during the Second World War, applied by Bevan, and exemplified especially in nationalized and regionalized hospital service. During the 1990s, the integration of ownership, planning, management and provision of services fundamental to Bevan's scheme has been replaced by the purchaser/provider system, which in many respects is a reinvention of the disastrously inefficient and defective arrangements the NHS was designed to replace. The regional hospital system constructed by Bevan has been allowed to disintegrate into its component parts, so replicating the anarchic situation among the voluntary hospitals before 1939. The commissioning authorities which purchase services are inferior to their pre-war counterparts since they possess no credible planning role or meaningful accountability to their local constituencies. From the current perspective it is a strange irony that the Conservative opposition's main attack on Bevan related to his 'mutilation of local government' and 'dangerous increase in ministerial power and patronage', when among the most conspicuous hallmarks of recent changes have been the elimination of local democratic participation and the huge extension of central interference and escalation of ministerial patronage.[30]

The recent precipitous disruptions in health care in Britain were entirely lacking in the kind of solid intellectual justification available in the case of Bevan. Whereas Bevan's scheme was sufficiently soundly based to prove viable without substantial alteration over a long period, the market system has needed persistent shoring up to prevent its complete collapse. Even now, after more than five years of constant tinkering with the market system, there is no appearance of stability. As best they can, the personnel of the service have protected the patient from the effects of the market system, but at the cost of traumatic damage to morale. Whereas Bevan's health service self-evidently yielded substantial benefits to the patient and greatly improved upon the performance of the previous unplanned system, despite huge amounts of research effort expended on justifying recent changes, there is still no unequivocal evidence that the reincarnated market system has brought about significant efficiency gains, expansion in services, or greater consumer satisfaction to compensate for its massively increased management costs.[31] It goes without saying that none of the succession of ministers responsible for marketing the recent government's health service policies has inspired anything like the degree of confidence achieved under Bevan's charismatic leadership. Bevan's reputation therefore amply stands the test of time. In the adverse conditions of post-war austerity, Bevan succeeded exceptionally well in his main practical objective to 'generalize' or 'universalize the best': making available to the entire population the first-class standard of medical service hitherto available only to the select few. Consequently, both the people and all those working in the health service came to share his confidence that they were collectively participating in the 'biggest single experiment in social service that the world has ever seen undertaken'.[32] Arguably for the first time in our history, Bevan successfully established health care as one of the highest priorities of modern government. As we approach the next millennium, and face new tasks of social reconstruction quite as formidable as those experienced after the Second World War, it will be instructive to observe how effectively future administrations give substance to Bevan's great ideal.

APPENDIX: *Bevan on Hospital Nationalization,*
October 1945[33]

The Minister of Health recalled that in the White Paper on a National
Health Service (Cmd. 6502) it had been proposed to leave the voluntary hospitals under their own independent management, though
subject to a certain measure of control in return for the assistance
which they would receive from the Exchequer and local rates. Estimates made by the Ministry of Health showed that, when the National
Health Service was established, at least 70 per cent, and in some cases
as much as 80 or 90 per cent, of the income of a voluntary hospital
would be derived from public funds. If income drawn from invest-
ments and past endowments were ignored, the current voluntary support given to voluntary hospitals would be negligible. Moreover, apart
from the big teaching hospitals, voluntary hospitals did not render a
satisfactory service and had conspicuously failed to provide the conditions necessary to maintain an adequate nursing profession. He had
accordingly reached the conclusion that there was an overwhelming
case for putting the voluntary hospitals under some form of public
control. If this was admitted, the first question was whether this
control could be exercised through some form of local government
machinery. The existing local government areas were neither large
enough nor so constituted as to suit the needs of hospital administration. He had considered the possibility of creating some new form
of local government unit for this purpose, but he could not find any
satisfactory solution either by the creation of new directly elected
authorities or by the establishment of joint boards. He accordingly
felt that the right course was to constitute a new National Hospital
Service which would take over both the voluntary hospitals and the
local authority hospitals, including sanatoria, mental hospitals and the
mental deficiency institutions. Safeguards against undue centralisation
would be provided by the setting up of a regional board for each
natural hospital region, and provision would be made for further

delegation to divisional committees where the geography of a region made this desirable. It was only by a scheme of this kind that it would be possible to give contributors an equal return for the equal contributions which they would be required to make under a new scheme of national insurance. His proposals would undoubtedly excite strong opposition by the voluntary hospitals and the local authorities. He was confident, however, that their opposition could be overcome; and his conversations with the medical profession, so far as they had gone, left him with the impression that, confronted with a choice between a primarily local government service and a primarily nationalised service, the great majority of the doctors would prefer the latter.

As regards the suggestion of the Joint Parliamentary Under-Secretary of State for Scotland that the voluntary teaching hospitals should be brought within the proposed National Hospital Service, it was not his intention that the big teaching hospitals should be excluded altogether from the Service, but only that special provision should be made for them within the scheme.

DONALD BRUCE

Nye

In the closing months of 1944 it became clear that an Allied triumph over Hitler and the German Reich could not be too long delayed. Despite the final fling of the German forces in pushing out a salient in the Allied Lines – the Battle of the Bulge – even making allowance for the inevitable war of attrition that was to succeed it, few of us in France doubted the approach of decisive victory. My thoughts as a British officer serving on General Eisenhower's staff became increasingly engaged on the prospects for a Labour victory as and when a general election was called.

I was not alone in thinking about Britain's political scene once hostilities had ceased. In French newspapers and, more particularly, in the US forces' newspaper *Stars and Stripes* there appeared an increasing number of political features. Some of these dealt with developments in Greece, where there was almost daily conflict between the left and the neo-fascists ostensibly in power which was not even mentioned in the UK newspapers available to us. I came to the conclusion that this printed material ought to be seen by someone in authority in the Labour Party, of which I had been an active member since November 1935. Aneurin Bevan immediately sprang to mind.

As a regular reader of *Tribune* I had long sensed an almost complete identity of view with Bevan's whole attitude towards the programme of change, not only in the conduct of foreign policy which might be followed by a future Labour government, but also the domestic programme to be pursued to revitalize democracy in post-war Britain by effecting fundamental and socialist changes in society.

An opportunity to contact Bevan soon occurred. In the course of the Allied advance eastwards and the retreat of the German army our forces had captured the Wehrmacht Chief Signals Officer, General von Braun, who had been transported to London to be housed in the POW 'cage' in the 'Ambassadors' Row' situated on the west side of Kensington Gardens in London. I was sent to London to interrogate the General and succeeded in obtaining what my Staff seniors considered to be a useful picture of the military structure and functions of the German High Command. While I was in London I sought out Aneurin Bevan in the Strand editorial offices of *Tribune* and, after securing a surprisingly easy access to his editorial room, introduced myself to him and placed on his desk a sample of the newspapers circulating in France. He did not appear at all surprised, although much later, in the 1945–50 Parliament, he admitted that he was highly suspicious of the appearance before him of a young Army major in full uniform and had thought initially that my visit might be a ruse of the Security Services somehow to entrap him. In the event, following my return to France, we corresponded occasionally and exchanged views. Much to my surprise I found that my own thinking was almost a mirror of that which Bevan derived largely, but not necessarily, from Marx, Lewis Mumford (the distinguished writer on town planning and social architecture) and John Maynard Keynes. I well recall being first introduced by him to Jennie Lee with the words, 'You see he is "another Mumfordite"!'

The next time Bevan and I met was in the House of Commons in August 1945, following the July election in which I became, by the narrow majority of 1,042 votes, MP for Portsmouth North. It can have been only a couple of days later when he and I met in the Commons Smoke Room – in those days often crowded and one of the key venues for informal talks and drinks among MPs. 'Donald,' he said as we walked along the corridor together, 'I should like you to be my PPS.' I immediately accepted, and walked back with him across Palace Yard and into the then Ministry of Health (covering health, housing and local government) on the opposite corner of Whitehall and George Street – now the Treasury.

Although the role of Parliamentary Private Secretary is of little official significance – indeed, then as now, PPSs were generally regarded (or perhaps 'affected to be regarded') as little more than bag and message carriers for their ministers – they were widely viewed as being in their confidence and felt considerably honoured on that account alone. As for me, the mere opportunity of serving a man whom I considered to be the greatest living socialist was, in itself, one of the high points of my life.

It has occurred to me only in recent years that my appointment, unimportant perhaps to anyone save myself, indicated a surprising aspect of Aneurin's political philosophy. Here was a former mine worker from South Wales, steeped in the miners' trade union traditions, who had played an active role in the battles with mine owners and in local government – and he had chosen an Army officer from the General Staff, and a chartered accountant to boot, to be his PPS. At the time I was innocent enough not to realize that many of my miner MP colleagues, and perhaps others, must have commented adversely on Aneurin's wisdom or credibility in choosing me. Certainly his choice can hardly have helped in easing the earlier perceived tension between himself and the powerful trade union leaders of the time – Ernest Bevin, Sam Watson and Arthur Deakin – and their unions' MPs in the House of Commons.

From the commencement of the 1945 Parliament Nye was under considerable personal stress. He was well aware that his whole political future rested on his ability successfully to manage the operation of the two great departments of state entrusted to him, as well as in his parliamentary skills both in driving and presenting Labour Party policies for ultimate enactment. In addition he was acutely aware of the heavy pressures which the withdrawal by the United States of Lend-

Lease facilities from the UK within eight days of the Labour Government taking office would bring to bear not only on the government itself but upon the country as a whole.

The negotiation by Keynes of the American Loan was to bring some relief and Bevan, like so many others, felt that there were few options open other than acceptance of its terms. I felt bound to advise him accordingly but cannot claim that I had any influence one way or the other. The main political consequence of the two episodes was to put the new Labour government, and its supporters, on the defensive. From then onwards the battle for the achievement of the programme set out in 'Let Us Face the Future' was an uphill one and it was not assisted overmuch by some of the parliamentary party's elegant theorists who were more interested in the nuances of theory than in the ordinary lives of people.

Within his two ministries Nye was actively involved every day from early morning. At first he had some difficulty in convincing his civil service chiefs that he was really determined to do what he said he would. I well remember the earliest stages of the formulation of what was to become the National Health Service. At the first series of staff talks over which Nye presided he gave a broad outline of what he considered should be the principles upon which the health service should be established and the nature of the organizational structure which would have to be developed to bring it to fruition. The Permanent Secretary (Sir Arthur Rooker, one time Private Secretary to Neville Chamberlain) was asked to provide a draft of outline proposals based on his minister's instructions. A few weeks later these were presented. I was not there myself but I was told that the proposals presented to Nye were almost the exact opposite of what he had requested and that Nye had roared with laughter on reading them. 'You can't do this to me, Sir Arthur!' he chided and sent him away to think again.

The Permanent Secretary was somewhat troubled by this response and invited me to lunch at the Reform Club to discuss the situation.

Indicating that he seemed to be getting at cross purposes with his minister, he asked my advice as to what he should do. In the course of our extremely hospitable and friendly encounter I thought I had convinced him that all he had to do was to do as he was told. Clearly, as events subsequently showed, I was not successful for, after a repeat performance some weeks later, Aneurin asked the Prime Minister to 'shift him'. Sir Arthur was duly removed to another job. Thereafter Nye had little difficulty in enforcing his will through the two ministries – after one similar small hiccup with Sir John Maude, in charge of housing and local government, who was moved across to the War Damage Commission for similar reasons.

Shortly after Nye's death I had a long session with Sir Wilson Jameson, the distinguished Chief Medical Officer during the 1945–50 government, who confirmed to me that Nye's tenure of office had been one of the most successful in his long civil service experience and that he had won the devotion of the staff. To a very large extent, he indicated, this loyalty arose because he invariably supported his own department's position at the numerous inter-departmental conferences held to ensure continuity and broad general policies applicable to other ministries or departments, particularly the Treasury. He would never strike bargains with other ministries, either separately or at Cabinet level, which would have the effect of altering fundamentally his own ministry's position as championed by his civil servants. They knew that the ground would not be shifted under their feet without prior consultation in depth. He was rewarded by their complete loyalty throughout his tenure of office.

Let it at once be conceded that the quality of Bevan's debating powers gives some considerable *prima facie* support to the concept of him as a violent and vitriolic personality. He was, of course, merciless in debate. In the earlier stages of the 1945–50 Parliament some members of the then opposition ventured a few experiments in individual inter-ruption and collective barracking whenever Bevan rose to address the

House. They soon stopped it. Their uncalled-for interpolations recoiled on their heads with such violence as to be a growing source of embarrassment to their own party.

Neither were there any half-tones in his method of expression. Here is his description of landlordism in the Welsh valleys, given in the course of a 1946 debate on the Acquisition of Land Bill: 'It is an area from which the landlord, who is the coal owner, has sucked the riches for the last hundred years. The area had created millionaires, and now part of it has been rendered derelict. The orange is almost dry. The sites are in the possession of the colliery owners but, like vultures, they will not desert the carrion for fear there might be the slightest bit of nutriment left.' And when threatening to make public the circumstances in which £2 million was spent, towards the end of the Second World War, in developing the abortive Portal House, he said: 'I suggest to hon. Members that it does not lie in their mouths to talk about commercial probity. They ought to be silent about it, or we shall exhume some other putrefying corpses.' This is hardly language likely to encourage amiable sentiments in the minds of one's opponents.

Such, of course, had never been his intention. For him no belief was worth holding unless it was held strongly. His bitter denunciations of what he believed to be wrong and his passionate advocacy of democratic socialism were a spontaneous expression of his deep conviction of the moral rightness of his cause. In the enunciation of *principles* any tepidness was contemptible and any compromise a weakness.

Most of the highly publicized excerpts from his speeches, not infrequently torn from their context, reflect this strength of belief. His participation in any public discussion, inside or outside Parliament, or on any important questions of principle, usually raised the temperature of the atmosphere in which it was ventilated, and invoked alike the fierce anger of his opponents and the warm enthusiasm of his supporters.

It is sometimes said that his readiness to participate in such fierce and often destructive polemics was a direct result of his harsh experiences as a boy and as a young miner; that the treatment endured by his family and friends at the hands of the mine owners had soured and embittered him, and that a class revenge in retribution was his dominating motive.

Nothing could be further from the truth.

For Bevan the principles of socialism were a matter of intellectual conviction which broadened and deepened after years of study. It was his reading and researches in the magnificent Tredegar Library, founded and financed by the miners themselves, and at the Central Labour College which first gave shape to his philosophy, rather than any emotional reaction to the conditions under which he had lived and had seen others live.

'The student of politics . . .', he wrote, 'must seek integrity and vitality. His Holy Grail is the living truth, knowing that being alive the truth must change. If he does not cherish integrity then he will see in the change an excuse for opportunism and so will exchange the inspiration of the pioneer for the reward of the lackey.

'He must also be on his guard against the old words, for the words persist when the reality which lay behind them has changed. It is inherent in our intellectual activity that we seek to imprison reality in our description of it. Soon, long before we realise it, it is we who become prisoners of the description. From that point on our ideas degenerate into a kind of folklore which we pass to each other, fondly thinking that we are still talking of the reality around us.

'Thus we talk of free enterprise, of capitalist society, of the rights of free association, of parliamentary government, as though all of these words stand for the same things as they formerly did. Social institutions are what they do, not necessarily what we say they do. It is the verb that matters, not the noun.'

Bevan himself very rarely referred to his experiences between the wars either privately or publicly. When he did so it was either in sheer indignation at the absurdity of 'good old days' talk in relation to the poorer section of the community, particularly the miners, or else by way of illustration of an argument to which his personal experience was relevant. 'I appreciate rather more than hon. Members opposite', he declared in July 1946, 'what lack of housing accommodation means. There are more people on our side of the House who have suffered from lack of accommodation than there are on the benches opposite. We do not need to be taught what lack of housing accommodation is. I was brought up, one of a family of twelve, in a four room house. I know what it is. When hon. Members opposite presume to teach us the humanities of housing, we regard it as cant.' If personal hardship, or intimate association with it, had influenced him then it served perhaps to intensify his deep appreciation of the lot of the poorer, weaker and more helpless sections of the community.

In 1934, writing in the *Westminster Gazette*, the then 36-year-old, six-foot, burly, grey-eyed miner MP had made his plea for the miners generally; and at a time when over 200,000 of them, or more than one quarter of the nation's mining skill, were out of work: 'We are told by many eloquent ones that the miner carries the rest of industry on his back. Yes it is true, but his back is bent with toil and weak with hunger, and only supreme courage keeps his head erect. I beg of you to succour him now in his travail, for if he falls he will bring down with him the proud nation which he now carries on his shoulders.'

Twelve years later, on the passing of the National Health Service Bill in 1946, it was the same voice speaking but in a wider context. To old colleagues it brought back old memories. From vehement Tory opponents it drew the tribute of silent respect. In a hushed House Bevan concluded his speech in these words:

The House of Commons only passes Bills, but it is the men and women outside who make them living realities. Now that we are reaching the conclusion let me hope that the echoes of controversy will die down, and that what will reach our ears will not be the declamations of the partisans but the whispers and piteous appeals of the sick people all over the country, of the weak and distressed, who are reaching out their hands to this House of Commons to give them assistance and succour in their difficulties. I believe that, eventually, it will be that small voice that will be heard and that will be most influential, and not the raucous declamations of controversialism.

In 1936 he had written: 'There is a loneliness to be experienced in modern society which the mere physical isolation of the past never produced. It is the loneliness of helplessness surrounded by indifference.' Eleven years later he was able to remedy an injustice to a particularly vulnerable and often lonely member of the community – the illegitimate child. In introducing the Births and Deaths Registration Bill of 1947, providing for a shortened birth certificate without mention of parentage, he referred to the subject in these terms:

If we can prevent injustice to one person we ought to do so. There is an old English roundelay which runs as follows:

> One is one and all alone
> And evermore shall be so.

It varies in different parts of the country but it is very old and shows how deeply sympathetic mankind is towards the isolated individual.

The year 1932 was the nadir of the Great Depression. On a dull, bleak November day Bevan rose in the House of Commons to denounce the Means Test regulations:

I can understand the bitterness in the breasts of people up and down the country today because of my own sense of humiliation when I had to go home and tell my mother, 'In future we shall have to live on my sister's earnings.' That is where the bitterness lies, that is the gravamen of our charge against this system – that you are saying to the working class families in Britain, 'Those at work and those idle must live on the Poor Law standard of subsistence.'

Fifteen years on, also in November, on the second reading of the National Assistance Bill of 1947, he was able to close the book of the past in these words:

The conditions in which the poor lived in the past were harsh and inhumane. Poverty was treated as though it were a crime. Those of us who have been associated with the Boards of Guardians will know how frightfully difficult it was to administer the law in a humane fashion ... These are not the things we are immediately leaving behind because we have left them behind for some little while; but this is the sort of thing upon which we are now finally turning our backs.

If this be the legacy of 'bitterness' over the years, many may think it is not an insubstantial contribution to the betterment of mankind.

It is not generally realized that Bevan, while Minister of Health from August 1945 to January 1951, was responsible for the passing of twenty-three Acts of Parliament on to the statute books. His ministry covered three broad streams of administration: health, housing, local government. This was subdivided into two separate administrations, Health, and Housing and Local Government – the latter also absorbing the truncated functions of the former Ministry of Town and Country Planning.

In addition to the more important pieces of legislation such as the National Health Service Act, the Acquisition of Land Act, the Local

Government Act, the Furnished Houses (Rent Control) Act and the National Assistance Act, he carried out a whole series of statutes covering such widely diverse matters as coast erosion, radioactive substances, prevention of river pollution, penicillin, births and deaths registration, and war damaged sites as well as measures concerned with midwives and nurses, the financing of the housing programme and the removal of some of the wartime restrictions on building works.

This achievement in its totality is roughly equivalent to the constructive legislation carried out by *all* ministries in previous Tory governments in a similar period of time. What is singularly significant about it is that the next Conservative government did not, until 1979, apart from the imposition of charges for treatment under the National Health Service, see fit to challenge the basic structure of Bevan's extensive legislative fabric.

In 1948 one of his bitterest political opponents, a measuring clerk in Bevan's old pit, told a press correspondent: 'The one thing I will not have is the story that Aneurin was lazy. He worked in places so bad that he had to keep blowing his lamp to give it enough oxygen to burn. Billy and he were the family wage earners.'

This same energy he brought to the Ministry of Health in 1945. From his arrival in Whitehall shortly before nine in the morning to the closing of the last Cabinet despatch box in his home at around two hours after midnight he was fully occupied in dealing with the problems of his own ministry and considering the broad national issues with which he was concerned as a senior minister. After two o'clock in the morning Jennie Lee, who had memories of his near-breakdown due to sheer exhaustion in 1936, used to assert her wifely authority and forbid further work. It was thanks largely to her unflagging support and careful household organization, helped by her mother and father who lived with them, that he emerged with his health intact, at any rate until the late 1950s, from the terrific strain that his activities in these years imposed upon him.

*   *   *

The vitally important attribute of a good administrator is the ability to make decisions. Bevan's ability to come to the core of a problem, to weigh up the issues in apparent conflict and to make a decision upon them earned for him the speedy and lasting respect of his senior civil servants.

Though many of the clauses of Bills introduced by him bristled with legal complexities he always insisted on mastering these personally. In the first place it was repugnant to him to have to place undue reliance, during debate, on prompting or advice from his senior civil servants and attendants in the officials' box. He was always well briefed prior to any important debate, but he rarely found it necessary to give more than an occasional and cursory glance at his notes. The principal points were invariably marshalled in his mind and in the correct order long before the time came for him to speak.

In the second place he had a distrust of the 'expert'. This was of long standing. In *Tribune* in May 1938 he wrote:

The people are excluded from forming judgement on various matters of public interest on the grounds that expert knowledge is required and that, of course, the people cannot possess . . . The debunking of the expert is an important stage in the history of democratic communities, because democracy involves the assertion of the common against the special interest . . . The first weapon in the worker's armoury must be a strongly developed bump of irreverence. He must insist on the secular nature of all knowledge.

This never inhibited him, however, from listening to the most expert advice he could obtain, whenever this was necessary. He just took pains to understand it, rather than allowing himself to be dominated by it.

He never permitted himself to forget the criterion by which all legislation and administration should be judged: its effect on the individual. 'I have heard', he said, during a speech on the second reading of the Local Government Bill in 1947, 'the most piteous complaints by representatives of local authorities that this or that local authority is being very badly treated. Now it is impossible to treat an authority badly; all you can do is to ill-treat a person. This is a perfect example of displaced terminology. We are primarily concerned with what happens to the individual.'

His insistence that local authorities should be more diversified in their housing schemes provides one of many examples of this concern:

> I hope that the old people will not be asked to live in colonies of their own – after all they do not want to look out of their windows on endless processions of the funerals of their friends; they also want to look at a procession of perambulators . . . The full life should see the unfolding of a multi-coloured panorama before the eyes of the citizen every day. Therefore I hope local authorities will arrange their schemes in this fashion.

The provisions in the Local Government Act of 1948 which permit local authorities to organize a wider range of amenities for the people than were previously possible are another example. Like many of us, Bevan took occasional alcoholic refreshment, though on any day when he was making an important speech he took none at all until after it was over. He did not care much, however, for the specialized nature of the ordinary public house:

> I believe that it would have a good effect on domestic relations, upon sobriety and upon the general standards of the community if a man were able to go with his wife into a proper place where if he wanted to have a glass of beer or lager, he could have this and his wife could have a cup of tea . . . The experience of most people is that domestic felicity would easily be advanced by it. Many of these public houses would be compelled to change their

character and become reasonable places if it were possible to have alcoholic refreshment in places with greater amenities . . . If a man does not want to have a drink he need not take it. Why should he be prevented from taking it because someone else does not like it? This is entirely a matter for the people in the locality to decide.'

Keenly interested himself in all kinds of cultural activity – he was a great lover of music and took a discriminating enjoyment in art – he was much concerned with the lack of proper local facilities for the encouragement of this aspect of social life: 'We want the local authorities to be armed with general powers to put up theatres of a kind that can also be used as cinemas. It is true that there is in this country to a very remarkable extent an intellectual and artistic renaissance . . . In many parts of the country there are to be found people who are hungry for the things that lie beyond the mere repetition of feature films day after day, week after week and month after month.'

The translation of these concepts into practice, the establishment of the National Health Service and the implementation of his policies on housing and other matters brought him into continuous conflict with entrenched sectional interests to whom his activities appeared as a menace, actual or potential, to their prospects of private financial profit. It was put about that he was rude and overbearing when receiving representations from interests likely to be affected.

This is quite untrue. He would, of course, refuse to negotiate with outside bodies as to the contents of a particular Bill. 'If there is one thing that will spell the death of the House of Commons,' he declared in 1946, 'it is for a Minister to negotiate Bills before they are presented to the House.' There were, nevertheless, many discussions with outside organizations; particularly those concerned with the health service and with housing. I was present at many of them. Unless a firm refusal to be intimidated by some of the highly voluble sectional interests pleading their own special cases, and in some cases making but thinly veiled threats, can be interpreted as 'rude' or 'overbearing', never, in my experience, did Bevan give personal cause for complaint. He was no more than firmly courteous in the face of what was sometimes considerable provocation.

His sense of administrative objectivity sometimes got him into trouble with his colleagues. He was firmly convinced that, for the health service to be a success, its regional and local organization would have to be entrusted to the most suitable and representative people regardless of their political affiliations, public or otherwise, and notwithstanding any avowed individual opposition to the scheme. In this, apart from minor exceptions, he was proved to have been right. But it incurred for him, at any rate temporarily, the hostility of many within his own party – usually the 'respectable' middle-of-the-roaders – who would not hesitate to press upon him the claims of this or that party or trade union official well beyond the limit which Bevan considered to be constitutionally proper.

With the National Health Service firmly established and pressure on Attlee to make changes in the Cabinet itself, Bevan with some reluctance accepted a transfer to the Ministry of Labour in early 1951. Thereafter he played a much larger part in continuing policy arguments on foreign policy and defence as well as on the internal economic and fiscal policies which engaged a government returned with such a slim majority after the February 1950 general election.[1]

Shocked by Cabinet and defence proposals involving an expenditure of £4,700 million Bevan, together with Harold Wilson, argued that it could not possibly be justified, nor could it be carried into effect. With the appointment of Hugh Gaitskell as Chancellor of the Exchequer in succession to Cripps, a move opposed by Bevan in the first instance, matters came to a head when Gaitskell decided, as part of the economies necessary to reconcile such a huge sum on defence, to impose charges for the provision of teeth and spectacles available under the NHS. For Bevan, who had been given an undertaking by

Attlee prior to his taking office as Minister of Labour that no charges would be imposed on such services, this was the final straw.

I well remember the telephone call I had early on the morning of 21 April 1951 asking me to come, with my typewriter, to 23 Cliveden Place for an important meeting. It took me some three-quarters of an hour to get there from my home in Hertfordshire. Nye and Jennie were in earnest discussion with a few others whose names I cannot now recall. Eventually I hammered out the letter, the original carbon copy of which I still retain and which read as follows:

2.30 p.m. 21st April 1951

The Rt Hon. C. R. Attlee C. H., M. P.,
10, Downing Street,
London, S.W.1.

Dear Clem,

In previous conversations with you, and in my statements to the Cabinet, I have explained my objections to many features of the Budget. Having endeavoured, in vain, to secure modifications of these features I feel I must ask you to accept my resignation.

The Budget, in my view, is wrongly conceived in that it fails to apportion fairly the burdens of expenditure as between different social classes. It is wrong because it is based upon a scale of military expenditure, in the coming year, which is physically unattainable, without grave extravagance, in its spending.

It is wrong because it envisages rising prices as a means of reducing civilian consumption, with all the consequences of industrial disturbance involved.

It is wrong because it is the beginning of the destruction of those social services in which Labour had taken a special pride and which was giving to Britain the moral leadership of the world.

I am sure you will agree that it is always better that policies should be carried out by those who believe in them. It would be dishonourable for me to allow my name to be associated in the carrying out of policies which are repugnant to my conscience and contrary to my expressed opinion.

I am sorry that I feel it necessary to take this step after so many years of co-operation in a Government which had done so much for the cause of Labour and the progress of mankind.

I need hardly say that my adherence to the cause of Labour and Socialism is stronger than ever and that I believe that renewed efforts by all of us will result in another thrust towards the goal of our hopes.

As is customary, I shall explain my position in greater detail in my speech to the House of Commons.

May I conclude by wishing you a speedy return to health and vigour.

Yours sincerely,

Aneurin

This was duly despatched to the Prime Minister who was in St Mary's Hospital, London recovering from a short illness.

It is necessary for me to correct the suggestion that Harold Wilson and John Freeman participated personally in the discussions that took place on this day. Nye telephoned Harold Wilson to tell him of his decision, and then John Freeman. Neither of these two equivocated; both offered their immediate support. Stories have been told that Wilson was tardy in his response and made long calculations as to how any particular stand made by him would affect his future political career. This was nonsense. However, I well recall the arrival of John Strachey, then Minister of War, who agonized over his own decision and, while paying tribute to Nye's 'courage', declined to follow him.

* * *

As the party's Foreign Office spokesman at the 1957 Labour Party Conference, Bevan astonished the delegates by his declaration in favour of Britain retaining a nuclear bomb as part of its own armament. 'Do not send me naked into the conference chamber!' he had pleaded.

This was interpreted by Jennie Lee as 'If you take the nuclear weapon from me *before* I go to international consultations, I shall not be able to negotiate for the best terms on which I can give it up.' A few months earlier Nye had visited Khrushchev, the then leader of the Soviet Union, with whom he had a long conversation as to ways in which world tensions could be eased. Security considerations prevented him, quite properly, from giving a public account of these detailed conversations and whether or not, as was customary at that time (and still is), the information was passed to the government itself.

My own view is quite clear. The Soviet Union was apprehensive lest the United States might consider allowing the Bomb to be put into German hands if Britain renounced the use of her nuclear weaponry. This situation, from a future British Foreign Secretary's standpoint, fully justified Bevan's advocacy of the Bomb's retention. Naturally it shattered the stance taken up by the Campaign for Nuclear Disarmament (CND) who thereupon set about attacking Bevan with a venom which certainly belied its peace-loving credentials. He was deeply hurt by these attacks, particularly as they came from *Tribune* and from those who had hitherto derived much of their own political status from their known association with him. It left a mark upon him and contributed much to the growing despair which, despite a final triumphant rallying of the entire party at the 1959 conference, undermined both his spirit and his health.

Shortly after the Labour government's defeat in the general election of 1951, Aneurin commenced work on what he described as a brief outline of his own political philosophy. Much of the work on *In Place of Fear* was carried out in the library of Buscot Park which his old friend, Lord Farringdon, had placed at his disposal so that he could be assured of a degree of uninterrupted privacy. I was able to visit him there from time to time and provide some of the statistical and other factual material from which he quoted where necessary.

The origins of Nye's political convictions were quite clearly Marxist. He wrote:

> In so far as I can be said to have had a political training at all, it has been in Marxism . . . Nor was I alone in this. My experience had been shared by thousands of young men and women of the working class of Britain and, as I have learned since, of many other parts of the world . . . The relevance of what we were reading, to our own industrial and political experience had all the impact of a divine revelation, fell into place. The dark places were lit up and the difficult ways made easy.

This belief, though fundamental to his thinking, was by no means unqualified. 'Quite early in my studies', he reveals in the second chapter of *In Place of Fear*, 'it seemed to me that classic Marxism consistently understated the role of a political democracy with a fully developed franchise. This is the case, both subjectively, as it affects the attitude of the worker to his political responsibilities, and objectively, as it affects the possibility of his obtaining power by using the franchise and parliamentary methods.'

Emphasizing the point further, if only by way of footnote, Bevan cited Frederick Engels's preface to the first English translation of Marx's *Capital* as giving an unequivocal summary of Marx's views:

> Surely, at such a moment, there ought to be heard of a man whose whole theory is the result of a lifelong study of the economic history and condition of England, and whom that study led to the conclusion that, at least in Europe, England is the

only country where the inevitable social revolution might be effected entirely by peaceful and legal means. He certainly never forgot to add that he hardly expected the English ruling classes to submit, without a 'pro-slavery rebellion', to this peaceful and legal revolution.

At this point, it becomes necessary to assess the relevance to Britain's needs of the various proposals put forward by New Labour under the leadership of Tony Blair.

'New Labour', a draft manifesto declares, 'is neither old left nor new right, for a very good reason. Neither remotely corresponds to the nature of the challenges facing us.' It continues: 'We have sought a new path between and ahead of the old left and the new right . . . in place of *laissez faire*, a new dynamism to modernise our economy . . . to set about rebuilding a new one nation society for today.' Later still we read: 'to say that Labour now offers nothing is absurd. It is to define radicalism by a policy agenda of 15 or 20 years ago and then claim any deviation from it is to ditch radical thinking.'

In fact it was less than twenty years ago that Neil Kinnock, Tony Blair's next but one predecessor (and now Britain's Commissioner in the European Community), wrote in his foreword to the 1978 edition of Nye Bevan's *In Place of Fear*:[2]

The self-proclaimed social democrats in Labour, Liberal and Conservative parties quail at the very thought of anything more radical than an ameliorating re-arrangement of society. They try to cajole capitalism into growth and responsibility whilst defending it as a virile guardian of liberty and mainspring of development. Their belief that they can make multinational companies give priority to the demands of democracy is as hollow as the idea that bookmakers are in the business for the advantage of the punters.

This characteristic expression of belief from the now derided 'old left' should be put alongside Mr Blair's sole reference to democratic socialism in the entire forty-page draft manifesto: 'Democratic Socialism is not about high taxes on ordinary people. It is about social justice and a fair deal.'

Bevan's *In Place of Fear* sets out a starkly different political perspective. Writing of the formative years in his political pilgrimage, Nye declared:

Society presented itself to us as an arena of conflicting social forces and not as a plexus of individual striving. These forces are in the main three: private property, poverty and democracy. They are forces in the strict sense of the term for they are active and positive. Amongst them no rest is possible . . . *Either poverty will use democracy to win the struggle against property, or property in fear of poverty will destroy democracy.*

He continued:

Of course, the issue never appears in such simple terms. Different flags will be waved in the battle in different countries and at different times. And it may not be catastrophic unemployment. There may be a slower attrition as there was in Britain before the war, but poverty, great wealth and democracy are ultimately incompatible elements in any society . . . This is the answer to so many people who see freedom in a vacuum. A free people will always refuse to put up with preventable poverty. If freedom is to be saved and enlarged, poverty must be ended. There is no other solution. The problem of how to prevent these sources from coming into head-on collision is the principal study of the more politically conscious Conservative leaders. How can wealth persuade poverty to use its political freedom to keep wealth in power? There lies the whole art of Conservative politics in the twentieth century.

It remains the firm belief of 'old Labour', including myself, that sooner or later the whole Labour movement will have to face up to the necessity, by parliamentary means, of challenging the capital-dominated order of society. The draft manifesto makes it abundantly clear that New Labour does not, even indirectly, seek to challenge the present dominance of capital (property) over the entire British economic and social scene. While making it clear that 'we *must* provide a labour force that is equipped to succeed, flexible and acceptable but also capable of being partners in the enterprise,' at the same time its attitude towards capital is permissive: companies '*should* be emphasising measures which enhance *people's employability. . . should* actively develop a new partnership with *their* workforce, which goes well beyond that of an ordinary buyer and seller of a commodity . . . Companies *should* be improving communications and participation.'

One seeks in vain for any intimation as to what will happen if companies decline to perform as they *should*. Instead every effort has been made by Labour to disarm capital (property) fears that anything untoward is likely to happen which might adversely affect their interests.

Concurrently with these developments there has been a deliberate effort by New Labour to distance itself almost completely from the trade union organizations which for a long time have played a dominating role in Labour politics. In pursuit of this 'stand-off' policy the present leadership can fairly claim that Nye himself dismissed their value as a political instrument for the achievement of socialism by parliamentary means. It is also reinforced by his refusal, while a Cabinet minister (1945–51), to accept trade union demands to legislate in any particular way put forward by them. Consult – yes; accept instructions – no. Even during the Labour government of 1945–51, this attitude did nothing to improve his working relationship with very right-wing trade union leaders such as Arthur Deakin and Sam Watson.

Historically speaking, the trade union reaction is hardly surprising in view of their day-to-day functions in securing the greatest possible benefits in terms of pay, conditions of work and future security from the capitalist employers of labour. Although, as founders of the Labour Party and providers of a significant amount of Labour's finances in the past, they were connected formally to the achievement of socialism in Britain, at the same time they felt dependent on the continuance of capitalism, and therefore of the employers of labour, as a fundamental condition for their continued relevance to their own members on whose behalf they were in conflict.

The unions themselves, perhaps with one eye on the fate of 'free' trade unions in the Soviet Union, had a deeply ingrained, though perhaps subconscious, uncertainty as to their prospects should a future Labour government venture to put a very substantial capitalist enterprise under the direct state control which they equated with the established concept of 'socialism'. There can be little doubt that with the publication – albeit subject to continual alteration and elaboration – of party policies by New Labour's leadership, trade union anxieties on that account ought by now to have been allayed.

As for Bevan himself, his continued advocacy of the achievement of a socialist society by the use of parliamentary democracy was drowned in a sea of Tory propaganda, not disowned by the right-wing members of the Labour Party or most of the trade union leaders who sometimes joined in the clamour that he was somehow a personal supporter of the Soviet system whose real purpose was to establish a Soviet dictatorship in Britain. The real truth is, of course, the exact opposite. Bevan was always highly critical of the Soviet dictatorship. He wrote:

Politics is an art, not a science. By the study of anthropology, sociology, psychology and such elements of social and political economy as are relevant, we try to work out the correct principles to guide us in our approach to the social problems of our time. Nevertheless the application of these principles to a given situation is an art. The failure to recognise this has caused the leaders of the Soviet Union to make blunder after blunder, not only in Russia itself, but more especially in their attitude to other countries.

And again:

We all know there are features of the Soviet system which are repulsive. The existence of huge forced labour camps, the ruthless punishments meted out to political offenders, the disappearance without trace of people who offend against the ruling clique, the appalling doctrine of 'associative crime', all these are deeply offensive.

More particularly, he was scornful of the endless description of the Soviet policies as 'Marxist'. He repeatedly made fun of MPs, including some Labour members, by challenging them to provide any writing of Marx advocating the pursuit of any defined political programme for any particular country or group of countries. The nearest thing to a policy ever advocated by Marx, and that was made jointly with Engels, he joked, was in the Communist Manifesto of 1848, in which they proposed the introduction of a graduated income tax and the nationalization of the Bank of England. Hardly revolutionary stuff.

Yet these puerile arguments became the vogue from the 1950s until Nye's death on 6 July 1960 and thereafter to the present day. Mainly this is due to an unwillingness, save for a minority of MPs and other political practitioners whether at national or local level, to make any sustained effort to read books. Instead there is a general acceptance of that which it is fashionable to believe at any given time and to rely on spin doctors, research assistants, speech writers and instant

TV snippets as a substitute for personal thinking and detailed examination. The half perception of this possibility is still evidenced by a vague sense of guilt reflected in the substitution of verbal and personal abuse for quiet, rational argument.

As Bevan wrote forty-five years ago:

> The British people have never been less informed about what is happening in the rest of the world. A large proportion of the tiny space now left to the national dailys and weeklys is devoted to deliberate pornography or to retailing the minutest details of the lives of the Royal Family. Indeed, the latter has now reached a point where it has become a national disgrace. It must be deeply repugnant to the persons immediately concerned, who are carrying out difficult duties with commendable dignity and restraint.

Bevan's involvement in international affairs and in disarmament is well known – particularly his support for Yugoslavia's independent stand against Soviet Russia and also his sympathy for the problems of India (strengthened by his and Jennie's close association with Nehru) and of the former colonial Commonwealth. Neil Kinnock, in his 1978 preface to *In Place of Fear*, emphasized the factors giving 'particular validity to Bevan's analysis, preoccupations and prophecies. They are not academic because they are related to experience, available proof and a historical perspective that is free of mythology. They appeal to common sense and acknowledge realities instead of rattling off dogma.'

Neil's tribute and testimony were of course given during the Labour Party's highly critical attitude towards the European Economic Community, as evidenced by its open opposition to the Single European Act of 1986. He was then mindful of Bevan's warning about the significance of international organizations. 'International organizations are continually passing the most idealistic resolutions that remain in the air because the statesmen subscribing to them are without the power to carry them out.' The assumption behind these activities is that the social and economic conditions derive from political constitutions. But the reverse is the case. An old teacher used to tell me concerning nations and constitutions: 'The man's clothes are there because the man is there, not the man is there because the man's clothes are there. A nation is a nation before it gets a constitution.' So much for the European super-state to which the Labour leadership is becoming progressively drawn.

I have deliberately quoted at length from *In Place of Fear* because, in my view, it ought to be read by every Labour MP (especially newly elected ones) as well as by party members and the wider public. At the same time I am aware of the difficulties attending the efforts that have to be made in studying such an important work. Forty-five years have passed since it was penned and many will need some convincing that its central themes are relevant today. The accelerating effects of improvements, some of them revolutionary, in information technology have resulted in our being able, literally, at the press of a button to gain access to areas of accumulated knowledge as well as to witness events as they happen on a world-wide, if selective, basis. The time for reflection on the significance of what we thus learn has correspondingly diminished, and with it the time available to us both to understand and to choose.

Yet choose we must. Bevan in his comparatively short life provided us with the moving parameters within which political, economic and, above all, democratic decisions vital to the enhancement of human life have to be made and the directions they must necessarily take – if civilization is to survive.

TESSA BLACKSTONE

The Boy Who Threw an Inkwell
Bevan and Education

Some people have the good fortune to be taught by inspiring teachers in attractive surroundings, mixing with fellow pupils with whom they make enduring friendships. They look back on their schooldays with nostalgic pleasure. For most people their schooldays are a more mixed experience, in which boredom and frustration feature as well as excitement and inspiration. For others the memories are profoundly unhappy: of being alienated from the whole process, even humiliated by teachers whom they loathed or feared, of learning little or nothing and of leaving school with profound relief. Such was Nye Bevan's experience. Michael Foot tells us that 'Aneurin hated school with an abiding hatred. He could hardly listen patiently to a discussion of formal education. Boys and girls should educate themselves as he did; any other method he was inclined to regard as newfangled and distorting.'[1]

His views on formal schooling were shaped by his elementary school headmaster, whom Foot describes as 'a bully and a snob'. Foot illustrates this with an anecdote about him humiliating a boy who had been absent from school because he had to share his shoes with his brother so that they were forced to take turns in going to school. Unable to tolerate the cruel mocking, Aneurin picked up an inkwell and threw it at the headmaster – apparently one of many incidents in which he fought this obnoxious figure of authority.

Somehow he learned to read but seemed to have acquired little else at school in the way of either skills or knowledge. Foot speculates that the terrible stutter he suffered from as a child may have contributed to his horror of school. His stutter may even have been brought about by the schooling he received: he was left-handed and forced to write with his right hand. His writing was sprawling and untidy and he never improved it; indeed he acquired a distaste for the physical act of writing which never left him, according to Foot. Certainly he was teased by his fellow pupils for his stutter and was what his sister Myfanwy called 'a lonely chap'. John Campbell speculates that, 'banned from the fellowship of the playground', this very loneliness drove him to voracious reading and, more unusually, public speaking, first at Sunday School and later at miners' lodge meetings.[2]

How strong the contrast was between his schooling and the informal teaching he received from his miner father, a romantic who loved music and literature, and from his mother, a skilled dressmaker and superb manager of a large family on little income. No teacher at Sirhowy School recognized his potential: indeed, his hated headmaster even kept him down a class with younger boys for a year, considering him to be lazy. So, unlike his clever elder sister, Myfanwy, who went to secondary school, he left school just before he was fourteen to go down the mine. By then he had joined the Sirhowy Bridge lending library and before long was reading at the Tredegar Workmen's Institute Library. Here, with the help of the librarian, he devoured books, reading into the night, in spite of the long hours at the pit. The learning he acquired was eclectic; he roamed widely across politics, history, evolution and natural history. He loved poetry and wrote it himself. To help cope with his stutter, he and a close friend, a fellow miner, with whom he tramped the countryside, borrowed Roget's *Thesaurus* and looked up synonyms for the words he found most difficult to pronounce. In doing so he built up a vast vocabulary, which fed his later oratory. When he went with his friend to Blackpool for a holiday, he took a case heavily laden with books.

He belonged then to that great tradition of working-class autodidacts who, in spite of huge obstacles, educated themselves through reading and absorbing what they read, arguing about it with others and relating it to their own experience. In his case that experience invigorated him as he moved around the pits of South Wales, becoming notorious for the way he challenged authority and stood his ground against the overmen and, indirectly, the colliery owners for whom they worked. At lodge meetings he took on the union leaders, too, urging them to fight harder for the men they represented. As Foot put it, 'no university could have taught him as much as life in the South Wales coalfields through those tempestuous years' of his young and early manhood. Small wonder then that he was dismissive later about formal education.

While his formal *schooling* stopped at the age of thirteen and he could justifiably claim that most of what he knew was self-taught, he did try, and succeeded in getting, some formal *education* as an adult. At the age of twenty-one he won a scholarship provided by the South Wales Miners' Federation to go for two years to the Central Labour College in London, which the Federation ran for young trade unionists to learn Marxist economics and labour history. The college's objectives were transparently revolutionary with a prospectus 'based upon the recognition of the antagonism of interest between Capital and Labour', declaring that its purpose was 'to equip workers to propagate and defend the interest of their class'. Its aim was clear: 'the abolition of wage slavery'.

What he gained from his experience there is a matter of some dispute. His own much later verdict was dismissive: it had been a waste of time; and Michael Foot accepts Bevan's version. But in a long footnote in the second edition of his biography, Foot admits that nothing in the first edition had stirred up so much controversy as his claim that 'his [Bevan's] two years at the Labour College left little mark', although Foot has also rather grudgingly admitted that 'almost certainly, he had sharpened his debating skill and his understanding of Marxism'. In the same footnote he quotes at length the views of George Phippen, a fellow student of Bevan's, who acted as secretary for the Welsh students in their relations with the South Wales miners. Phippen knew Bevan well and claimed that the benefits for Bevan were far greater than Foot implied. First the curriculum was broader than the college's aims and prospectus suggested. The students were taught sociology, economics, philosophy and history. Teaching by the college's staff was supplemented by experts from outside, lecturing on a diverse range of subjects from literature to local government. In addition students were encouraged to go to LCC evening classes. Bevan apparently took up the opportunity, going to classes in Fulham on finance, banking and foreign exchange. Presumably he wanted to find out more about how capitalism worked.

As is almost always the case in adult education, Bevan also learned from his fellow students. Phippen implies this without saying so explicitly. Bevan had come from a homogeneous community. At the college he met miners from all over the country and men from other occupations, railwaymen, engineers and dyers, for example. Many of the men he met there went on to become leaders in the British working-class movement in the trades unions and the Labour Party. In his second year he also taught an evening class himself in North London, about which he expressed doubt as to his capacity to do it. He persevered and succeeded. He was also helped by the college's visiting elocution teacher finally to overcome his stammer. Like so many adult students the experience of studying with others, in a more formal structure than sitting alone reading at night, gave him confidence, forced him to discipline himself in what he read and listened to, and widened his horizons.

If Bevan even partially acknowledged this, he would surely have embraced today's movement for lifelong learning and the campaign to give adults more opportunity to pursue education, either full or part-time, as mature students. As someone with prodigious energy and drive himself, he would also have identified with and recognized the qualities of adults with jobs who study in the evenings and at weekends. He would, I think, have argued for investing more in such people and for widening opportunities for adult learning, in spite of, or perhaps even because of, his rather despairing view of conventional schooling. It is for this reason that I have devoted this chapter to exploring the view that the only proper concept of education is lifelong.

Slowly but relentlessly the predominant view of education as the preparation of young people for adult life is being replaced. What is emerging instead is a new concept of education as an experience that never ends but continues throughout people's lives. This is a much more dramatic change than appears at first sight. Indeed it is every bit as significant as the introduction of universal education in industrial societies in the latter half of the nineteenth century. For around a hundred years education has been focused on children and adolescents and a small minority of young adults. It has had a clear beginning in early childhood and a clear end, although the cut-off date has varied according to social class, gender and ability. It has for the most part been institutionalized in schools, colleges and universities and clearly separated from other activities; the task of education has largely been in the hands of full-time trained professionals.

During the 1970s various changes in education took place across the developed world. Education was extended downwards to younger children, challenging assumptions about an appropriate starting age of five or six years old. Of course the idea of educating very young children outside the home was not new. Pestalozzi, Froebel, Montessori and others in the nineteenth and early twentieth centuries all advocated the partial relinquishment of the family's responsibility for the early socializing and education of children, and devised institutional structures and curricula for this purpose. Moreover, in the Welsh valleys, there was a long tradition of children starting school before the age of five. However, the movement for universal nursery education did not have much success until the late 1960s. Influenced by both new forms of feminism and, from the left, the drive to equalize opportunities through educational reform, for the first time it started to move towards centre stage in policy debates. Psychological studies revealing the rapidity of learning in very small children also had an impact and the idea that children were ready for schooling only at a certain age was challenged.

More or less simultaneously education was also being extended beyond the secondary school for far larger numbers than ever before. The expansion of higher and further education was rapid in most OECD countries as well as in the fast developing countries of the Pacific rim, during the 1970s and 1980s. The biggest beneficiaries of this expansion in many countries have been women. One facet of the changing position of women has been to open up educational opportunities to them that were closed in the past – in spite of girls' superior performance to that of boys at the primary and secondary stage. Whereas in the 1950s and 1960s many parents expected that their sons would go into higher education but that their daughters would seek lower-level qualifications, by the end of the 1980s these different expectations for male and female children had largely disappeared.

The huge increase in the participation of school-leavers in post-school education during this period helped to expose the extent to which not just Bevan's generation of school-leavers, but those which followed, had missed out on the chance to study at a more advanced level. As this became more and more apparent the demand for university and college places from mature students in their twenties, thirties and forties grew. Much of this demand has taken the form of a wish to study part-time, combining it with full-time employment or the care of children. A new climate developed in which the combination of the pursuit of formal learning with other adult responsibilities, notably jobs and families, became commonplace, whereas earlier it had been a rarity.

The rapidity of social and economic change was at the same time becoming more and more apparent. This cast doubts on the effectiveness of an education system which ended most people's access to it well before they were twenty and, even for the minority who successfully completed higher education, two or three years after they were twenty. The need to update skills and knowledge later in life became a more and more frequent refrain. The growth of high-tech industries and the information technology revolution in the service sector reinforced the need to acquire new skills. At the same time the demand for unskilled labour collapsed in many advanced economies. All these changes have helped to shape the educational revolution I am describing. Since this revolution is by no means completed, it is continuing to be affected by these economic and technological changes.

Other changes both in the nature of employment and in social structures are playing their part. In particular, adults have time available to pursue education in ways that were much more difficult in the past. A few determined autodidacts like Bevan himself were always willing to sacrifice the limited leisure they had as adults to learn. For most people, however, long working weeks and domestic responsibilities made the night school, or reading alone in the local library, a tough assignment that few could muster the energy and enthusiasm to take on. As the working day has shortened it has become easier to do a job and to pursue education at the same time. The trend towards more flexible hours, more part-time jobs and more working from home will make it easier still. Flexible retirement, earlier retirement and in increasing numbers much earlier retirement will enhance the opportunities of middle-aged people to continue their education into later life. It is nevertheless unlikely that Bevan would have seen these increased opportunities for late education as adequate compensation for the enforced retirement of so many people in their fifties.

In the post-war years right through to the early 1970s, most young men and women married in their early twenties and had their first child soon after. Marriage and the creation of a family more or less coincided with the end of education. Working-class young people who for the most part completed their formal education sooner than their middle-class peers married and started a family earlier than those who extended their full-time education beyond the secondary school. Later marriage or long-term cohabitation and the substantial delay which now takes place before the first child is born have led to a disconnection between the end of education and parenthood. The average age of becoming a mother for the first time in Britain is now twenty-eight. Many young women and their partners do not now contemplate parenthood until their thirties. This too creates time in early adulthood for the pursuit of education during the first decade of working life, time which did not exist on a large scale before. Childless couples are more likely to have the energy, the time and the resources to continue with various forms of part-time education and training than those with small children.

The breakdown of many marriages, leading to separation and eventual divorce, may also lead to more adults seeking to change their lives outside the domestic sphere. One route to such change is the pursuit of education and training. The end of a relationship is quite often cited by mature students as a reason for enrolling on a course. How much of this is compensatory behaviour to fill in the time otherwise taken by the departed spouse or partner is unclear. For some it may be straightforward liberation – a new-found freedom to pursue interests they had been wanting to pursue but felt constrained from doing so by a relationship. For others it may represent a need to start afresh and fill their time with new activities; some may even hope to find a new partner by this route.

A job for life, a career for life, a husband or wife for life, once taken for granted by many people, can no longer be assumed. Discontinuities at work and at home in which people's lives have a more episodic character to them are more and more commonplace. Serial employment, based on short-term contracts, has started to replace the permanent career, sometimes in a single organization, often in no more than one or two, in the past. More frequent job changes require the ability to adjust to new environments and work structures and to enrol for further education and training to ease the process.

What evidence is there that education systems are responding to these changes? The changing nature of student profiles in many countries is one indication of the way they are responding. The conventional stereotype of the student as an eighteen-year-old male, more or less straight out of secondary school and studying full-time (in fact playing quite a lot of the time) with no involvement in the labour market, is now out of date. In the UK there has for some time been a disproportionate increase in the number of applications for an undergraduate place in a higher education institution from mature men and women. In the five-year period between 1987 and 1992 applications from people over twenty-one increased by 215 per cent, whereas applications from those under twenty-one increased by only 66 per cent. Around a quarter of all applicants were over twenty-one in 1992 and around 12.5 per cent were over the age of twenty-five, an increase of 262 per cent since 1987. Over half of all students actually studying now are over twenty-one. Many older students study part-time, combining jobs and courses. The proportion of first degree and diploma students studying part-time has doubled since the late 1970s. By 1993 12.6 per cent of these students were studying part-time. However, the proportion of *all* students, including postgraduate degree and diploma students, studying part-time is much higher: by 1993 a third of all enrolments were part-time.

After an unprecedented growth in higher education which greatly increased access for eighteen-year-olds as well as older students, many commentators are predicting a slow-down in further growth for school-leaver entrants. Such predictions are tricky, if only because they depend on institutional factors as well as underlying demand based on perceptions of the value of higher education. At present the proportion of school-leavers with two A Levels going into higher education has virtually reached saturation point; nearly all young people who manage to stick it out at school and get two A Level passes get a place somewhere. The proportion of young people with A Levels has grown from 11 per cent in 1962 to 32 per cent today. Some experts believe that further growth is unlikely to be spectacular.[3] The broadening of A Levels, to which the Labour Party is committed, could, however, alter the situation. Nevertheless, it seems reasonable to assume that a good part of the further growth of universities will be to provide for adults returning to study some years after leaving school or, in the case of postgraduates, some years after graduating. Some of the old universities were initially slow to adjust their provision to take adults returning to education into account, while in contrast the new universities have always catered for substantial numbers of part-time undergraduates. Today nearly all universities are aware of the importance of their adult clientele, although many old universities concentrate their provision for mature students at the postgraduate level.

An analysis of the continuing differences in access at eighteen for young people from different social backgrounds is illuminating and has implications for future growth in provision for mature students. Participation in higher education is still considerably higher among the children of professional and managerial groups. Were Bevan alive today he would certainly rail against this as a manifestation of the perpetuation of class privilege. It would also have reinforced any doubts he might have had about education as a vehicle for social change or a means of redistribution. Two-thirds of those offered places in the old universities were from social class I and II in 1992 and 55 per cent of those offered places in the new universities came from similar backgrounds. However, an examination of the trends over time does reveal some catching up by young people whose parents are in manual or clerical jobs. In the seven-year period between 1985 and 1992 in the old universities the participation rate for young people from social class IV and V increased the fastest, followed by those from social class III N (non-manual) and III M (manual). The slowest growth was in the professional managerial groups. It is also noteworthy that participation rates for the children of manual workers are higher in the new universities than the old. In spite of these relative increases in participation, and the significance of the new universities for young people from social backgrounds with little tradition of entering higher education, the proportion of young people entering universities whose parents are manual workers, whether skilled, semi-skilled or unskilled, is still much lower than for their middle-class peers.

Bevan would surely have welcomed the fact that the fastest growth in eighteen-year-old participation will come from these under-represented groups, if current trends continue. Much will, of course, depend on the success of the education system in retaining these young people until they are eighteen and on the openness of higher education institutions to recruit those with vocational rather than conventional academic qualifications.

There is therefore still scope for growth in the demand for places from older men and women from lower-middle- and working-class backgrounds who missed out earlier. There will be many such people in their late twenties and thirties who will observe their younger relatives going to university, even though they did not. Some of them will aspire to higher education as a route to promotion into lower- and middle-level management positions in the service sector where they are already employed. Others will wish to escape from routine manual jobs whether in manufacturing or service sectors, where job prospects are poor and opportunities for promotion are limited. Many of these people will be aiming for vocational qualifications which look as if they will help them most in the labour market. There will, however, continue to be adults from these social groups who want to enrol for traditional academic courses with no particular vocational route in mind. These are people whose secondary school experience may have been negative and whose family background provided little encouragement to pursue higher education on leaving school.

Birkbeck College, focusing on research-based teaching in the arts, social sciences and natural sciences, is full of such people at the undergraduate level. But even at Birkbeck, which, compared with the new universities, provides few directly vocational courses at first-degree level, new degrees in law and business studies have proved phenomenally attractive. These vocational courses are probably at the top end in terms of the academic demands they make on students. A growing part of higher education is likely to be vocational courses, both for those without graduate qualifications and those with them, who wish as adults to equip themselves for particular occupations. They will range widely, from catering to computer applications to the care of the elderly.

Subjects such as pure science and mathematics will decline in numerical importance, as universities continue to expand to meet the demands of older students studying, for the most part, on a part-time basis. Opportunities for lifelong learning in these subjects must be maintained both for the small minority of those wanting to start these subjects from scratch as adults and for those graduates returning to bring themselves up to date with new developments in their field. But, given the poor take-up of science places by eighteen-year-olds, those seeking to upgrade and renew their knowledge and skills in the sciences will also be a minority. Conventional wisdom has it that the lack of people coming forward to study science and mathematics, and incidentally engineering too, is a matter for concern. Those conventional concerns are, however, misplaced. Education in science and engineering at higher levels is very expensive and the number of jobs available for graduates in these fields is relatively small and likely to continue to be so. The old Soviet Union trained large numbers of scientists, many of whom ended up in unproductive work in research institutions, which are now collapsing as the vast public subsidies which sustained them vanish. Advanced economies need top-class scientists and engineers, but only in small numbers. Both cost constraints and the shift towards lifelong education will mean the proportion of people studying science in universities will go on declining. Hand-wringing about this will be out of place.

No assessment of the factors affecting the future of education and the move away from rigid structures confining it to young people can be complete without considering the potentially revolutionary impact of the information super-highway. Earlier I touched on some of the social and economic factors leading to the de-institutionalization of education as we know it. Technological change is likely to be even more important in bringing this about. Surfing the super-highway can be translated into pursuing a course in the virtual classroom at the virtual university on the Internet. How Nye would have responded to this is anyone's guess! He might have seen the new technology as a New Jerusalem providing exceptional opportunities for the lonely learner in charge of his or her own destiny rather than being dependent on teachers and the formal educational system. Alternatively he might have feared that genuine learning would be degraded by the 'cherry-picking' made possible by the Internet. There are currently around thirty million users of the Internet world-wide of whom around one million are in the UK. It is predicted that by the turn of the century there will be 750 million account holders, opening up access to new forms of information world-wide to vast numbers of people. The more people who can afford to have the necessary equipment in their homes, the greater the likelihood of large-scale de-schooling – at least for adult learners.

Back in the 1960s Ivan Illich wrote a book in which he advocated the break-up of conventional schools and colleges and the creation of new forms of learning in the home, the workplace and the community.[4] Given Bevan's dislike of formal education, he might well have found these ideas refreshing. At the time Illich's blueprint seemed idealistic and unlikely to materialize. Today it looks distinctly possible, if not for young children and adolescents, at least for young people over the age of about sixteen and for adults. Even younger children might be able to spend less time in the classroom and more time on the computer at home. However, the question of who supervises them would arise. Schools were invented in the first place partly to keep children off the streets, when it was no longer possible or acceptable to employ them. Unless the labour market were to be changed in dramatic ways to allow parents to stay at home for longer hours, schools will go on being needed. But teachers may have less control over what children learn as their pupils surf the super-highway outside school hours.

For adults the scope for de-institutionalized lifelong learning is greatly enhanced by the new technology. Illich quotes Fidel Castro, who predicted that the time would come when all universities in Cuba could be closed with the de-schooling of society. This looks a little less far-fetched than it did at the time, though today's university teachers need not anticipate being out of a job quite yet. My own institution, Birkbeck College, has, in fact, initiated the first ever British course to go on the Internet. It is on the Principles of Protein Structure and uses the World Wide Web in association with the Globe Wide Network Academy (cyberspace's virtual university). The jargon may be a little off-putting but the possibilities offered by courses delivered in this way are breathtaking. It allows the instant creation of an international community of scholars: 250 students enrolled last year from twenty-seven countries all over the world. It makes it possible to construct a course with contributions from experts or 'consultants' who log in material from all over the world. Thus not only was course material provided by scientists from Birkbeck's renowned Crystallography Department — some thirty experts in protein structure also fed graphics and textual material into the course and involved the students in technical discussions about it via e-mail. Moreover, the students themselves can interact with each other via their keyboards in the virtual classroom in which a number of participants can be logged into the same remote computer. Many of the participants produced material for the course in the form of web pages on their 'personal' protein or area of interest.

It will surely not be long before hundreds of other courses are developed for the Internet: in 1997 space can be rented for as little as £40. The courses have the advantage of being available at any time of the day or night, so that the student can study when he or she wishes rather than at the hours dictated by institutional timetables. As a man who read through the night, Bevan would certainly have appreciated this. The Internet could eventually reduce the need for institutional facilities, such as classrooms and libraries. Looking up a definition or following a link to more material can be just a mouse click away. It will also reduce the need for students at advanced levels to travel to other countries to study in institutions with well-established reputations in their field. This could be of considerable benefit to the developing world. Potential students of any age in any part of the globe can enrol.

There is, of course, one key proviso: they must have access to the required equipment. Such access, particularly in the third world, depends heavily on the costs entailed. Presently the price of a personal computer is coming down by 50 per cent every two years. At 1997 prices, to get into the Internet requires buying a modem (around £200), £10 per month rental and the cost of time on line; £30 a quarter purchases quite a lot of time. The cost of this investment is, of course, beyond the reach of most third world students. It is, however, much less than the cost of providing for them at a UK university. As such it poses a challenge to donor countries in formulating new kinds of development aid.

To summarize, there are social, economic and technological forces at work which will transform education from institutionally based provision largely confined to young people to one in which many people are being educated and re-educated throughout their lives and doing so without necessarily turning up somewhere where they sit at a desk and take notes from someone who 'teaches' them directly. This raises a number of important policy questions, which have so far not been given much consideration. The policy agenda is still preoccupied with a range of problems concerning the expansion of the *existing* system, how higher education should be funded, the relationship between research and teaching, the quality of courses and how this should be monitored. There are worries about whether diversity should be encouraged or whether convergence is an inevitable consequence of giving more and more institutions the status of universities.

These are all legitimate matters for debate. Higher education is a big and expensive industry costing around seven and a half billion pounds per annum in the UK. Nearly a third of all eighteen-year-olds now go on to full-time study at a university. In 1900, when Bevan was a small child, it was 1.2 per cent; by 1938 it had doubled to 2.4 per cent; by 1962 it had reached 6.5 per cent (including teacher training at colleges of education). Where just before the Second World War there were fifty thousand students of whom half were at Oxford, Cambridge and London and a quarter at the Scottish universities, today there are approximately three-quarters of a million. If part-timers, postgraduates and overseas students are included, the figure is nearly one and a half million. However, the debate about expansion centres too much on whether more school-leavers should be admitted to first degree courses. Various organizations, including the Confederation of British Industry and the Committee of Vice-Chancellors and Principals, are calling for a 40 per cent target for young people graduating by the year 2000 and 50 per cent or above a little later. However, experts have estimated that young people now have a 60 per cent chance of going to university at some time in their life if opportunities for part-time or full-time higher education for mature students are taken into account.

The question that is rarely asked is whether there are advantages in some people starting a course in their twenties or thirties rather than in their teens? Should we be relentlessly continuing the expansion of the number of eighteen-year-olds going into conventional forms of higher education? Would it instead be better if more of them delayed study at first degree level until later? Can we motivate half

171

or more of all young people between the ages of sixteen and nineteen to do the necessary preparatory study for a degree at today's required standards? To ask such a question may be perceived as reactionary by some people. If, however, lifelong learning is to become a reality there should be a genuine choice for the individual about when to come in and out of it. And the policy-makers need to consider whether to encourage more provision immediately on leaving school or more later. If the achievement some obtain is much greater as a result of starting studies at this level when they are older and more mature, then there is a case for developing policies which make increases in mature students more likely.

At present the way in which students are financed militates against genuine choice. All full-time students – the vast majority of whom are young people in their late teens and early twenties – receive free tuition in British universities. All part-time students, most of whom are in their late twenties and thirties, though in some cases even older, have to pay fees, which contribute to the cost of their tuition. They are also ineligible for any kind of maintenance grant or for the government loan scheme, even if they are unemployed. This inequity in the treatment of part-time older students is difficult to justify unless we wish to put a premium on starting study at eighteen rather than at twenty-five or thirty and to discourage later starters.

The expansion of higher education has, however, led to serious questions being raised about its future funding, as its potential cost to the taxpayer escalates. For some time economists have pointed out the regressive nature of higher education funding in which the poor and the disadvantaged, who do not have much chance of going to university, pay taxes towards the education of a relatively privileged group of young people, who get the benefit. Under the present system, if it were to expand to a 50 per cent participation rate for eighteen-year-olds, that would still leave half the population either getting nothing at all, or having to pay either for courses in the FE system or for part-time courses in higher education later. Bevan at his most idealistic would no doubt have argued for free education for all with equal access to it. However, there has never been free post-school education for all; what is more, the privileged have free access and the less privileged pay. But largely because of escalating costs to the public purse, rather than on equity grounds, new forms of funding are now being proposed. Students would be asked to repay at least some of the costs of their higher education later, through various income-contingent repayment schemes. Bevan the pragmatist would, I think, have supported reforms of this kind. He would have seen the case for recovering part of the cost from those who have benefited from higher education when their earnings are above an agreed threshold. He would certainly want to make the system less inequitable.

If students have to repay later, any one of the following changes could happen. First, more undergraduates may wish to remain at home to save on repaying their maintenance costs. The university as an expensive boarding school, in which older adolescents spend substantial amounts of time at play in subsidized facilities as well as studying, has many attractions, not least for their parents. It is, how-ever, immensely expensive; around one-fifth of the total cost of higher education goes on student maintenance. A lot of university real estate is made up of residential accommodation for students. A further 25 per cent expansion of the existing system (to get to the target of 40 per cent of eighteen-year-olds) would entail building a lot more halls of residence. Expansion weighted towards older students who live in their own homes would avoid this. The abolition of maintenance grants which do not have to be repaid will also cut costs because of more home-based students as a consequence.

Second, changes in funding entailing repayments from graduates may also lead to a break-up of the three-year honours degree system. In order to reduce costs some students may want to opt for 'sprint' learning, going for fast, intensive courses, totally immersing themselves in study and reducing the time spent on play. Others may want to combine study with full or part-time jobs to avoid the need for a loan for their maintenance costs. This might lead to a demand for strung-out courses lasting for several years, giving the part-time student a lot more time for leisure than at present when the completion of the equivalent to a three-year full-time course is expected of them in only four or five years part-time.

Third, students who get used to studying and working at the same time while doing undergraduate courses are likely to return as part-time students later, either to do a master's degree or a Ph.D. or to pursue a vocational diploma or certificate or to do short courses even more directly related to their employment. Indeed, it is not altogether fanciful to envisage a future in which growing numbers of people are permanently pursuing a series of part-time courses of some kind. Many of those who studied full-time initially will also study part-time later. Part-time study can be as addictive as jogging or aerobics, and probably better for us too. Once the habit has been acquired, withdrawal symptoms can occur when a course ends. If this leads to re-registration at a more advanced level or in a related or different field, so much the better. The Learning Society will have arrived.

The Council for Industry and Higher Education recently published a policy document arguing for new forms of learning to complement the older ones.[5] What was meant by this was a growing focus on applied studies related to the world of work. The council argues cogently for the acceptance of vocational qualifications for entry into university courses, better links with FE colleges and their courses, a review of the balance between practical and theoretical work and new criteria for defining quality. These criteria include data appreciation, teamwork, tackling unfamiliar problems and, interestingly, preparation for lifelong learning. Their report underlines the importance of inspiration, stating that 'The content of courses and the way they are taught must be chosen above all so as to inspire students with a passionate inquisitiveness to continue learning through life. Learning and enthusiasm for learning are bound together, learning is an attitude, perhaps implying a set of skills, that can itself be learned and taught.' Bevan would surely have agreed that learning and enthusiasm for learning are bound together. Regrettably some recent government policies on teaching in primary and secondary schools fail to understand this and seem to want to return to the kind of teaching Bevan himself endured. In their ill-considered attack on progressive teaching methods, they have fallen back on adopting a Gradgrind approach that ignores the importance of motivation. Whether it is possible in post-school education to teach a set of skills that will encourage learning to be an attitude is perhaps more debatable. But the point about inspiring 'passionate inquisitiveness' is well made. Bevan was lucky to have acquired it outside school, probably from his father; others are less fortunate, as he would have been the first to recognize. Certainly effort can and should be put into developing a climate in which lifelong learning becomes universally accepted by those studying for degrees, whatever their age.

More emphasis on applied and vocational study will be attractive to employers, who want better-trained and more highly qualified employees. During Bevan's lifetime, and well beyond it, close contact between universities and employers was thought to be rather unseemly. Academics ought to be involved in the pursuit of knowledge for its own sake, and their students likewise. The job market was an irrelevance. In the 1980s much higher levels of unemployment dispelled these attitudes. Students are more concerned about being prepared for work because, not surprisingly, they usually want a job when they leave. More older part-time students at undergraduate or postgraduate levels have led to more thought being given to links between employment and study. None of this implies that the content of higher education should become narrowly vocational, focusing on competencies and defined tasks. Employers must resist the temptation of asking or expecting universities to go down this route. Work-based training is where these can be learned. Occupationally related learning in higher education is not new: in law, medicine, accountancy and engineering, it is well established. It will be further enhanced in many other fields as the principle of lifelong education becomes established and more and more employers engage in the process, supporting and encouraging those who work for them to go on learning.

Lifelong education puts a premium on universities being accessible throughout the week and throughout the year to allow people to fit in their study at times when they do not have to be at work. Whether universities will be able to hang on to an academic year in which they are semi-closed for some twenty-two weeks annually is questionable. The university of the twenty-first century will probably be open for students for fifty weeks of the year. Traditional academics, concerned about their research, need not be frightened by this. It does not imply that everyone is teaching for fifty weeks of the year. What it does mean is that buildings and plant are more intensively used and more accessible and that different groups of teachers are working at different times. For example, the year might be divided into five ten-week teaching blocks, in which staff are committed to teaching during three of these blocks.

University teachers are already a more diverse group than they were. Universities of the future seem likely to employ a wider range of people to teach than used to be the case. The traditional full-time academic, pursuing research and scholarship at the same time as teaching, will probably be supplemented by people whose teaching is experience-based rather than research-based. Many more part-time teachers could be employed who have other jobs. Just as barristers contribute part-time teaching to law degrees, so may television producers to courses on the media, data-system specialists to courses on computing, or museum curators to art history degrees.

Patterns of employment are undergoing profound changes and however great the resistance may be, universities cannot expect to be immune from them. Contract work, a portfolio of several different jobs and working from home are all becoming more common. Combining professional or business positions with some higher education teaching will be an attractive option for some people. It may also benefit students who will thus be exposed to a wider range of people with an input to their course, bringing in different kinds of expertise and experience. If this occurs there will be a de-institutionalization of staffing structures in which many different kinds of contract are held by those teaching in higher education. Pressure from governments to keep costs down as the system expands will also increase the likelihood of this happening. Full-time academics teaching relatively few hours per week have high overheads and while their pay may be deplorably low they do not come cheap in other ways.

All these changes will pose enormous problems for the management of higher education institutions. They will require a transformation of institutional structures, forcing them to be far more flexible, imposing substantial pressures on administrative staff as well as on academics. Considerable leadership skills will be needed to bring them in without demoralizing effects on those used to a rather cosier and perhaps less threatening system. Questions of maintaining quality will certainly arise. New forms of learning on the information super-highway probably pose the most difficult problems of validation and monitoring for quality. While courses have a clear institutional base it is easier to evaluate them and get a view about standards and quality. On the Internet, particularly if these courses multiply rapidly, the potential student may be faced with a bewildering choice and little guidance about which course is best. It could be equally difficult for employers and higher education institutions trying to rate courses and decide what credit to give to people who have completed them. Courses provided on personal computers also raise as yet unresolved questions about how to assess what those who take them have learned.

Not all learning needs to be graded and assessed. This is particularly true of graduates taking courses later in life, who neither need nor want pieces of paper saying they are qualified. Indeed, there are frequent complaints from such people about the mainstreaming of extra-mural courses, in which the drive for accreditation has forced study for pleasure into study for diplomas with exams and other forms of assessment en route, something which Bevan too would probably have disliked. Higher education has a vital part to play in enhancing life chances but it could also play a role in nourishing life styles. In other words it is a consumption good as well as an investment good. Paid educational leave may also have a consumer element to it in the same way as paid holidays.

To conclude, the way in which higher education is delivered is likely to be as diverse as the people in receipt of it. Some will want face-to-face teaching of a traditional kind with a qualification at the end of it. They will want structured study and to share the experience with others with whom they can discuss their problems and socialize on a regular basis. Some will want to go with members of their family to a course in the evening provided in a local college or community centre. Others will prefer to sit in front of their PCs sometimes in the middle of the night, sometimes on a Sunday afternoon. They will want to do their learning in their own time and at their own pace and possibly to plug into something provided by a college in California or a company in Australia. One thing is certain. In thinking about our policies for higher education we must accept that its provision is increasingly going to be both 'out-sourced' and on a global basis and adjust what we do accordingly.

As a politician, Bevan took little or no interest in education. His biographers do not cover it, other than to mention in passing his disdain for formal schooling. In the 1945 Labour government, education, unlike health, was not at the cutting edge of the ideological debate; a political consensus had already been built round the 1944 Education Act. It is possible, therefore, only to speculate that, were he alive today, Aneurin Bevan would have embraced the idea of lifelong learning and the transformation of our existing education institutions to help it happen.

MICHAEL FOOT

Bevan's Message to the World

Whenever Prime Minister Jawaharlal Nehru paid a visit to London in his later years, he would look for a meeting, before he saw anyone else, with Aneurin Bevan. Considering how out of favour Bevan so frequently was with his own government or even his own party in London, it was a remarkable choice. Over the years and across the continents, each had constructed a special faith in the judgement of the other about the way the world was going.

It was not so surprising that the man who had played the foremost part in the achievement of Indian independence should have won such an admirer; he was for sure one of the great men of the century. But the other side of the friendship reveals a less familiar record and one without which the world politics of our century could have been turned to tragedy. The tradition which Aneurin Bevan represented saved us at moments of crisis when not so many others were prepared to sustain it. Fortunately for us all, and for the joint causes in which our two countries believed, Nehru saw that Bevan was the man he could trust and that particular confidence helped to save us all.

The first common cause which stirred their sympathy was not directly an Indian or a British affair; it was the outbreak of the Spanish Civil War in the late 1930s, which British experts of one breed or another chose to dismiss as a faction fight or a religious conflict just as other experts would dismiss as immoral or insoluble the ancient rivalry between Hindu and Muslim in the Indian empire. Jawaharlal Nehru was already a leading figure in the Indian Congress but he was still treated as a rebellious troublemaker by members of the British government and, most especially, by the British Foreign Office. When he travelled to London via Madrid in 1938 and saw for himself how perilous but still not hopeless was the Spanish Republican cause, his offence cut deeper still in British official circles. British policy was to let the factions fight it out to a finish, even though one side was the aggressor and the other democratically elected. By the time Nehru had taken the trouble to see for himself what was happening, growing sections of British opinion, headed by the British Labour Party, were reaching the same conclusion.

The common interest which the two men showed in the possibility of a victory for Spanish democracy had several subtle undertones which illustrated their respective political character and outlook. What Bevan admired in Nehru, what especially the world at large came later to admire, was the spectacle of a great leader on the world stage carrying into effect the ideals and resolutions of his youth and early manhood. He translated his dream of Indian independence into reality, and then offered the additional boon that these blessings could be applied across larger spaces still. Only Mahatma Gandhi himself had, maybe, a longer vision, and for him the chance of fulfilment was destroyed by the assassin's bullet. The peril was thus all the greater, but Nehru's achievement was made the greater still too. By the time of his death, the statesman's achievement was acknowledged in the most unlikely places – Winston Churchill had hailed him 'the star of the East'. It was altogether fitting that, at the new moment of crisis, it was the voice of Aneurin Bevan, speaking in person in the Indian Parliament, which tipped the balance in favour of the new India choosing to stay within the Commonwealth, and tipping the balance too across a wider sphere which seemed threatened by a new form of destruction, a new Hiroshima or Nagasaki. If that peril was averted, it was partly because Nehru and Bevan had a similar political education and one which sharply divided their outlook from that of almost all other practitioners on the world stage.

Theory and practice, the idea and the deed; no other British politician of comparable stature and achievement in this century weighed in the scales so carefully and conscientiously his declared principles and his success or failure in carrying them into practical effect. (The most likely comparison is that with Winston Churchill and we shall take a fresh look in that direction a little later.) His own conduct in the establishment of the National Health Service is the most obvious proof of this proposition. True, he made some concessions to win the support of sections of the medical profession and some others which impaired the democratic rights of local authorities. Both of these failures, if failures they were, could be remedied in later years. But what he fought for especially and without which there could be no truly national health service, was comprehensive action to cover all ailments and all kinds of patients. Despite all the mean-minded assaults upon it over the years, the main edifice still stands. It is still the National Health Service which he described in his Second Reading speech on 30 April 1946 – as Charles Webster describes in this volume or, more appropriately still, in the chapter Bevan wrote in his own *In Place of Fear* on the free health service. He described there afresh the principles which he had sought to translate into practice and which, after the commotions surrounding his own resignation, seemed to shine more clearly than ever. Politicians, Labour politicians especially, must keep their pledges – not in obedience to some electoral pedantry but as an essential strand in the compact between elected leaders and their followers. It was the seeming careless regard for this breach of principle in 1951 which made him so furious with his fellow ministers. Of course, he knew as well as anyone that Labour governments would always have to make difficult choices between competing demands; he himself invented the phrase 'the language of priorities is the religion of Socialism'. But he was suddenly confronted with the demand from his Cabinet colleagues to accept a breach in the principle – to save a paltry £13 million in the national budget which could easily have been found elsewhere.

The establishment of the National Health Service and the defence of it against attack from all quarters was his chief achievement as an administrator. But during his period as Minister of Health he had several others to add to it. Against all the odds and expectations, he proved himself a first-rate administrator, if an entirely unorthodox one. Owing to his lack of any normal schooling, owing perhaps also to the physical handicap of not being able to write with the hand he was taught to use at school, he had to perform all the most important of his ministerial functions with the same mouth and ear which had enabled him to captivate the House of Commons. Civil servants soon discovered that they were dealing with a more sensitive, responsive instrument than they had ever encountered before. He quickly won the fascinated allegiance of all or almost all the top civil servants with whom he had dealings. All became converts to the adventurous tasks to which they were committed. When the best civil servants seek to do their job properly, they may appreciate most of all the influence which their minister can exert throughout the whole administrative machine from the Cabinet downwards. At least a dozen of the ministers in the Attlee Cabinet had more administrative experience than he had, and the post which he had been allocated required the speedy and persistent mastery of inordinate detail. Many observers prophesied that he would never survive and that he would lose any firm foothold of principle amid such storms. Yet he withstood them all through six years of office and then through another ten years of rearguard action. The National Health Service, designed by Aneurin Bevan, became the best in the world, the finest model of an institution shaped and established on a democratic socialist foundation. A good enough monument for anybody, even if later hands were to disfigure some of its especial beauties.

However, the same Aneurin Bevan applied the same principles in other periods of his parliamentary life: not with the same stunning legislative success but in the long reckoning with no less momentous consequences. He was a Cabinet minister for six years, a Member of

Parliament for thirty. What he did for his people and his party in Parliament was as important as what he did for the health service. Most political leaders of all political parties are judged by what they do in office. But the manner in which they prepare the challenge or defend it later can be hardly less significant. The British Parliament has its own traditions. A few, a very few, have made or sustained their reputations and their causes in opposition, and the occasions when they have done so in extremity have been the most testing in our history.

The most famous example is that of Charles James Fox who first succeeded in making the backbenches of the House of Commons more potent than the front; with no more than a handful of associates he first challenged the outrageous regime of George III, and then, amid the bitter tensions provoked by the Revolution in France, kept alive the hope of English liberty. Richard Cobden performed a similar role in the next century. He never had a seat on the Treasury Bench but he challenged, in long campaigns, the almighty power both of the landlords and of the warmongers who would have destroyed the hopes of a liberal Europe; his old opponent, Disraeli, recognized his supreme qualities, which suited the spirit of the age. Aneurin Bevan was the politician who best matched these achievements in our century, lifting the argument for democratic socialism to its proper heights, insisting at moments of crisis – a series of them – that it was the true international creed which could save mankind.

His first essay on this theme – a ten-year-long apprenticeship in the Commons – was his response to the collapse and betrayal of 1931, an intellectual abdication so complete that it seemed nothing worthy of the name of democratic socialism could ever be revived. Across the European continent, fascists and communists both felt that the field would be theirs. They could fight out the issue between themselves, with any pretence of democracy banished for ever. None of the supposedly democratic parties or countries looked as if they had a remedy for mass unemployment and the miseries it brought in its train. Both communists and fascists claimed that they did have the remedy. All through his adult political life – which started in a colliery at the age of fourteen – Aneurin had been obsessed by the spectacle of mass unemployment and its attendant miseries; the waste, the stupidity, above all, the cruelty which means-tested benefits inflicted on individual families. And Bevan's home town of Tredegar had been most directly afflicted by this curse. He never forgot or forgave. Almost all his early speeches returned to the theme. For him, 1931 was not merely a political betrayal; it was a betrayal of the men and women who had sent him to Westminster. He could speak for them not only with the knowledge but with the savagery which the case required. He looked also for full-scale socialist remedies, the readiness of Parliament to use its full power for the purpose. The official Labour Party was turning its back on these remedies, but Bevan scorned its timorous tone.

The year 1931 branded itself on the mind of socialists of Aneurin Bevan's generation with a searing indelibility. It was not only the desertion of a political leader to the enemy which seemed so portentous. Several of the leaders who stayed seemed to share the responsibility for the feebleness and failure of the Labour government. It was Parliament itself, the British brand of democracy, which had failed and showed no prospect of revival. The huge Tory majority which swamped the new House of Commons had no capacity or desire to see what was happening in industrial Britain. Parliament seemed rather to be recreated in the detestable image of Neville Chamberlain who in the late 1920s had been the chief tormentor of the unemployed men and women in Bevan's own Tredegar. Labour's representation in the Commons was cut to ribbons and the numbers in the unions outside fell to the lowest total recorded in the century. Representation in the House of Commons itself was reduced to a few handfuls from Scotland, Wales and the East End of London. Among these last were two – George Lansbury and Clement Attlee – who were to play a particular part in Bevan's own political career. Lansbury was elected to lead the little rump of the party which was left. He had a fighting spirit all his own, and if he had been allowed to exert it in the previous administration, the tragedy might have been avoided. Lansbury, with Stafford Cripps, one of the other few survivors from the 1931 debacle, was determined to mount a genuine defiance of the bitter decrees especially against the unemployed and their families which formed a principal part of the government's programme. It was the moment of the harshest application of the hated Means Test. It looked as if all forms of resistance could be swept aside amid the same hysteria which had dictated the terrible verdict at the polls.

And yet a resistance was mounted even in that battered, beleaguered Labour Party in the House of Commons. Aneurin Bevan had learnt no respect for the place. It was the scene where the great betrayal had been staged. And yet now, under a new leadership, against the odds, and from the backbenches especially, a few spokesmen raised their voices who knew what cruelties and indignities were being inflicted on working-class homes. Day after day, night after night, the case was put, even if the votes were lost. Bevan spoke in that Parliament more than any other backbencher. It was a wonderful awakening to hear Lansbury and Cripps speak in the same vein from the front bench. A few flickers of revival seemed to indicate that parliamentary democracy was not quite dead.

And yet these spasms of resistance and revolt could hardly be dignified by the name of democracy. When the opportunity for a recovery at the polls came in the British general election of 1935, Labour made some recovery from the deepest failure of 1931, but the solidly entrenched Conservative government was hardly disturbed at all. Neville Chamberlain and all he stood for was more formidably established than ever. The challenge to democracy even in its most elementary definition seemed stronger than ever, with a British conservatism content to play no part in the resistance and thereby to assist the storm. When the news filtered through that storm troops in Hitler's Germany were repeating the kind of tactics which

Mussolini had practised in Italy, British ministers protested that it was none of our business. An early flagrant attack occurred in 1934, when a fascist-catholic regime sympathetically friendly with the fascist regime in Mussolini's Italy turned its guns on working-class flats in Vienna. No one in the ruling circles thought they should move to defend democratic rights there.

Aneurin Bevan understood the fight for democracy for his own people; he would never forget. But the democratic socialism which he had been taught or fashioned for himself was an international creed, and he would never forget that either. The infamies which were now being practised in Europe and which our own rulers seemed to mark with a sinister callousness opened for him a new dimension in his politics. He wanted to see a Britain, but first of all a Labour Party, which would play a leading part in resisting the new attacks on civilized life and shaping a new world. How to perform these contrasting roles was not so easy. His own beloved leader, George Lansbury, was a Christian pacifist and therefore quite unfitted, despite all his other virtues, to deal with the new desperate challenge. Bevan hated the brutal manner in which Ernest Bevin secured the removal of Lansbury from the leadership, but it had to happen. A new policy had to be devised which would construct a European alliance, but Ernest Bevin showed himself no more ready for that course than Lansbury.

But then suddenly, overnight almost, a new challenge and a new hope presented itself, a new development which placed a genuine fight for democracy at the very centre of the European political stage where it ought to be. The Spanish war transformed everything. The newly elected Spanish government was a truly democratic one, representing all shades of liberal opinion. It was attacked by fascist forces which would not accept the vote, backed by assistance from fascist Italy and fascist Germany. So sudden and ruthless was the attack that many observers, including the British Foreign Office, calculated that it was bound to be successful. But the new Spanish government had a much stronger hold on the Spanish people and on military resources than these observers could appreciate. Despite all diversions or internal tensions, that new Spanish regime survived for nearly three years, and could have crushed the rebellion altogether in 1937 or 1938, if it had not been for the reinforcements for fascist forces which poured in from Germany and Italy. Most of the Western powers enforced a policy of non-intervention, that is, no supply of arms to either side, which meant in practice that the balance was surely shifted in favour of the invaders.

For a few wretched, shameful months at the beginning of the war, that policy of non-intervention was supported even by the Labour Party leadership. But political pressure, a storm at the party confer-ence, above all, the successful democratic resistance in Spain itself, changed the prospect, and Attlee and the others honourably sought to execute the new policy of outright support for Spanish democracy fighting for its life. But the British government would not alter its course by one jot, even when Mussolini despatched Italian troops to take part in the conflict or the Germans bombed Guernica. In the last desperate hours of the conflict, when Spanish forces were stream-ing across the frontier into France, a craven British Foreign Office felt it would be unwise to intercede on their behalf for fear of offending the new fascist rulers in Madrid.

As the policy of appeasement towards the fascist onslaught was directed even more openly by Neville Chamberlain, Bevan partici-pated in the great argument with a rising sense of outrage. He thought his Labour Party could have acted more boldly as they should have done at the outbreak of the Spanish war. He wanted to mobilize the full strength of the Labour movement against the Chamberlain administration. He joined a campaign for a united front of socialists, communists and other left parties to unseat the Chamberlain govern-ment. When that failed, he joined with Stafford Cripps and some others to form a popular front, as Leon Blum had done in France, against Chamberlain, and he found himself expelled from the Labour

Party in the process. Nothing could persuade him that the cool temper with which some of his leaders watched these events was right. A more vigorous democracy could have stopped the war in Spain. A more vigorous democracy was needed to overthrow Chamberlain and all he stood for.

The House of Commons at its best helped to save the nation – and Aneurin Bevan at his best helped to save the House of Commons. Neither of these claims is always properly recognized, but both should be. Without the removal of Chamberlain, Hitler could have won the war or at least dictated a European peace on his own terms. Even after Churchill was in office, the Chamberlainites, headed by Halifax at the Foreign Office, were ready for a new deal with the aggressors. But the House of Commons, having tasted victory with the heroic overthrow of Chamberlain, would not have lapsed back into habits which had so nearly encompassed our destruction. If there had been any such attempt, a vigilant Churchill, a revived Labour Party taking its proper place in the War Cabinet, and a revived House of Commons would have stopped it. That House of Commons was required to undertake an entirely new range of duties for the successful conduct of the war itself. As the months passed, Aneurin Bevan took the leading role in these activities, either acting on his own with a few of his closest friends or with the sympathy or backing of the Labour members on the opposition benches.

He had not embarked on this course as a deliberate strategy; he was not setting himself up as the leader of any group or faction, he was much more still the advocate of the poorest sections of the community who had no other voice of their own, but as the issues in the war became more complex, as the direct Labour contributions to the debates in the Commons became more muted since their leaders were in the Cabinet, as the necessary international implications of war itself became more far reaching, so the House of Commons must retain or enlarge its power to debate the issues. Thanks to the belated exercise of the powers of the House of Commons, the nation had been saved. All the more was it necessary that that same vigilance should be preserved in the future. No other country engaged in the war had such a vigilant, powerful body debating and scrutinizing these events. Few other cities suffered such punishment as was inflicted on London, Plymouth and Coventry. No other country mobilized so effectively. And one reason for these triumphs was not merely the freedom for which the nation fought but the freedom which it practised – the conduct of the war itself. And the prime defender of that parliamentary freedom from 1939 to 1945 was Aneurin Bevan.

He started the war an outcast in his own party but with a firm knowledge of the blunders and crimes which had led to the disaster. By the end of it, he had become the most formidable debater in the place, capable of challenging his own leaders on what he conceived to be their frequent failure to measure the surge of democratic fervour which was sweeping the country, or, as he believed more essentially, Winston Churchill himself on the conduct of the war and the making of the peace. It was his daring assaults under this second heading which brought the most bitter counter-attacks. Critics should try to keep their mouths shut in wartime, and what did he know about war, anyhow? He was the most amateur strategist who ever staked his military reputation. And yet, as the years passed, more and more people in the country at large and a few in the House of Commons started to listen. He himself knew that the domestic and the world-wide arguments were more and more merging into one another.

What he was interpreting better than any other observer or partici-pant was the momentum of the democratic revival which was sweeping across Britain, across Europe, across the Atlantic, across the planet. When he talked about what was happening, in the pits or among the victims of the social security system, they knew he was speaking from first-hand experience; they had to listen. He was telling them how *his* people could help win the war. When the debates turned to the great questions about what was to happen afterwards – as they did from about 1942 onwards, following the publication of the Beveridge report – his voice grew stronger still. He wanted to see his Labour Party, including ministers in the Cabinet, taking the lead in all these matters. His pressures and prophecies on this theme became stronger month by month. Of course, there were a multitude of other voices pressing the same claims. That was part of *his* case, but somehow he seemed to use the platform of the House of Commons more deliberately and effectively than anyone else. And one reason why he did command that ever-larger audience was precisely because he would not leave the great questions of war and peace to be decided by Winston Churchill and his War Cabinet. Churchill in 1940 had played a splendid part in saving the nation. The Labour Party had played its proper part in putting him there but even without Churchill the British people's rejection of all Neville Chamberlain stood for would have come. The popular tide, the rejection of fascism in every guise, seemed to give a fresh impetus and strength to the idea of democracy itself. What was staged before our eyes in 1940 was not only the indispensable British resistance on which all else turned, but also the beginnings of the international civil war which would bring to us the allies needed for the final victory.

The essence of Chamberlainism was that no such allies were needed. Britain could stand alone. He and the Conservative majority which he still commanded in the House of Commons brought us near to absolute destruction. Churchill was much wiser and it is an insult to mention them in the same breath. At the moments of crisis he had some brilliant insights into the kind of allies we *did* need – the French in 1940 or the Russians in 1941, or the Americans through the whole period. We owed much to Churchill's wisdom. Of course, he could command public support for what he was doing, but that does not diminish the credit. At the crucial moments he acted with an international statesmanship without which our whole cause would have foundered, and we may add the parenthesis that the three countries who became our allies had been the peculiar targets for Chamberlain's insults.

But Churchill had his blind spots too, not merely passing aberrations but deep-seated political prejudices which might suddenly rise to the surface and destroy his judgement. Especially in the war, when he suffered from such seizures it was necessary that he should be challenged. Aneurin Bevan was prepared to make those challenges more boldly and persistently than anyone else, either with a growing approval from the Labour benches or with only a handful of supporters on his side. So he was often accused of being mischievous or worse and sometimes, for sure, he had misjudged the pressures on the War Cabinet. But mostly he was applying his democratic principles more faithfully than those ranged against him, with Churchill at their head.

One of Churchill's own original blind spots had been Spain. First he tried to dismiss the conflict as a faction fight, but generously acknowledged his error when the Germans were bombing Guernica. Even after the momentous greetings which he gave for the alliance with the Soviet Union on the night of Hitler's invasion, he was still too deeply convinced that the Russians would be defeated to carry through the change in strategy which the moment required. His own chiefs of staff backed him in his caution but there were other military experts, most notably among the American chiefs of staff, making a wiser judgement on the prospects. So when Bevan constantly attacked him on this issue in the Commons, Churchill knew that Bevan had allies in high places in the US administration who shared the criticism and looked for a better strategy. A constant anxious peril was that the Allied High Command in Washington, upon whose decisions the final outcome of the war would depend, might make the fateful choice to transfer essential resources from the European to the Far Eastern theatre of war. Bevan attacked the Churchill strategy not out of some sentimental association with the Russian communists, but through a serious estimate of the competing perils in either strategy.

However, other Churchill blind spots, particularly as he surveyed the new victors emerging from the international civil war, seemed to expose him as a figure who still hankered after the methods of the old world rather than one preparing for the new. The worst example of it, and the most menacing for the future, was the manner in which he persuaded his War Cabinet to treat the great question of India. India's participation in the war was decided in Whitehall; the offence was especially bitter since almost all Congress Party leaders, headed by Mahatma Gandhi and Jawaharlal Nehru, would not and could not sign on a Churchill dotted line. No one could forget that it had been Churchill himself who had shown the most ferocious opposition to any move towards Indian independence throughout the 1930s. Some cooler heads in the Whitehall machine, knowing how deep had been the Indian hostility towards similar conduct in a previous war, tried to advise a wiser diplomacy, a different approach altogether. But all objections from them were swept aside as were the all too feeble protests from the Labour members of the Cabinet. When the announcement was made in the Commons about the imprisonment of Mahatma Gandhi and Jawaharlal Nehru, Bevan's voice was the strongest raised in protest, but he was not alone. The case for full scale Indian independence was more powerfully advocated in the Labour Party than ever before.

The new nations emerging from the thralldom of fascism or more ancient tyrannies were insisting on their elementary democratic rights; their rights to settle their problems at the ballot box. Most of the different peoples concerned, especially if they had just succeeded, in the most desperate circumstances, in organizing partisan resistance against their immediate tormentors, felt they were properly qualified to adopt the full democratic system. Many of these partisan revolts had been brilliantly organized affairs – in Yugoslavia, in Italy, in Greece, Aneurin Bevan had been especially eager in supporting these movements either directly in the House of Commons or in the columns of *Tribune*. Several socialist parties in France, Spain and Italy played a leading role in these heroic endeavours. Across the whole stricken continent it did look as if a new democratic dawn was breaking. This for sure was what the British people had fought for. Despite all the original imbecility and cowardice of their leaders, despite the horrors of the war itself, they had won the right to shape the future themselves.

Aneurin Bevan had experienced a different war from anybody else. He had had the chance to turn himself into the most effective debater in the House of Commons, and the most powerful advocate for democratic socialism. But as the war drew to its close and as the war leaders met at Yalta to settle the post-war world, he detected a darkening cloud which might still mar the victory. The reports reached him as they filtered westward that fellow socialists in Poland, Czechoslovakia, Italy and Yugoslavia, who had played the leading part in the resistance movements, were themselves being turned upon by their communist compatriots. At the Yalta Conference, the leaders seemed to turn their blind eyes to these offences against those who died defending their democratic rights. Bevan himself would not join them. One reason was that he himself had been responsible for hiring a writer called George Orwell to write a column in *Tribune*, called 'As I Please'. Orwell's anti-Soviet temper seemed to grow sharper week by week, as the news grew darker. But when readers protested, as many of them did, it was Bevan especially who insisted that the promise to allow him to write as he pleased must be kept.

Tribune, on Bevan's insistence, had given shelter to George Orwell soon after he had given up his job in the BBC and when he was the victim of a fierce political ostracism – his *Animal Farm* had been rejected by a series of publishers' readers, the most eminent of them being T. S. Eliot. But all through the war up to the moment of Orwell's arrival at *Tribune*, Bevan himself had been blacklisted by some bosses at the BBC. Curiously, Orwell made no mention of this shocking piece of censorship at the time, and the revelation came only with the publication of W. J. West's book about Orwell, *The Truth Betrayed*, in 1987.[1]

With the development of BBC broadcasting during the war, the radio came into its own as never before. Winston Churchill used the instrument to the full, often most skilfully to circumvent debates in the House of Commons. Some others made new reputations or rediscovered old ones in the same way – most notably J. B. Priestley, whose postscripts came to rival Churchill's, or the creators of the original BBC brains trust, Professor Cyril Joad and Julian Huxley. All the more surprising is it to recall that the Aneurin Bevan who was making a new reputation, both inside and outside the House of Commons, had as yet no access to this main instrument of public debate. It was to the platforms outside that people had to go if they wanted to hear him.

With the coming of the 1945 election and the establishment of the Labour government, he became and remained the most controversial figure in British public life. He had the chance to turn his ideas into deeds in a manner he himself could hardly have dreamed possible. Much of this present volume is devoted to a discussion of how well he did it: his gift for practical statesmanship. But after a few years of high office, he became deeply dissatisfied with his own and his own party's achievement. He thought he should be doing much more. Even before he actually resigned in April 1951, he had often talked of resigning on the more general pretext that he wished to use his influence to give a fresh socialist impetus to British politics and world politics. He could not have guessed as much at the time, but the place from which he had to do it was that same backbench in the Commons.

One half of Aneurin Bevan's 1951 resignation speech was devoted to his defence of the National Health Service. The other half (the first half) was a critique of British foreign policy, Labour foreign policy, past, present and future. Some of his critics dismissed this section as an afterthought conveniently revived to bolster the other half of his weak case and since this view seemed to be confirmed by a statement from Prime Minister Attlee, the political world was eager to accept that as the final verdict. However, the Cabinet minutes published thirty years later – first used effectively by Kenneth Morgan in *Labour in Power*, published in 1984[2] – fully confirmed Bevan's contention. But the questions involved are by no means confined to matters of historical accuracy. Where Attlee turned a deaf ear to his warnings and prophecies, his followers at the time and many others in the world at large listened more carefully and responded to his invocations. Inside the British Cabinet and out of it, he was constantly searching for the principles on which democratic socialism should act. For him, domestic policy and foreign policy perpetually interacted. He never took the view that sound policies abroad could compensate for the failures at home; rather the other way round: socialist victories at home could bring the bonus of unexpected advantages abroad. Even in that resignation speech he especially lamented the failure of other Labour leaders, Hugh Gaitskell in particular, to take a special pride in the National Health Service: how it was enhancing Britain's reputation among the nations in a manner Tory patriotism could never comprehend.

Democratic socialism must find its own way and apply its own principles, seeking to understand, but never bowing the knee in subservience to either of the two great powers which had emerged in such ascendancy from the war. It looked at times as if conflict between them was inevitable, and since the world was also learning the ever mounting potential menace of the nuclear weapons exploded at Hiroshima and Nagasaki, the demand for real peacemaking became more urgent than ever. Bevan understood the urgency – he never made a speech on such issues for the rest of his life without a sense of the peril – but he understood also how pressures and persuasions must be applied to each of the two giants on behalf of the multitudes of peoples who refused to place themselves in either camp. He would like to have seen a Labour government in Britain still performing that role. In some of those respects the government elected in 1945 had played its part well, even if in some others it had failed. In the crises of 1950 and 1951, that administration had somehow lost its balance, but he still hoped it would recover. A Labour government could perform the task better than any Conservative one, but even in opposition, thanks to its achievements in the war and in the 1945 government, the Labour Party could speak with a special resonance and help tip the scales towards a real peace.

Throughout the rest of his life, he was offering his judgement on this mightiest of all matters, and it was a judgement worth hearing. What he sought to discover was not some middle ground between the two giants – he was never much in favour of middle-of-the-road journeys anywhere; such travellers were in danger of being run over – but an intelligent diplomatic stance based not on a stereotypical interpretation of the two competing systems but a proper modern appreciation of their weaknesses and strengths. If the course of world history was to be shaped by the Soviet Union's verdict on the United States or the United States' verdict on the Soviet Union, we should all be doomed.

At times he appeared to be directing his criticism especially at the dangers of United States policy; in his resignation speech one climax condemned the peril of Britain being 'dragged too far behind the wheels of American diplomacy'. The United States administration had made its own response to Soviet actions in the Far East, and then required that its allies should respond too, even if the first conclusions of the American diplomats or the American generals appeared misjudged. What he argued for and what he thought had been originally agreed among the allies was a measured response to fit the challenge, both in terms of the military response in the Far East and the scale of rearmament in the defence system as a whole. To such proposals from Washington the Labour government had readily agreed, and Bevan himself, as Minister of Labour in that government, had skilfully defended the new policy in the House of Commons. He started to elaborate then his own estimate of Soviet strategy which governed his thinking. Of course, all attempted Soviet aggressions must be resisted; that was essential in Korea as it had been in Berlin a little earlier. But an intelligent calculation of what the Soviets could or would do did not mean that their armies poised in the East would soon attempt a full-scale march across Europe. They had not the military strength to do it – not even sufficient steel production of their own or which they could capture to make the invasion possible. Yet this was the kind of concept to which some of the supposed military experts subscribed more readily in Washington than in London. To offer the military shield necessary to prevent such an onslaught would certainly bankrupt economies like the British one which had not escaped the burdens of the last war.

For some two or three years before the resignation speech, Aneurin Bevan had been shaping and presenting his ideas in the Cabinet, and he continued to advocate and elaborate them with what looks now an astonishing consistency for the next ten years. The consistency bore not the slightest resemblance to 'the hobgoblin of feeble minds' as denounced by Thomas Carlyle. It was rather the expression of how surely politicians must seek to put principles into practice or they would find themselves blown off course by every passing breeze, particularly those to which Labour politicians just arriving in office were most subject. For a little more than half that period, he was once more speaking from the backbenches of the House of Commons, a position for which he had now acquired considerable respect; it enabled him to choose his moments and his time for speaking. Then, for a few years, he was back on Labour's front bench or on the platform at the Party Conference, speaking with growing effect on every occasion. It was sometimes lamented that Attlee had made a big mistake in selecting Hugh Gaitskell rather than Aneurin Bevan to succeed Stafford Cripps at the Treasury. Looking back now, it is even more lamentable that when the chance arose a little later to appoint a successor to Ernest Bevin at the Foreign Office, he chose Herbert Morrison for the task instead of Bevan. Morrison proved to be a shaming failure at the Foreign Office. Having no coherent principle of his own which he wished to apply, his patchwork soon fell apart. In or out of office, Aneurin Bevan could have continued to develop the grander perspective which the age required. When he had spoken as Minister of Labour in February 1951 in a peculiar way all his own, he had taken over the highly necessary task of defining and expounding a new foreign policy. He defended the first proposals for a moderate, controlled rearmament, enough to help deter the aggressor but not so much as to wreck the whole economy. As he reached the end of it and was turning to chide the Tories, from Winston Churchill listening intently on the opposition front bench came a famous interruption: 'Don't spoil a good speech now.'

Churchill was right about that speech. It had the right tone and temper and statesmanlike content for dealing with a rapidly worsening world crisis. Everyone who heard it thought he must be the best man for the job of taking over the foreign secretaryship or the leadership of the party. But in a sense these personal reflections were trivial matters compared with the outline of a new, intelligent, dignified foreign policy for the country at large. Sooner than any prophets could have foretold, Churchill himself was returned to office, and the subject in which he was quickly most interested was the direction of foreign policy and the particular matter of the intensifying conflict between the United States and the Soviet Union, and how Britain could still play some part in stopping a headlong clash between the two. Churchill in office soon recognized that Bevan's figures were more accurate than Gaitskell's, that his proposed next steps were a good deal more hopeful than Morrison's, that his foreign policy altogether was more ambitious than Attlee's. He could not quite express his preferences thus, but the evidence is overwhelming.

Out of office, embittered as his enemies both inside his own party and outside might suggest by his failure, quite unable for sure to derive any comfort from Churchill's patronage, he achieved a renewal of spirits, a flowering of his political genius which he turned especially on the world scene. He saw the danger more starkly than ever before and from fresh angles; he made a company of new friends and spoke on their behalf too, but seemed more excited than ever before by his intellectual liberation. So little was he truly a man driven by his own diseased ambition, the wicked caricature first drawn in Hugh Dalton's diary and later in Hugh Gaitskell's.

He went on travels where he had longed to go before – to Yugoslavia, to Egypt, to Israel, to India. Many political leaders in these varying political climates would listen to his accounts of what was happening in the cold war, the incipient nuclear arms race, more carefully than the Labour Party leaders at home. What he described fitted the facts much more readily than the propaganda machines' outpourings from Moscow or Washington, especially when the latter assumed the accents of John Foster Dulles. Dulles preached even more raucously than the presidents he served the absolutist doctrine that between the great powers no such phenomenon as neutrality was to be tolerated. In Belgrade, New Delhi, Cairo even, that was a doctrine of despair, and Bevan's voice raised against it was a wonderful promise of a new departure. In one continent after another, he argued not that these alliances should be suddenly surrendered – that might merely spread fresh alarm – but that the giants must not be allowed to exert their strength to the limit. That could mean total war and total extinction, and yet there were moments when Dulles preached that doctrine more violently than Stalin himself. Bevan happened to be in New Delhi when the news came through of Stalin's death, and he was able to discuss directly with Jawaharlal Nehru himself how auspicious for the world at large the moment might be. Friends since they had first met in London in 1938, their alliance had been vastly consolidated when Bevan protested with all the power at his command at Churchill's imprisonment of the Congress leaders in 1942. Here in 1953 they were making a common plea to the same Churchill – not knowing, then at least, that Churchill was the most eminent convert to their side of the debate. But if a Conservative government was made so cautious by its alliances or whatever else, all the more reason why the Labour leadership should seize the initiative. Sometimes they did; Attlee initiated a debate in which the great nuclear argument was properly presented. But there were lapses too, lapses in which the Labour leaders might find themselves entrapped in policies which derived from the Dulles doctrine itself. One such policy was to form a so-called South East Asia Treaty Organization to match the NATO alliance which had certainly deterred the aggressors in Europe. But the proposed SEATO was flawed from the start, since it accepted the exclusion of India, the most important country in the area. When Bevan heard that the Labour Party leadership had appeared to accept the Conservative government's proposition without demur, he made his own protest in the Commons and resigned from the Shadow Cabinet. His conduct was condemned within the party, but much better understood in the countries which he had been visiting. Many people throughout the area which the pact was supposed to cover felt that the Dulles doctrine was deeply divisive, and they were glad that so powerful a voice had been raised on their side of the argument. Many of these themes, both on domestic policies and on foreign policy, were incorporated in *In Place of Fear*, completed on his visit to Yugoslavia and published in 1952. He did not find the actual process of writing an easy one, but he was fascinated by argument, especially philosophical argument. He liked to stretch his own capacities to the limit and reach out for the formulation of new ideas. *In Place of Fear* contained his definition of democratic socialism, and the mood and temper in which democratic socialists must be prepared to act. The wisdom which he preached more assuredly than ever in the last decade of his life was a cool and collected product of all his thinking which, however, must always have the courage to translate theory into action.

Some time later in that last Churchill administration, their paths crossed even more memorably. The subject was the same one, the relationship between the great powers, but the tension had been vastly increased by the development of nuclear weapons. It looked like a reckless race in which nothing like enough was being done either in Washington or Moscow or London, for that matter, to bring the great powers to their senses in the search for an escape from global madness of an unprecedented character.

Voices of protest were raised across the planet – not yet in the form which the Campaign for Nuclear Disarmament shaped and dictated but still in accents resonant enough. Bevan's was the most fervent among many in the Labour Party calling for high-level talks to seek diplomatic agreement to stop the race. When Stalin died in 1953 and seemingly new, untried men had come to power in the Kremlin, an obvious, urgent fresh occasion arose for seeking such talks. Bevan and his backbench friends pressed the case: sometimes Attlee and Co. seemed lacking in a proper sense of urgency; was that due to his natural temperament or a real deficiency in comprehending the scale of the new challenge? As the House of Commons turned its mind to the matter in the two-day debate in March 1955, the pressure for a much stronger initiative grew still more intense until, sensationally, Churchill himself added his weight to it. His response came in the middle of Bevan's own speech and in response to his direct question: 'Why were the negotiations delayed? Could it be that Churchill wanted to meet the Russians but that the United States would not let him – a sombre thing to say and a wicked thing to believe – that we have now reached the situation where Great Britain can, in a few short years, run the risk of the extinction of its civilization, and we cannot reach the potential enemy in an attempt to arrive at an accommodation with him because we are at the mercy of the United States?' That was the question which brought Churchill to his feet in his last major debate in the House of Commons. His intervention in Bevan's speech was more significant than his own earlier introduction of the subject. He spoke for the first time in public of the stroke which he had suffered and how it had interfered with his own cherished hope to secure high-level talks to deal with the greatest danger mankind had ever faced and the risk his own country was taking to back an American policy which had ceased to command his confidence. Quite a moment in the history of Anglo-American relations since the testimony came from the Winston Churchill who was accepted to be the most fervent upholder of the alliance, and he was accepting the criticism of the man who was posing the most important argument since Britain had agreed to establish United States nuclear bases on its soil.

Everyone who actually heard the Bevan–Churchill meeting of minds on the supreme question of the age was shaken and deeply moved. We heard at first hand how the old rivals had given their best combined thought to the problem and had come forward with a common solution. High-level talks between the heads of governments did not always produce solutions, and ever since Yalta, Bevan himself had expressed his suspicions about them, especially when Churchill might be involved: he had been known to resort to them as an escape from reality. However, as the perils in the nuclear arms race intensified, each was impelled, along varying paths of reasoning, to the same urgent conclusion. The arrival of new leaders in the Kremlin surely made it all the more necessary that new possibilities should at least be tested. Churchill was especially aggrieved that his old wartime colleague, now President Eisenhower, would not respond to his overtures. Either our own obstructive Foreign Office was not presenting the case with sufficient force or Eisenhower was submitting too readily to the pressures of what he himself called 'the military industrial complex' in the United States – the modern term for the United States diplomatic-cum-military machine which Bevan himself had discerned at work in the 1950–1 crisis. What Bevan had so constantly argued for and where Churchill in office heartily concurred was a major political initiative to take control out of the hands of the military whose answer to all problems was merely to ask for more.

It could make all the difference actually to *hear* him; not only because his voice could be sweet and strong at the same time, not only because of his idiosyncratic but still natural choice of language, with the stutter itself adding quite unselfconsciously to the effect, not only because the raillery and the invective could set out to explore quite unexpected destinations; not only for all these assembled arts which it might be supposed he had perfected over the years, but rather for the exactly opposite reason. No one who heard any of his great speeches in the last decade of his life, including this last exchange with Churchill, could imagine that he was driven by some personal spleen or pursuing some individual vendetta. It was the drama of world events, with the nuclear peril casting the blackest cloud across the whole stage, which governed every action he took and every word he uttered. His capacity as a debater had never been sharper and he could wield it without mercy against the opponents in his path. Those of us who had cheered most lustily when we saw it scatter our enemies should not have complained when just occasionally the blade fell across our own backs. We should have known – a few of us – that it was still the same Aneurin Bevan who was summoning his combined courage and imagination to the highest pitch, to save us if he could. The two together, never one without the other: the imagination to comprehend what was happening to our world and the courage to search for the awkward solutions. Some of us squeezed into Trafalgar Square to hear him, at the height of the Suez crisis when the news filtered through the crowd that the Soviet armies, partly unleashed by Britain's own Suez aggression, were storming into Budapest. No one unravelled so well as he the connection between these two aggressions and the nuclear threat itself. He wanted to see his Labour Party leading to that promised land, and a new world order. His speech in Trafalgar Square marked the way. He would not absolve from their share of the guilt any of the parties who had brought the universe to the edge of disaster – neither the Egyptians nor the Israelis nor the Americans, least of all the ministers in Downing Street who, if their own professions were true, were too stupid to be in charge of great affairs.

The manner in which he spoke to that seething mass at the mighty Suez demonstration should have been a lesson to us all. He was much more interested in raising the argument about the nuclear arms race to its proper height than he was in any cheap debating victories over the little men in Downing Street. If we could drop a bomb on Cairo or Alexandria, someone else could drop bombs on us; it was not only the echoes from the outrages being perpetrated against the Egyptians and the Hungarians which sent the shudder through the square that shameful afternoon. It was the exposure of the wanton risks our rulers had run in a world which had become infinitely dangerous. But his was the voice that could save us – not that of some individual hero, nor some inspired guru; he had always despised such claims – but rather, more than ever at that moment, a spokesman who drew every sinew of the strength in his mind and body from the Labour movement in which he had been reared and from the doctrine of democratic socialism which must form the essential part of the new world order.

If there had been any political justice in our world, the Aneurin Bevan of Trafalgar Square would soon have been transformed into the Foreign Secretary in a new Labour government. His three speeches in the House of Commons itself clinched the case. He marshalled the full argument against the crime and folly of the Suez expedition better than anyone else. He exposed the collusion between the guilty leaders in London and Paris long before the historians were able to verify it. But he strove also to translate the exposure of the present catastrophe into future constructive action. The whole world could witness the benefit of a Labour Party uniting to uphold its highest tradition: the demand for collective action to save the peace. If such a Labour Party had been able to take power at that moment, one result for sure would have been direct action for the high-level talks for which he had pleaded most consistently, and, as mankind was to discover a little later, some new hopes were being born in both camps of the great powers: in Washington President Eisenhower would be issuing a warning against the exorbitant claims of the military-industrial complex and the new man in the Kremlin, Nikita Khrushchev, was indicating that there could be beneficial cracks in the communist monolith. It was not at all the sign of a full-scale readiness to stop the arms race which came from Mikhail Gorbachev in the same Kremlin thirty years later. But it could have been and should have been the moment when the leaders of the Western powers seized the initiative to drag mankind back from the nuclear precipice. Aneurin Bevan saw that possibility more clearly than anyone else and in a sense sacrificed his own life to secure it.

The aftermath of Suez was something different from that which even the most malign god might have decreed. The most eager first sponsor of the military expedition, Harold Macmillan, became the chief beneficiary of its failure. When Bevan himself heard that Macmillan rather than R. A. Butler had been adopted as Prime Minister, he was amazed: he had always thought Macmillan was a mountebank. As for the new-found unity in a great cause discovered by his precious Labour Party, he could not believe – especially after the display of British patriotism throughout the Suez crisis, some of it monstrously distorted but nonetheless real, which he understood better than most – that the British people would vote for a party committed to an immediate programme of unilateral nuclear disarmament. If that appeal was attempted and failed, he knew that the chance of a high-level agreement on the supreme issue of nuclear weapons would be cast aside; the opportunity would trickle through our fingers. He faced all these interlocking tests at the Brighton party conference in 1957. He felt he had to win that debate too, and who today would say that he was wrong? He had given his whole mind to the greatest question of all: how the nuclear threat was to be banished for ever across every continent.

One sentence in that 1957 Labour Party conference speech at Brighton became more famous than any other: his plea not to be sent 'naked into the conference chamber', his passionate demand that a new Labour government should not shackle itself in advance and thereby frustrate the whole enterprise. He pursued the same goal wherever he went and spoke thereafter – in the House of Commons itself, in the Indian Parliament, in the British general election and in its aftermath, when amid the bitterness of the party's defeat he did more than any single individual to restore the shattered hopes of democratic socialists not solely in Britain but across every continent where men looked for the combined inspirations of political freedom and collective action. One without the other could prove a monstrous delusion: the two ideas welded together became more than ever the essence of Aneurin Bevan's doctrine and he wanted everybody to hear it. And when his constituents wanted to provide a permanent memorial to him, they placed on the mountainside where he would address his May Day meetings four great sandstones, three of them commemorating the three towns which comprised his constituency, Tredegar, Ebbw Vale and Rhymney, with the fourth stone inscribed thus: 'This was the place where Aneurin Bevan spoke to his constituents and the world.' The last three words were included on the suggestion of Jill Craigie, who thereby added the final international flavour. He does still speak to the world at large.

ALAN WATKINS

The Greasy Pole:
Bevan and the Leadership

The Welsh medieval poet Dafydd ap Gwilym gave his readers the somewhat impractical advice not to die in the summer. Aneurin Bevan died in the summer of 1960. If he had lived, he might well have stood against Hugh Gaitskell in the autumn of that year. As things turned out, a reluctant Harold Wilson – shamed into standing by the initial candidature of Anthony Greenwood, who then withdrew – won 81 votes to Gaitskell's 166. By then Bevan would have been nearly sixty-three, which would have been considered on the elderly side even in those more tolerant times. In retrospect it can be seen that he should have been given the chance to contest the leadership at some time during the 1951–5 Parliament. C. R. Attlee should have retired. He stayed, not to keep out Bevan but to keep out Herbert Morrison.

After the 1945 election, Morrison and Harold Laski had tried to supplant Attlee and promote Morrison by seeking to have the leader re-elected by the new parliamentary party. This was one reason for his suspicion of Morrison. In addition, as he observed – rather pettily, one may think – to the journalist Leslie Hunter: 'He stood against me in 1935, didn't he?'[1] In 1952 Attlee agreed with Hunter and his wife Margaret Stewart (who was also a journalist) that the party would elect Morrison if he retired: 'That's the one thing that worries me. I'd go at once if I thought Morrison could hold the party together, but I don't think he can. He's too heavy-handed, you know, and he might wreck the whole show. I may have to hang on a bit and see.'[2]

Five years earlier there had been a revolt against Attlee which Morrison was asked to join, but he refused. This did nothing to increase Attlee's charity. 'He never knew the difference between a big thing and a little thing,' he told Hugh Dalton later. It is probable but by no means certain that Morrison rather than Bevan would have won the leadership if Attlee had retired during the Churchill government of 1951–5. It is more difficult to make out the same case if we are thinking of the period between May 1955, when the recently appointed Anthony Eden won again for the Conservatives, and December 1955, when Attlee at last retired. Dalton believed that those who thought Morrison would have succeeded shortly after the 1955 election underestimated the damage which had been done to his reputation by his tenure of the Foreign Office in 1951. This most unsuccessful period of Morrison's political career would have been even fresher in the memories of those exercising the parliamentary party's franchise after 1951 – even though they would have been more of Morrison's generation.

The idea that Attlee hung on after the 1955 election, just as he had in 1951–5, partly to keep out Morrison is deeply entrenched in the mythology of the Labour Party. Hunter certainly thought so: indeed, it is the principal theme of his book *The Road to Brighton Pier*, which Richard Crossman reviewed in 1959, leading to the following exchange with Attlee:

Crossman: I've just been reviewing a book about you.
Attlee: Ah yes, I know. He says I hated Herbert. It's quite untrue. I pitied him and pity is a kind of affection. His trouble was vaulting ambition, which o'erleapt itself. Of course [referring to Hunter's book], it's all a pack of lies.[3]

This view of Hunter's work is incorrect. Most of his facts are right: it is his interpretation that is wrong. Attlee certainly disliked Morrison, wanted to keep him out of the leadership of the Labour Party and almost certainly put off his resignation in Labour's first post-war period of opposition to serve this end. But by May 1955 Morrison's decline in the party's esteem was already well advanced. Earlier, Attlee had wanted Aneurin Bevan to succeed him. In 1952 he had shown a clear preference for Bevan 'if only he wouldn't play the fool so much'. In March 1955 he said to Crossman: 'Nye had the leadership on a plate. I always wanted him to have it. But you know, he wants to be two things simultaneously, a rebel and an official leader, and you can't be both.'[4] As late as November 1955 he said to Hunter: 'I'd like to see him get it. Trouble is he's so unstable, all over the place and you never know where you are with him. Anyway he's cooked his goose for the time being and the party would never stand for him.'[5]

If Attlee had indeed possessed such a high regard for Bevan, he could have appointed him Chancellor of the Exchequer in 1950, before his resignation from the government. Many of the Labour Party's troubles in the 1950s flowed from this decision. In 1954–5 Bevan was perhaps in his most awkward and prickly phase. He resigned from the Shadow Cabinet over the South East Asia Treaty Organization, and was replaced by Wilson, greatly to his annoyance – though Crossman approved. In the autumn he was comprehensively defeated by Gaitskell for the Labour Party treasurership. This was largely an honorific, even symbolic position, though Gaitskell did not treat it wholly as a sinecure. Its principal advantage was that it carried with it an automatic seat on the National Executive Committee.

Gaitskell would not have won the treasurership so easily if he had not possessed the support of the big unions or, rather, of their leaders: Arthur Deakin of the Transport and General Workers, Tom Williamson of the General and Municipal Workers, and Will Lawther, the miners' president. Bevan, as a former miner from Tredegar in Monmouthshire, was particularly hurt by the hostile position of the miners' union. In a sense, he had only himself to blame – though he did become treasurer in 1956, when a peace of sorts had been imposed on the party. Ever since his arrival in the House in 1929, he had tended to avoid the miners generally and the Welsh miners particularly. Naturally, this created some resentment. His close relationships with Lord Beaverbrook and others, combined with his taste for the better things of life, gave the impression that he had now detached himself from the working class. But the miners or, at any rate, the Welsh miners (in the 1940s and 1950s still a powerful group) would not have cared about his expensive restaurants, tailored suits and strong spirits if only he had paid them some attention. This he refused or neglected to do. If he had, they would have seen to it that he became leader.

The union leaders' hatred (it is not too strong a word) of Bevan did not mean that they were passionately attached to Gaitskell. That is the other myth about the succession to Attlee: that the unions 'made' Gaitskell leader. How could they, when they did not have any votes? They had to wait till 1981 and the succeeding decade before that power was bestowed upon them. The union leaders had never loved Morrison, but he was still their candidate to succeed Attlee. When, as late as October 1955, Crossman asked George Brown, a former transport workers' official, why a 'gaga Morrison' was preferable to a 'gaga Attlee', Brown replied that under Morrison's leadership the unions 'would be able to reassert their authority and smash the intellectuals'. This, of course, may have reflected no more than Brown's dislike of (and desire to annoy) Crossman, who was certainly of that group which awaited Brown's hostile actions. Nevertheless, it does show that Morrison was still regarded by some trade unionists, who included Brown, as the natural successor to Attlee.

This is what Gaitskell thought too. In autumn 1954 he topped the poll for the Shadow Cabinet jointly with Jim Griffiths. Bevan, having resigned in April 1954, did not stand in the autumn. Gaitskell certainly saw himself in 1954–5 as a major figure in the party and a future leader. But he thought of himself in the first stage as deputy leader under Morrison. He genuinely had to be drafted. In March 1955 Anthony Crosland, Roy Jenkins and Woodrow Wyatt wrote to him arguing that the leader should have the support of the centre 'which Herbert has not got'. But Gaitskell refused to canvass in the Tea Room. He left that to Dalton, who was described by Mrs Dalton as being 'like an elephant going through the jungle – clumsy, trumpeting but sly'.[6]

By March 1955 numerous figures in the party – certainly Gaitskell and Deakin, probably Morrison and Williamson as well – had convinced themselves that Bevan would have to go. Attlee thought that Gaitskell and Morrison, either of whom might succeed him, wanted to inherit a disciplined party and that consequently both wanted Bevan eliminated (in the Labour Party's gentler usage of that word) well in advance. Attlee was half-hearted about the operation from the very beginning. Gaitskell was not, and composed an indictment for Attlee in which he set out the counts against Bevan. There were three of them. They were all based on his conduct in the House in 1954–5.[7]

First, in April 1954 Attlee had indicated his approval of the government's support for a new anti-communist alliance in South East Asia, SEATO. Bevan then rose and questioned his leader in a way which implied a lack of confidence in him. At a meeting of the Shadow Cabinet on the next day, Bevan was rebuked, though not formally censured, for his behaviour. He responded by announcing his resignation from the Shadow Cabinet.

Second, in January 1955 Bevan had proposed that Labour should table a motion calling for talks with the USSR before ratification of the treaty on German rearmament. The parliamentary party rejected Bevan's proposal but nonetheless his allies had it placed on the Order Paper, as they were perfectly entitled to do. Gaitskell, however, wrote that, though 'technically' there had been no breach of the Standing Orders, this was 'certainly contrary to their spirit'. A special meeting of the parliamentary party was called, when Bevan and his supporters were condemned for refusing to support majority decisions.

And, third, the parliamentary party had decided shortly afterwards to support the government over the construction of the hydrogen bomb. In the subsequent debate Bevan questioned the decision. He said that he and his friends would have to do the work of opposition in default of anyone else. Within hours he was interrogating Attlee vigorously in the House about whether the opposition agreed with the policy of making a nuclear response to a conventional attack. In the division, he and sixty-one others abstained on Labour's official motion.

A special meeting of the Shadow Cabinet was summoned. Gaitskell, Morrison and a youthful James Callaghan pressed for the withdrawal of the whip. Attlee demurred but was overruled. The majority decided to make the question one of confidence. The whole Shadow Cabinet would resign if its recommendations were rejected by the parliamentary party, which met on 16 March 1955. Bevan was unrepentant. Opinion was evenly balanced. A compromise motion proposed by Fred Lee, calling for censure instead of withdrawal of the whip, was defeated 138–124. The Shadow Cabinet's motion was carried 141–112.

The question was what to do next. Standing Orders said that the matter should be referred to the National Executive Committee. The majority of the Shadow Cabinet wanted to do this so that Bevan should be expelled by the committee (with, however, a right of appeal to the conference, which Bevan might well have exercised successfully). The majority argued that withdrawal of the whip merely divested him of his duty to comply with it and imposed no real penalty upon him. He was bound to be readmitted to the parliamentary party – to have the whip restored to him – before the election. So to the NEC the matter duly went.

The trade unions, through their representatives on that body (almost always the second-in-command figures), were now directly involved. Gaitskell, the treasurer, himself believed, as he was to write in his diary, that the unions would be less munificent in disbursing the workers' pennies at the forthcoming election if Bevan remained unpunished. In explaining Gaitskell's conduct, there is no need to go quite so far as Brian Brivati who, in his life of Gaitskell,[8] accuses him of carrying out Deakin's instructions.

The resolution to expel Bevan considered by the NEC was framed in terms of his refusal to comply with majority decisions rather than of his affronts to Attlee. When it began to look probable that Bevan would be expelled, Attlee stopped doodling and proposed that a special sub-committee should be set up to interview him. This was carried by fourteen votes to thirteen. Bevan's pursuers had lost him to a temporary sanctuary which had been erected by Attlee and was to turn out to be permanent. At the sub-committee Bevan was accused of persistent attacks on party and union leaders, repeated refusals to accept majority decisions and the formation of an organized group with its own press (that is, *Tribune*). However, at the reconvened meeting of the NEC, Griffiths moved and Attlee seconded a motion approving the withdrawal of the whip from Bevan but accepting an apology from him (which had already been cleared with Attlee) together with an undertaking of future good conduct.

Attlee and Griffiths were the peacemakers; both Gaitskell and Morrison wanted Bevan's extirpation. The union leaders blamed Attlee, for Griffiths then occupied the same position in the Labour Party as the Queen Mother was later to fill in the country. They thought Attlee had mishandled the situation. This was one reason why they wanted him to depart after the 1955 election. In late April the whip was quietly restored to Bevan in preparation for this contest.

In the election of 26 May 1955 the Conservatives won 344 seats, Labour 277, the Liberals 6 and others 3. To Gaitskell's surprise, it was an election defeat that did not swing the party to the left. Even Bevan commended Labour's 'good domestic programme' which, though not 'exciting or ambitious', was 'definite and practical'. After the election Dalton began what he called his 'Operation Avalanche' to clear out the 'old gang', in which he included himself – he resigned from the Shadow Cabinet – but not Attlee. Dalton wrote to Attlee that his own position was 'a very special one'. It was his 'strong hope that in the interests of party unity' he would continue as leader when the new Parliament met. The hope was shared, he knew, by many of their colleagues. No one else of whatever age could 'do this difficult job' as well as he could.

Bevan was, if anything, even keener for Attlee to stay. On 8 June 1955 the Shadow Cabinet, without a dissentient voice (for Morrison kept quiet), urged him to continue. Attlee said he would go on until October 1955, the time of the party conference, but no longer: the party, he said, must have a younger leader 'soon'. At this stage the Labour politicians thought the session would end in October 1955 and that they could then contemplate matters afresh in time for the parliamentary party's sessional elections in November. Instead the Eden government decided to prolong the session until autumn 1956. On the next day, 9 June 1955, Attlee announced to the parliamentary party meeting that he had told the Shadow Cabinet he wanted to go at once but had been asked to stay. Bevan urged him not to fix a date for his departure. That would lead only to 'speculation and intrigue'. An affecting exchange followed:

Bevan: Clem, I implore you, put no limit. Just go on. (*Cheers*)
Attlee: Is that the general wish? (*Cheers*) Anyone against? No? Very well.[9]

Dalton noted that this was 'almost entirely the end of Morrison' as a future leader. He was 'too old to succeed Attlee now'.[10] The thought in many minds that day was that Bevan had ditched Morrison by prolonging Attlee's reign beyond the next twelve months and that, when Attlee finally went, Bevan would succeed him. However, things worked out quite differently. Though Gaitskell was to prove the eventual beneficiary, it is clear that Attlee was not staying on specifically to keep out Morrison. In June 1955 – and up to the date of his departure in December – it was Bevan and his acolytes who wanted Attlee to stay on precisely for this purpose. On 21 June Attlee wrote to his brother Tom: 'It's high time the party found a new leader. I am too old to give a new impetus. I hoped to force their hand by fixing a date for retirement, but they would not have it. Twenty years is quite long enough, I think.'[11]

Bevan's biographer and friend, Michael Foot, writes of a plan by the anti-Bevanites to push Attlee out and Morrison in and of Attlee's moving with 'astonishing agility' to safeguard his position.[12] This is not borne out by the evidence. Certainly Morrison's friends wanted Attlee to leave in June or July 1955, allowing Morrison to take over in the autumn. This was before it was realized that the session would continue into 1956. But Morrison's friends were no match for Gaitskell's friends, notably Dalton. By encouraging Attlee to stay, he intended to provide time to build up Gaitskell's strength. This conflicted with Attlee's own wishes about his retirement. In the session of summer 1955 Morrison, Attlee thought, tried 'too hard' in the House.

Dalton refused to come to a firm conclusion about whether Attlee delayed to keep out Morrison. What he did know (he wrote) was that Attlee did not regard Morrison as likely to make a good Prime Minister or Labour 'a happy ship'. He was also dismissive of the view, advanced then and since, that Attlee's resignation was hastened by pressure from trade unions or from newspapers – some wanting Gaitskell, others wanting Morrison, none (apart from *Tribune*) wanting Bevan. Dalton doubted whether there was much in this. He thought Attlee's health, and his wife's influence in the interests of his health, provided a much more likely explanation.

Indeed, on 8 August 1955 Attlee suffered a slight stroke, and his eczema recurred. Unlike Winston Churchill's more serious incapacitation of two years before, this was not kept secret. Speculation about his leadership increased. It grew still more in September when Percy Cudlipp – then writing a column in the *News Chronicle*, and brother of Hugh – visited Cherry Cottage in Buckinghamshire and was granted an interview.

Labour, Attlee informed the readers of the paper (officially an independent Liberal organ, in practice advocating a kind of enlightened Lib-Labbery), must have at the top men brought up in the present age, not, as he had been, in the Victorian age. The party had nothing to gain by dwelling in the past. Nor did he think it could impress the nation by adopting a 'puerile left-wingism'. He regarded himself as to the left of the centre, which was where a leader of the party ought to be. The world was constantly presenting new problems. It was no use asking what Keir Hardie would have done. He had 'had a long innings' and would be glad when he could hand over to a younger man. This appeared not in the Percy Cudlipp column's usual place but as the paper's main story headlined ATTLEE IS READY TO GO.

Later that month, however, Barbara Castle told Crossman that she had seen Attlee, who had said he was willing to carry on for twelve months: 'With Barbara one is never sure whether Attlee hadn't merely grunted at intervals while she told him what to think. I tested her view by myself talking to Attlee . . . He certainly has not committed himself to staying for the whole twelve months but merely to staying on if the party insists, which is slightly different.'[13]

The party conference opened at Margate on the surprisingly late day of 10 October 1955. At this point Gaitskell hoped only to replace Morrison as deputy leader when Morrison replaced Attlee. He agreed with Patrick Gordon Walker that this outcome would be best both for the party and for himself. The big trade unions wanted Attlee to go because he had, they considered, been 'weak' in not expelling Bevan from the party in April 1955. They were moving towards Gaitskell as a successor – though they had no *locus* in choosing him

– on account of Morrison's age and his ever-increasing apparent feebleness.

The *Daily Mirror* wanted Attlee to go and Gaitskell to succeed him. The paper's editorial director, Hugh Cudlipp, later wrote that Attlee, 'the chief architect of defeat', had to go, but that Bevan was not fit to take over the leadership. Gaitskell, according to Cudlipp, supplied 'the brains and the zest' – the last not perhaps the quality which first came to the minds of those attempting to describe this intelligent, serious but prickly product of Winchester and New College. Unhappily, Gaitskell 'did not understand the *Mirror*. He assumed, rather imprudently, its automatic support as if it were a popular version of the less popular *Daily Herald* [then Labour's official newspaper].'[14] The *Mirror* gave Attlee the name 'Lord Limpet'. Foot wrote that the paper made his position 'intolerable'. Attlee, who wanted to go anyway, was perfectly capable of standing up to the *Mirror*.

Foot is, however, frank that the Bevanites, of whom he was a leading figure, wanted Attlee to stay to give their candidate a better chance of succeeding him. By 1957, they thought – at any rate, hoped – Gaitskell's bubble, which weekly in 1955 they could see assuming alarmingly balloon-like proportions, would have burst. At the pre-conference demonstration Mrs Castle, another leading Bevanite, issued a fulsome invitation to Attlee to stay as long as he wished or could. As Anthony Howard put it in his life of Crossman, she 'drew a touching picture of evil forces being prepared to hustle poor deserving Clem Attlee off the stage before he was ready to go'.[15] Gaitskell again defeated Bevan for the treasurership. For this reason and others, Bevan exploded. He chose the private session on the Tuesday afternoon (the traditional time in the conference calendar for such debates) which was ostensibly devoted to Wilson's report on party organization. Hugh Massingham recorded in his column in the *Observer*, which in those more self-effacing days he wrote as 'Our Political Correspondent', that 'A time-bomb went off with a shattering explosion. It was the fearful noise of Mr Bevan blowing his top at what was comically called a private session. As every window was open and the loud-speakers on, even the quiet fishermen at the end of the pier could catch every word.'[16] According to Foot: 'Delegates thumped out their enthusiasm so violently that the reporters who thought they might have had an afternoon off came rushing back to discover what explosion had shaken the Margate pavilion.'[17] Crossman's version was:

> In the course of twelve minutes I do not recall Nye mentioning the [Wilson] report. He merely replied to Webber [William Webber, a trade union member of the National Executive Committee] on the subject of his expulsion, on the hypocrisy of the debates, on the trade union oligarchy and on anything else which came into his head. It was a brilliant and spontaneous tour de force and as Nye returned to his seat he was nearly mobbed by the delegates.[18]

Though Bevan won the cheers from the constituency delegates, his support in the parliamentary party was not increasing, while former supporters of Morrison were moving to Gaitskell. Dalton asserts that, when the conference dispersed, Gaitskell had decided to stand. This is doubtful. Gaitskell's aim was to stop Bevan. He consented to stand himself only when Morrison's political reputation and parliamentary performance had declined so far that this course became the best means of accomplishing his end. Alfred Robens (now Lord Robens) said in a speech at Manchester that Attlee would retire ten days after Parliament reassembled. Eight MPs wrote from the Council of Europe in Strasbourg urging Gaitskell to stand. The *Daily Herald* was so excited that it despatched its political reporter Hugh Pilcher to interview Attlee in Malta, where he was on a brief visit. Attlee's denial of any intention to resign was curiously equivocal. He said: 'I have no intention whatever of resigning at the present time. There is nothing on the agenda of the parliamentary party meeting about it. I have heard of no one who intends to raise the subject.'[19]

Morrison was urged by his friends, who were worried by Gaitskell's growing support, to tell Attlee that, unless he resigned, most of the Shadow Cabinet would resign instead. But though he was anxious for Attlee to depart, Morrison himself – partly, no doubt, out of loyalty, partly out of feebleness – was reluctant to cause a split.

Gaitskell's speech in the autumn budget debate marked the end of 'Butskellism' – the word coined by *The Economist* to denote the alleged unity of economic views between Gaitskell and the Chancellor, R. A. Butler. It was also the moment when Gaitskell himself became the clear favourite to succeed Attlee. Crossman noted that Gaitskell's unwonted aggression towards Butler 'made the headlines and in fact made his speech'. He had taken the opportunity to destroy once and for all the figure of Mr Butskell. This demolition was essential if he was to become leader of the party. This was a significant entry in Crossman's diary. It demonstrated that by late October 1955 he (a Bevanite, or a Bevanite of sorts) was prepared not only to contemplate the likelihood of Gaitskell's becoming leader but also, by implication, to welcome that outcome.

Attlee was equally pleased. He told Hunter that Gaitskell had 'done very well' and 'come on a lot'. Though he had the best chance, the party would have to decide. Herbert Bowden, the Chief Whip, approached Wilson and told him that Attlee was delighted. Now that Wilson and Gaitskell were working so well together, he said he was ready to go. Attlee's biographer, Kenneth Harris, writes that it was at this point, in late October, that Gaitskell made up his mind to stand for the leadership. This may be so. Nevertheless, as late as 2 November Gaitskell would write to Douglas Jay that, though there was a continual fuss going on, as far as he could see Attlee had no intention whatever of moving on and consequently the discussion was all rather academic as well as regrettable. After Gaitskell's triumph in the budget debate came Morrison's failure in the censure debate.

Crossman agreed with Bevan 'in feeling sympathy with the old boy for the treatment he got. The Tea Room [shorthand for the solid centre of the party: the Bevanites, like the Conservatives, favoured the Smoking Room] was utterly heartless. They were really like the spectators in a bullring, booing a matador who is past his years.'[20] It was after this failure that Gaitskell finally decided to stand.

Both Morrison and Bevan took alarm. On 3 November they met together in the Smoking Room. Morrison authorized first Eddie Shackleton and then Richard Stokes to negotiate with Bevan's representative, Leslie Hale. Bevan sought the advice of a Conservative minister, James Stuart, later Lord Stuart of Findhorn. It was to 'disentrench' his troops opposing Morrison and realign them in support of the older man in order to defeat Gaitskell.

This was the first of two plots involving Morrison and Bevan which are often confused, partly, no doubt, because they contemplated the same outcome: that Morrison should be the Prime Minister in some future Labour government, unhappily as yet unelected, with Bevan as his Foreign Secretary, and that, after two or three years, Bevan should succeed him as Prime Minister. In this first plot, the assumption was that Gaitskell, Morrison and Bevan would all stand. The further assumption was that Bevan would come bottom of the poll: a creditable third, but bottom nonetheless. Neither Gaitskell nor Morrison would have won an absolute majority. If Morrison were first, Bevan's votes, redistributed virtually en bloc to him, would guarantee him the succession. If, however, he was second and Gaitskell first, Bevan's votes would still give him a sporting chance. It was this double miscalculation – that no one would win an absolute majority, and that Bevan would be bottom of the poll – which kept Morrison in the contest, despite the advice of many of his friends that he should withdraw before he subjected himself to further needless humiliation.

On 16 November Bevan berated Crossman for the line he had been taking that it would be a disaster if Morrison succeeded Attlee.

According to Crossman, this led logically to accepting Gaitskell as the next leader, 'though I never say so'.

> *Bevan*: You can't force the party to accept Gaitskell, and I must warn you that, if he is leader, I might not be able to collaborate.
> *Crossman*: But what's the alternative?
> *Bevan*: Well, there are times when no decision is best. The right thing to do now is to wait. After all, something may turn up. (*As an afterthought.*) Gaitskell might be more acceptable in nine months' time than now . . .
> *Crossman*: But you've got to understand that many of us know all the drawbacks of Gaitskell but accept him as inevitable because you've ruled yourself out.[21]

The whole conversation, Crossman records, was conducted in a perfectly rational way between friends. Towards its end Crossman blurted out to Bevan what he claimed never to say: that Gaitskell was the logical or inevitable successor. Both Bevan and Morrison were still resolved to prevent this from happening.

Later in the month Attlee called in Bowden, said he was going and asked him to fix a date. Bowden said they should get it over before Christmas and suggested 7 December. Attlee agreed. Bowden asked whether he, as Chief Whip, should tell the contenders privately. Attlee told him to tell Gaitskell. Morrison was understandably piqued and said, with a humour which was admirable in the circumstances, that he 'felt like Princess Margaret' (who had just renounced Group Captain Peter Townsend as a suitor). It was 'a bit hard' that he should be the only person that Attlee had not consulted in any way. He thought Attlee would go next day, 7 December, 'but he hasn't mentioned it to me'. He was 'a rum fellow'. He could, he said, tell his interlocutor Crossman 'a lot more about that if I wanted to'. On 6 December Attlee wrote to his brother Tom: 'I am tomorrow giving up the leadership of the party. As you know, I wanted to go after the last election, but stayed on to oblige. There is, however, so much speculation as to the next leader going on that I think it best to retire now. The party is in good heart.'[22]

Irrespective of whether the version given by Michael Foot and the Bevanites is accepted – roughly, that Attlee was forced out by a combination of popular newspapers and brutish trade unionists – it is evident that, having reluctantly agreed to continue as leader in June 1955, Attlee expected to carry on till the end of the session. This, through the decision of the Eden government, would occur in 1956, not, as had first been thought by Labour politicians, in 1955. When Attlee announced his resignation to the parliamentary party on 7 December, he said it was regrettable that since June scarcely a week had passed when one prominent member of the party or another did not talk about his resignation. That certainly did not help the party. He said 'Thank you' and left the meeting. Morrison took the chair. It was decided that nominations for the election would close on Friday 9 December at eleven. Later that day, 7 December, it was announced that Attlee would be going to the Lords.

On the evening of Attlee's resignation, Morrison and Bevan dined together. Next day's events, Dalton wrote, seemed to stem from 'this surprising love feast'. Bevan told the press on the Thursday that he would willingly accede to a proposal of ten MPs that he and Gaitskell should withdraw and allow Morrison to become leader unopposed. The scheme originated with Emanuel Shinwell, a Morrison man; its supporters included David Grenfell, Richard Stokes and Tom Williams. This was the second Morrison–Bevan plot. The first one, as we have seen, was that on any second ballot Bevan's votes would be switched to Morrison. Now Bevan's votes could not be switched because Bevan, together with Gaitskell, would not – so it was vainly hoped – be contesting the election at all.

To Morrison's biographers, this was a 'curious and desperate manoeuvre'.[23] To Bevan's biographer, however, it was a 'feasible plan'.[24] The plan, manoeuvre or plot certainly did not arouse much enthusiasm at the time. Twenty MPs who had formerly been Morrison supporters approached Gaitskell on the opposition front bench and urged him not to withdraw. More supporters of Gaitskell appealed to him in the Division Lobby. Lena Jeger, then a young, leftist MP, had been present at the Morrison–Bevan dinner. She promptly told Harold Wilson (as a young, leftist MP likewise), who went immediately to see Gaitskell, said he was 'nauseated' and promised that, if Gaitskell withdrew, he would stand himself. Morrison himself remained hopeful and went off to see his tailor at the Woolwich Co-op. Mrs Castle continued to be his loyal supporter, explaining 'passionately' to the journalist Leslie Hunter that, though she had disagreed with many of his ideas on policy in the past – which was something of an understatement – his record had earned him a short period as leader. Attlee was 'crazy' if he imagined the party would accept Gaitskell.

Mrs Castle rebuked her friend Crossman for his unsteadiness. On Thursday 8 December he had no doubt that Bevan and Gaitskell would both stand too. She reproached him with the rumour that he was going to vote for Gaitskell, which Crossman attributed to George Wigg. At this stage Crossman thought there was no problem. On the first ballot, with three candidates standing, it was essential that the left should poll its full strength. If Gaitskell did not obtain the absolute majority on the first ballot, and he and Morrison remained in the contest, he would either vote for Gaitskell or tear up his ballot paper. Accordingly Wigg (if it was he who had started the rumour) was already half right. In any case, Crossman's proposed actions were clearly contrary to the Bevanite line: that, if Gaitskell and Bevan both remained in the contest, the correct course to follow was to vote first for Bevan and then for Morrison but on no account for Gaitskell.

As he left the Smoking Room, where he had been having tea with Mrs Castle, Crossman ran into Bevan and said impetuously that he heard there was a 'ridiculous rumour' that he was going to vote for Gaitskell against him. This was 'completely untrue' and he would like Bevan to know it was so. In his diary Crossman confessed himself 'a little bit baffled' that, though Bevan smiled, 'he looked a bit embarrassed but said nothing whatsoever and walked down the Lobby'. Bevan was presumably being bashful about the Morrison–Bevan pact which, had it been successful, would have imposed the (by Crossman, at any rate) hated Morrison upon the party. The pact, though it did not come to anything, provided Crossman with the pretext for voting for Gaitskell rather than for Bevan, a course he had really wanted to follow all along. He as good as announced his intentions in a special column in the *Daily Mirror* (for which he was then writing a regular column) on Saturday 10 December, four days before the MPs voted.

The proposed pact, Crossman wrote, obviously put Gaitskell in an extremely embarrassing position. He was far too deeply committed to consider Bevan's offer. The contest went on. Like many other left-wingers he himself would have preferred Bevan to have the leadership until he 'threw it away'. He could not support Morrison because he did not believe that the Labour Party in its present state of health was 'strong enough to stand two or three more years of disintegration at the bottom and infighting at the top'. The next day Hugh Massingham, the *Observer*'s political columnist, who was close to Bevan, Shinwell and Wigg, wrote more sympathetically of Morrison's decline: 'Those who owe everything to Mr Morrison, who would not even be in the House without his patronage, have deserted to Mr Gaitskell. No doubt they have their reasons, but it is not a pleasant spectacle and it is not a pleasant fact to record.'[25]

The parliamentary party met at seven on the following Wednesday in Committee Room 14. Attlee was not in the chair on account of his precipitate ascent to the peerage. Morrison was there in his place. The result was: Gaitskell 157, Bevan 70, Morrison 40. Gaitskell had won an absolute majority, Bevan had polled better than expected and Morrison had been humiliated. Attlee wrote to Gaitskell: 'I was delighted with your vote which was just about what I had anticipated.

It was a pity that Herbert insisted on running. He had, I think, been warned of the probable result.'[26]

He concluded with the 'hope that Nye & Co will now go all out to support you'. Nye and Co. showed no such disposition, at any rate to begin with. Indeed, Bevan conducted himself with a conspicuous lack of grace or good humour. Gaitskell's succession, he wrote immediately afterwards in *Tribune*, was the result of an 'unworthy conspiracy'. Labour would 'rue the day' when it permitted 'the least reputable among newspapers' – the *Daily Mirror* – to 'fill the role of kingmaker'. He did, however, announce that he would not stand against Morrison for the deputy leadership.

This small gesture of magnanimity proved barren. For Morrison slunk away like an old wounded animal. Bevan later stood against Griffiths in January 1956 and lost 141–111. If Attlee had made Bevan rather than Gaitskell Chancellor of the Exchequer in 1950, or Bevan rather than Morrison Foreign Secretary in 1951 – Morrison was appointed in March of that year, whereas Bevan resigned from the government in April – matters might have turned out differently. As things were, Gaitskell was never forgiven for defeating Bevan so comprehensively in 1955. Though there was a period of factitious concord in 1957–9 in readiness for the election, peace was restored only with the death of Gaitskell in 1963 and his succession by Harold Wilson.

WILL HUTTON

The Scene Shifts – the Legacy Remains

'The National Health Service would never have been established in 1948,' declared Aneurin Bevan in a crowded Manchester hall eight years later, 'in the mood of the Labour movement of 1956.' If he thought that in 1956, he would have thought it many times over about Labour in 1997. Today the new convention in the Labour Party is to return fire, and scorn the apparently quintessential 'Old Labour' categories in which Bevan thought; after all they had brought the party to a new low ebb. But Bevan's thinking was more subtle than such categorizations imply; the Old Labour tag too simple.

He was an advocate of nationalization, yet also a stern critic of how public ownership had manifested itself in reality. His belief in planning made him a powerful critic of the endemic short-termism and lack of co-ordination in British government, notably at the Treasury. And he understood more clearly than many others the role of ideas and argument in sustaining political legitimacy, and how their lack would rot Soviet communism. If he was a quintessential class warrior, his passionate commitment to the cause of the working class gave him the fortitude, political direction and courage to take on powerful adversaries and construct one of the great British institutions of the twentieth century – the NHS. There are lessons in his brand of democratic socialism from which today's Labour Party, despite very different circumstances, might profitably learn – and parallels in the two disparate traditions that neither side might wish to acknowledge.

At first sight it is Bevan's legacy from which the Labour Party has been trying to escape. Here was a passionate believer in Clause IV, a man who considered that the transfer from private to public ownership was what gave socialism its teeth. Here too was a committed disarmer instinctively hostile to nuclear weapons, yet realistically distanced from unilateralism. He believed not in 'One Nation' politics but in the urgent necessity to establish the dominance of the working class and to promote its interests in national life. Taxation had to be high enough to provide for the goods that the public needed, and economic policy should be as redistributive as possible. He had no truck with the nostrums of *laissez-faire*, and famously regarded the Tories as vermin. The historic mission of democratic socialists was to transform the operation of capitalism – to plan, to nationalize, to redistribute income and wealth, and, of course, to disarm.

It was this portfolio of views that, when hardened into the Labour manifesto of 1983, proved to be the party's electoral undoing – the 'longest suicide note in history' as it was memorably dubbed. In that sense Bevan's legacy was malign, creating the intellectual tradition that would ultimately cause Labour to split – perhaps the single most important reason why the Conservatives so effortlessly won four general elections. On the other hand he was the creator of the National Health Service, the embodiment of collectivism – the citadel around which the tide of markets and individualism washed but never succeeded in breaching. Indeed the NHS marked the limits of where the free marketeers could go; even John Redwood has had to accept that the principles of the NHS are inviolate. This was one of the foundations upon which Labour and the ideas of the left managed to sustain their appeal even at the moment of the right's apparent intellectual supremacy.

But the substantial point is that Bevan, an endlessly inventive man who was crucially aware of the need for any democratic politician to be abreast of contemporary trends, would not have put his name to a policy programme that in 1983 was so essentially backward looking – or at least he would have attempted to shape the programme so that it was more modern and connected to realities while retaining its essential components. In this respect he would have agreed with Labour modernizers: socialism Labour-style had by the early 1980s become intellectually ossified and seriously out of touch with the lived experience of ordinary people. It was more like a religion than a system of living political ideas; its adherents demonstrated their 'radicalism' by making ritual obeisance to great socialist nostrums – public ownership, planning, equality – without succeeding in showing their relevance to the here and now. It was one of Bevan's strengths as a politician that he was forward rather than backward looking; an optimist about progress rather than a guardian of never-ending socialist icons. He was an archetypal modernizer.

His approach to nationalization typified the complexity of his thinking. He was wary of wholesale nationalization for its own sake, but more importantly he was critical of the Morrisonian model on which nationalization had been constructed. He was acutely aware of the way these essentially bureaucratic monopolies were over-centralized, offered no genuine participation to the workforce and were indifferent to the needs of the consumer. It wasn't good enough merely that they were in public ownership; that had to mean tangible benefits or else the whole socialist project would be delegitimized. By the mid-1970s the left's unwillingness to think creatively about how the nationalized industries might be made to work better for consumers and workers alike left the field open to the right, with well-known consequences – mass privatization. By not daring to develop the idea or recast it – for example by contracting out the management of nationalized industries to private managers, or developing the companies as mutual societies, or finding ways for the workforce to have some stake in the enterprises, or exposing them to competition – Labour was left as the defender of the indefensible. It was a political outflanking that Bevan would have fought to avoid.

However, the social landscape of the industrial society with which Bevan was so familiar and relied on to make his case has changed immeasurably. He could take it as axiomatic that there was a working class present in factories, mines, docks and railways whose economic function was unchanging. This class was readily organizable into trade unions – and had a value system in which collective action and class solidarity were taken for granted. Although some of his writing was remarkably prescient, he did not anticipate how de-industrialization and rising incomes would generate an individualism which made both the economic structures and accompanying value system hostile to trade unionism and, indeed, socialism.

And if he was anxious to link the Labour Party with strong progress-ive social forces, that wasn't a difficult task in the 1940s and 50s. The strongest social force was the trade union movement, so the political task was clear. In 1997 the trade unions are weaker, and progressive social forces are fragmenting into single-issue pressure groups; these groups are instinctively less willing to subsume their interests under the banner of the Labour Party, in a wider common cause. And no longer do politicians gain their purchase on public opinion through great street rallies and platform speeches in crowded halls; the mass media, notably television, is the vehicle for shaping the political agenda. The world is moving on, and Bevan would now have to accept that the Labour Party could no longer rely on a trade-union base to provide the core of its political support. The building of new coalitions, including more upwardly mobile individu-alistic voters in the Labour cause, would have required him to make important changes in ideology and the way arguments are presented. Like John Prescott, he would have been prepared to move with the times.

The political agenda and the battle for men and women's minds is fundamentally about success in argument. This was a core Bevanite canon. Much of his economic analysis had more Marxist than Keynesian roots, but he abjured the political absolutism of Marxism. He believed in democracy, in the rule of law, in the winning of argument; not for him the dictatorship of the proletariat and the view that the state could and should become its puppet. There had to be democratic institutions, free votes and competing political parties – and he saw socialism as constant work-in-progress always responding to changing circumstances; in this respect he foreshadowed the appetite of the constitutional reform movement around Charter 88, in that he saw vividly how the concentration of executive power in London throttled the democratic spirit. Power had to be won, and then given away – and he would have heartily approved of this element in New Labour's political programme. Lord Irvine, Donald Dewar and Tony Blair are in this respect more Bevanite than they could imagine.

The difference between them and Bevan lies in their approach to capitalism. Bevan was inherently suspicious of private enterprise and the free market. For him private firms were of necessity exploitative and short-term, anxious to construct monopolies and ignore organized labour if they could. Moreover market economies were unstable and prone to systemic breakdown. There had to be a spine of planning if they were to prosper, and the commanding heights of the economy had to be in public ownership. Demand management, Keynesian-style, was a palliative and a cover which allowed the big issues of capitalism to remain unaddressed, in particular by creating conditions under which free trade might prosper so the prospects of sustaining socialism in any one country would be undermined.

Forty years later such fears appear both wise and foolish. Socialism has proved impossible to sustain in a free trade world as Bevan feared, but free trade itself is more obviously a transmission mechanism of growth and employment than it appeared to him, steeped in the disasters of the early 1930s. Keynesian demand management has broken down, exposing the innate tendencies of markets more cruelly – but while there is an increase in job insecurity, low wages and monopolies, capitalism shows a vitality and energy beside which the planned economies have been exposed as ineffective. The job is not to transform capitalism, but to work with its grain to civilize and humanize it – a rather more modest ambition than Bevan allowed when alive, but one to which he would have subscribed as at least offering some way forward. He would have seen the point of stakeholding – a contemporary means of giving workers a voice in the running of a firm, of securing human values in the workplace and of raising investment – even if it falls far short of some of his loftier aims. Tony Blair's reference in his famous Singapore speech to stakeholding as a means of resisting the commodification of labour would have immediately struck a chord with Bevan – and he would have seen how to locate the idea in his conception of democratic socialism much more readily than many current left-of-centre thinkers.

It was the possession of such an ideological template coupled with his passion to advance working-class interests that gave Bevan his energy as a left politician; this combination underpinned his resolution to deliver a better world to working people. An effective stakeholding position in 1997 demands a readiness to stand up to powerful vested interests in the City and industry, and to reshape law and the financial system so that they provide an architecture in which it can take place. That takes political courage and nerve of the type Bevan displayed when driving through the NHS. The idea of nationalizing Britain's hospitals and turning self-employed doctors into civil servants was opposed root and branch in 1947 and 1948, just as it would be today. To hold his nerve and go ahead under such circumstances required deep inner conviction, and that in turn demanded an intellectual rationale and a passion for justice. Bevan had them both, and his legacy is the NHS – whose continuing legitimacy is a tribute to the still-powerful undercurrent of belief in collectivism that exists in British life. Indeed the hostile reaction to the way marketization, spending limits and the private finance initiative are undermining a true national service gives the lie to the idea that the British have turned their backs on all attempts at justice and social solidarity. Bevan believed that ideas had to be made flesh in functioning institutions and defended in democratic debate, and the NHS is living proof of his convictions – the most successful initiative by the left this century. It is a spirit and approach upon which his successors today might ponder.

Notes

GEOFFREY GOODMAN:
The Soul of Socialism

1 Aneurin Bevan, *In Place of Fear* (Mac-Gibbon & Kee, 1952; with a foreword by Jennie Lee, EP Publishing, 1976).
2 Ibid.
3 John Campbell, *Nye Bevan and the Mirage of British Socialism* (Weidenfeld, 1987).
4 Anthony Crosland, *Socialism Now* (Cape, 1974).
5 Hansard, 3 November 1979.
6 *Daily Mail*, 7 July 1960.
7 Bevan, *In Place of Fear*.

BARBARA CASTLE:
A Passionate Defiance

1 William Warbey was prospective parliamentary candidate for Wimbledon during the war. In 1945 he won Luton for Labour, but lost his seat in 1950. He returned to the Commons in 1953 as MP for Broxtowe, later for Ashfield, until he retired in 1966. He died in 1980.
2 Hugh Dalton, *Call Back Yesterday. Memoirs 1887–1931* (Frederick Muller Ltd, 1953).
3 Roy Campbell's verse 'On Some South African Novelists', reproduced in the *Oxford Dictionary of 20th Century Verse*, 1973.
4 Winston Churchill, war memoirs, *The Second World War*, vol. 1, *The Gathering Storm* (Cassell & Co. Ltd, 1948).
5 Michael Foot, *Aneurin Bevan*, vol. 2, *1945–1960* (Davis-Poynter, 1973); John Campbell, *Nye Bevan: A Biography* (Hodder and Stoughton, 1994).
6 Denis Healey, *The Time of My Life* (Michael Joseph, 1989).

DAI SMITH:
'The Ashes onto the Wind': Bevan and Wales

1 Jim Griffiths, *Pages from Memory* (Dent, 1969).
2 Peter Mandelson, *The Blair Revolution* (Faber & Faber, 1996).
3 Aneurin Bevan, *In Place of Fear* (Mac-Gibbon & Kee, 1952).
4 Dai Smith, *Aneurin Bevan and the World of South Wales* (University of South Wales Press, 1993).
5 Chris Williams, *History Workshop Journal*, vol. 41, 1996.
6 Sue Demont, *Tredegar and Aneurin Bevan: A Society and its Political Articulation, 1890–1929*, unpublished Ph.D. thesis, University of Wales, Cardiff, 1990.
7 Gwyn Thomas, *Return and End* (unpublished) and *A Tongue for a Stammering Time* (unpublished).
8 Trevor Griffiths, *Food for Ravens* (working title) screenplay for BBC Wales, 1997.

NOTES

JILL CRAIGIE:
Political Blood Sport

1 Michael Foot's biography, *Aneurin Bevan*, vol. 2 (Davis-Poynter, 1973), gives a well-documented account of Nye's fight for the National Health Service; see also Nicholas Timmins, *The Five Giants: a history of the welfare state* (HarperCollins, 1995).

2 In the Poritt report, commissioned by the Conservative government of 1962, the name 'Bevan' does not even appear in the introduction headed 'Survey of the Historical Background'.

3 The same phenomenon was experienced by the suffragettes. Crowds flocked to the meetings out of curiosity to see the 'amazons', 'screaming sisterhood', 'women starved of a natural outlet for their emotions' and were then amazed to discover that they were ordinary women talking better sense than many of the politicians.

CHARLES WEBSTER:
Birth of the Dream: Bevan and the Architecture of the National Health Service

1 Michael Foot, *Aneurin Bevan*, vol. 2 (Davis-Poynter, 1973), chapter 3. For subsequent commentary, see for instance F. Honigsbaum, *Health, Happiness, and Security. The Creation of the National Health Service* (Routledge, 1989); R. Klein, *The New Politics of the NHS*, 3rd edn (Longman, 1995); J. E. Pater, *The Making of the National Health Service* (King's Fund, 1981); C. Webster, *The Health Services since the War. Volume I. Problems of Health Care. The National Health Service before 1957* (HMSO, 1988).

2 H. Eckstein, *The English Health Service.*

Its Origins, Structure and Achievements (Harvard University Press, 1958), p. 3.

3 For details, see appendix to this essay (p. 128).

4 K. O. Morgan, *Labour in Power 1945–1951* (Clarendon Press, 1984), pp. 151–7; Webster, *Problems of Health Care*, pp. 84–8.

5 For a useful summary, Honigsbaum, *Health, Happiness*, pp. 172–4. See also N. M. Goodman, *Wilson Jameson Architect of National Health* (Allen and Unwin, 1970); Lord Taylor of Harlow, 'The Birth of a Service 4. The Making of the Act', *Update Review*, vol. 18, no. 5, March 1979.

6 Webster, *Problems of Health Care*, pp. 22, 26–7, 33–4, 80–4.

7 *Lancet*, 1942, ii, 614–15, 21 November 1942. The prime mover for Medical Planning Research was Stephen Taylor.

8 'Regional Economics', *The Economist*, 13 June 1942, pp. 816–17.

9 *The Economist*, 24 April 1943, p. 523.

10 'Local Authority Finance', Parts I and II, *The Economist*, 25 September and 2 October 1943, pp. 421–2, 452–3, drawing upon J. R. Hicks and U. K. Hicks, *Standards of Local Expenditure*, National Institute of Economic and Social Research Occasional Papers, No. 3, Cambridge University Press, 1943.

11 'Local Authority Finance', Part II, *The Economist*, 2 October 1943, p. 453.

12 'The Site of Government', *The Economist*, 22 April 1944, pp. 524–5. For a similar conclusion, 'The Administration of Policy', *The Economist*, 12 August 1944, pp. 208–10. See also 'The Health Controversy', *The Economist*, 5 August 1944, pp. 176–7, which is more pragmatic, albeit accepting that a 'completely national solution is the ideal'.

13 *The Economist*, 24 February 1945, p. 238.

14 'Local Government in England and Wales', *The Economist*, 6 January 1945, pp. 3–4.

15 'Counties and County Boroughs', *The Economist*, 24 February 1945, pp. 237–8.

16 *The Economist*, 26 May 1945, pp. 695–6.

17 *The Economist*, 30 June 1945, pp. 887–8.

18 *The Economist*, 25 August 1945, pp. 259–60.

19 *The Economist*, 20 October and 10 November 1945, pp. 548–9, 668–9. 'The Problem of Rates', Parts I, II and III, *The Economist*, 17 November 1945, pp. 710–13, 24 November 1945, pp. 741–3, 1 December 1945, pp. 782–3.

20 E. Russell-Smith to R. A. Russell-Smith, 27 July and 3 August 1945, Durham University Library.

21 E. Russell-Smith to R. A. Russell-Smith, 21 August 1945.

22 E. Russell-Smith to R. A. Russell-Smith, 22 August 1945.

23 E. Russell-Smith to R. A. Russell-Smith, 1 March 1946.

24 Cabinet Office, Cabinet Secretary's Notebook, 11 October 1945.

25 CM(45) 40th mtg, 11 October 1945, CM(45) 43rd mtg, 18 October 1945, CAB 128/1.

26 Cabinet Office, Cabinet Secretary's Notebook, 20 December 1945.

27 CM(45) 65th mtg, 20 December 1945, CAB 128/1.

28 Webster, *Problems of Health Care*, pp. 94–103.

29 C. Webster, 'Overthrowing the market in health care: the achievements of the early National Health Service', *Journal of the Royal College of Physicians*, 1995, vol. 29: pp. 502–7.

30 Webster, *Problems of Health Care*, p. 99.

31 R. Robinson and J. Le Grand (eds), *Evaluating the NHS Reforms* (King's Fund Centre, 1993); R. Klein, *New Politics of the NHS*, pp. 223–57.

32 Bevan, speech to Executive Councils Association, 7 October 1948, cited from Webster, *Aneurin Bevan on the National Health Service*, p. 140.

33 Statement by Bevan, recorded in the final Cabinet Conclusions, 11 October 1954, CM(45) 40th mtg, PRO, CAB 128/1. The relevant memorandum by Bevan, 'The Future of the Hospital Services', 5 October 1945, CP(45) 205, 5 October 1945, PRO, CAB 129/3, is reproduced in Webster, *Aneurin Bevan on the National Health Service* (Oxford, Wellcome Unit, 1991), pp. 31–40.

DONALD BRUCE:
Nye

1 I myself was defeated by 948 votes in this election and thereafter served Nye in a private capacity.

2 Aneurin Bevan, *In Place of Fear* (with a foreword by Neil Kinnock, (Quartet Books, 1978).

TESSA BLACKSTONE:
The Boy Who Threw an Inkwell: Bevan and Education

1 Michael Foot, *Aneurin Bevan*, vol. 1 (MacGibbon & Kee, 1962).

2 John Campbell, *Aneurin Bevan* (Weidenfeld, 1987) ch. 1, n. 3.

3 Smithers and Robinson, Council for Industry and Higher Education Executive Briefing, 1995.

4 Ivan Illich, *Deschooling Society* (Calder & Boyars, 1971).

5 Council for Industry and Higher Education, 'A Wider Spectrum of Opportunities', March 1995.

MICHAEL FOOT:
Bevan's Message to the World

1 W. J. West, *The Truth Betrayed* (Duckworth, 1987).

2 Professor K. O. Morgan, *Labour in Power* (Oxford University Press, 1984).

ALAN WATKINS:
The Greasy Pole: Bevan and the Leadership

1 Leslie Hunter, *The Road to Brighton Pier* (Arthur Barker, 1959), p. 130.

2 Ibid. p. 123.

3 R. H. S. Crossman Diary, 6 May 1959: *Backbench Diaries*, ed Janet Morgan (Cape and Hamish Hamilton, 1981), p. 746.

4 Crossman Diary, 19 March 1955: *Backbench Diaries*, p. 406.

5 Hunter, *Road to Brighton Pier*, p. 159.

6 Hugh Dalton Diary, 28 April 1955: Philip M. Williams, *Hugh Gaitskell* (Cape, 1979), p. 364.

7 Eric Shaw, *Discipline and Dissent in the Labour Party* (Manchester University Press, 1988), pp. 39–42.

8 Brian Brivati, *Hugh Gaitskell* (Richard Cohen, 1996), pp. 202–13.

9 Hugh Dalton Diary, 9 June 1955: *Memoirs*, vol. 3 (Frederick Muller, 3 vols, 1953–62), p. 422.

10 Ibid.

11 Kenneth Harris, *Attlee* (1982 rev pb edn 1995), p. 535.

12 Michael Foot, *Aneurin Bevan*, vol. 2 (Davis-Poynter, 1973), p. 489.

13 Crossman Diary, 23 September 1955: *Backbench Diaries*, p. 441.

14 Hugh Cudlipp, *Walking on the Water* (Bodley Head, 1976), p. 212.

15 Anthony Howard, *Crossman* (Cape, 1990), p. 197.

16 *Observer*, 16 October 1955: Williams, *Gaitskell*, p. 356.

17 Michael Foot, *Aneurin Bevan* vol. 2, p. 492.

18 Crossman Diary, 16 October referring to 11 October 1955: *Backbench Diaries*, p. 448.

19 Harris, *Attlee*, rev pb edn, p. 539.

20 Crossman Diary, 4 November referring to 31 October 1955: *Backbench Diaries*, p. 451.

21 Crossman Diary, 16 November 1955: ibid. p. 453.

22 Harris, *Attlee*, rev pb edn, p. 451.

23 Bernard Donohue and G. W. Jones, *Herbert Morrison* (Weidenfeld, 1973), p. 339.

24 Foot, *Bevan*, vol. 2, p. 496.

25 *Observer*, 11 December 1955.

26 Harris, *Attlee*, rev pb edn, p. 542.

Index

237

INDEX

INDEX

INDEX

240